HeartWiseGuy

How to Live the Good Life
After a Heart Attack

GARY CARTWRIGHT
Foreword by Ann W. Richards

St. Martin's Press ❧ New York

Design by Bryanna Millis

Some parts of this book were previously published in articles in the
December 1986, January 1987, and June 1997 issues of *Texas Monthly*
and are reprinted by permission.

Library of Congress Cataloging-in-Publication Data

Cartwright, Gary
    HeartWiseGuy : how to live the good life after a heart attack /
Gary Cartwright ; foreword by Ann Richards.—1st ed.
        p.   cm.
    ISBN 0-312-18591-X
    1. Cartwright, Gary—Health.   2. Myocardial infarction—
Patients—United States—Biography.   3. Myocardial infarction—
Patients—Rehabilitation.   I. Title.
RC685.I6C356   1998
362.1'961237'0092—dc21
[B]   98-10193
                                                                CIP

First Edition: May 1998

10   9   8   7   6   5   4   3   2   1

Books are available in quantity for promotional or premium use. Write
to Director of Special Sales, St. Martin's Press, 175 Fifth Avenue, New
York, N.Y. 10010, for information on discounts and terms, or call toll-
free (800) 221-7945. In New York, call (212) 674-5151 (ext. 645).

FOR MONIQUE, WHO MADE THE MAGIC HAPPEN

Contents

FOREWORD

$\mathcal{S}$everal years ago, Gary and Phyllis Cartwright, Bud Shrake, and our mutual agent, Esther Newberg, were having lunch with me at the Governor's Mansion. Gary looked terrific, which was amazing for someone who had undergone a heart bypass and had more plumbing problems than the Mir space station. For a while, it seemed as if no matter what they cut on or medicated, some other ailment would crop up that Gary had to deal with. I can't say that his hijinks in the early years were the cause, but I'm sure they didn't help.

Back to the fact that he looked terrific. He started talking about his regimen of exercise and attention to food, and I suggested that his story ought to be told, because he had become a poster boy for looking good, feeling good, and enjoying life. This book is a result of that conversation.

Gary Cartwright is one of the funniest, zaniest, most delightful people I have ever known. It wasn't just that he was willing to do any goofy thing that was proposed, but that he was good at thinking them up too. We were all pretty good at entertaining, but in honesty our goal was to entertain ourselves and each other . . . and we did a really good job of it. We were perfectly content to listen to stories told over and over again, embellished and enhanced, which was okay because everyone had a different version of what really happened the night before. Some of that highwire artistry is retold in this book. Be aware that all the rest of us have a different version that makes Gary look worse and us look better.

Since I have just celebrated my fifth annual sixtieth birthday, I like the "here's how your body works" and "here's what to do about it" parts best. It is really good stuff. It should send you running to a gym and a trainer and start you paying attention to your five food groups and how many cups it takes of each to stay healthy.

Sobriety and sanity are better, and so is growing older. Gary Cartwright is a living, breathing example.

—Ann W. Richards
August 27, 1997

HeartWiseGuy

Introduction

Okay, I'm a mess is one way to look at it. You'd be, too, if you'd kept up with me. This has been rough and rocky traveling—great fun but trickier than I had anticipated—and the fact that I went forty-something years doing every fun thing that I damn well pleased and 98 percent sure I was bulletproof didn't help. But I finally got it semiright—that's the point and the reason I'm writing this book.

High blood pressure was my first clue. Twenty years ago, when a doctor first warned me that my blood pressure was too high, I blew it off. Hell, being high was what it's all about, eh? But two years later I finally had to admit that I was in trouble—serious trouble, judging from the look on the faces of the doctors and nurses around me at the time. High blood pressure—or hypertension, as they call it over at Austin Diagnostic Medical Center—could kill me any second, with very little outside help. That was the message. Still, it was hard to accept. You don't *feel* hypertension. It's like drinking a cup of decaf with skim milk and Equal, make-believe stuff, and that's what makes it so deadly. But the numbers on the blood pressure machine don't lie. Since accepting that hypertension is a disease, I've swallowed enough pills to stuff the Goodyear Blimp, and will continue to take a handful every morning for the rest of my life. Pills and regular checkups are part of the deal. I finally got around to buying a blood pressure machine that I could figure out how to work—or rather Phyllis did—just a few months ago, when she discovered that she also suffers from hypertension. It's a common affliction in most people over age fifty. Treating the disease has become part of our marriage ritual: we take each other's bp, remind each other to take our medication, and order our margaritas without salt. Phyllis got into the routine right away, but, as I say, it took me most of twenty years.

Then there was the heart attack and the quintuple bypass in 1988, a direct consequence of high blood pressure, though again I didn't make the connection back then. It has been nearly ten years since my bypass. At first it got my attention in a big way, but it didn't keep it. Like some of my friends who have had the same problem (or set of problems), I gradually drifted back to most of my old habits, drinking and eating pretty much what I wanted, spending weekends on the couch reading and petting my dogs, getting fat and soft and cuddly as hell. Smug in the knowledge that I had survived the Big One.

Two years after the bypass I was back in the emergency room. Seems I had blacked out while interviewing this young man from Odessa who believed he had proof that his father was the hidden sniper who killed John Kennedy. Though the interview in itself was enough to make a block of granite dizzy, it turned out that my heart was not regulating itself as it should have. My heart's natural pace-maker no longer sent the proper signals that kept the heart pumping at a regular rate. Tests proved that I needed an artificial pacemaker to do the job. I spent two days in the hospital having the gadget in-stalled, and I have to have it checked four times a year. But it's no big deal. Then in 1992 another meddlesome doctor discovered that I suffer from a kidney disease for which there is no cure. Nephrotic syndrome, it's called. The most encouraging thing he could tell me was that the odds were fifty-fifty that my kidneys would fail within ten years. Organ donor groups have stopped calling.

The seasonal allergies that plague nearly everyone who lives in Austin, Texas, have after all these years developed into asthma. A drag, to be sure, but nothing that can't be factored into the larger equation. But, as you can see, my medical problems had started to mount a formidable offensive. I'm a believer in playing the odds. One or two serious problems *might* kill me. But five or six? Pick 'em up, kid, you're history.

I finally got religion, as it were, in 1993 when my current doc-tor, Thomas Blevins, an endocrinologist who takes a scientific inter-est in treating cases that other doctors have ruled hopeless, gave it to me straight and hard. My options were *(a)* lose forty pounds—the twenty that I intended to lose after bypass surgery, plus another twenty that I had gained while pondering weight-loss solutions—and simultaneously change my eating, drinking, and exercise habits *and* lower my blood cholesterol at least a hundred points, or *(b)* die. He didn't actually say die, but I got the message.

A few days later I sat down with a dietitian, who put me on a diet that was surprising easy to follow and maintain. Essentially, it was the oldest and cheapest diet on the books, the Food Guide Pyramid, published by the U.S. Department of Agriculture. In four months I had reduced my weight from 215 to 175. At the same time I joined Big Steve's Gym, a discipline that in my wildest dreams I never imagined I would practice, especially at age fifty-nine. While dieting, exercising, and moderating my drinking habits, I also took a cold, hard look at my basic attitude. I'll go into detail later, but what I discovered is that of all the lifestyle alterations a citizen might attempt in his pathetic urgency to add good years to his wasted and miserable life—moderation in eating and drinking, exercise, having regular checkups, and following the advice of his overpaid doctors— the single most important is attitude.

So after all these years of hard travel and bad choices, am I better than ever? In my opinion, definitely! Life has never been so full, so sweet, so rich. Modesty prevents me saying that I've never looked better, but I can assure you that I have never been trimmer—175 pounds, thirty-four-inch waist, the same as it was when I was discharged from the Army at age twenty-one. Less fat, more muscle, a general feeling of well-being. Though my weight has varied as much as eight or nine pounds since my initial weight loss—it always goes up after lengthy vacations or holidays—I have had no difficulty recovering my target of 175 pounds. I haven't given up eating or drinking well, I've merely refined my habits.

As for sex (you knew I'd mention sex, didn't you?) . . . how to say this? Well, what we have here is something heretofore beyond my experience. Is it legal for two people carrying AARP cards to feel giddy?

For now, I'll tell you just one thing: Phyllis and I keep falling in love all over again, at least four or five times a year. I mean quantum leaps of passion and appreciation—wild, hot teenage monkey love! Three years ago we rented an apartment for a week in Paris. Since that week she has called me Frenchy and I have referred to her as Monique. *N'est-ce-pas?* (meaning: "If you catch my drift").

In the belief that it might be instructive to others, I offer in the pages that follow my own history of failed opportunities and dogged stupidities, along with some constructive tips on how to correct your own mistakes and reinvigorate your life.

However, in no way is this intended as a medical how-to book. Readers are advised to consult with a physician or other qualified health professionals regarding treatment of all of their health problems or before acting on any of the information in this book. I'm simply writing of my own experiences and how I dealt with them. Attempting to stay current on medical research and advances is nearly impossible, since new discoveries are being made almost daily. All the supplements mentioned in this book—even such apparently harmless substances as vitamins—should be used with caution, and on the advice of a doctor, especially since the manufacture of supplements is not subject to the oversight of the Federal Drug Administration. Let the patient beware!

Part One:

GETTING THERE

One

Considering my raucous lifestyle and unrestricted appetites, nobody deserved a heart attack more than me. Nevertheless, it surprised me. As far as I knew, there was no history of heart disease in my family. Nor did I have any warning symptoms that I associated with heart problems. What I had was chronic heartburn, which I attributed to a diet of chicken-fried steak and Mexican food, washed down with heroic quantities of beer and tequila. I now understand that chronic heartburn isn't something that can be corrected with over-the-counter remedies, but back then I didn't have a clue about heart disease or damn near anything else.

Growing up in a small Texas town didn't prepare me for the possibilities of Greater Texas, much less the life and temptations I would discover as a journalist and writer. Except for the time the Baptist church burned, nothing exciting or memorable ever happened in Arlington. Located in the exact center of what is now the Dallas–Fort Worth Metroplex, it was a rural town of middle-class, mostly white families, living uneventful if not boring lives, on neat rows of quiet residential streets with names like Oak, Pecan, and Mesquite. Arlington had a railroad track, a junior college, a retirement home for aged Masons, another home for aged members of the Eastern Star, three cafés, three drugstores, a pool hall, a village idiot, and enough foul-smelling subterranean mineral water to last the world for the next four centuries. Downtown Arlington was rather quaint and picturesque. The curbs were elevated two feet above the pavement, turn-of-the-century-style, with embedded iron rings where anyone who still preferred riding a horse could tie one. There wasn't a central square but a sort of open circle, arranged around a still-functioning mineral well, which was housed in what looked like the cottage where Hansel and Gretel were born.

All in all, I can see now, it was a good place for a kid to grow up. Nobody in Arlington ever locked a door, though that was generally true in any small town fifty years ago. Nobody got shot or knifed, at least in our part of town. Drugs were unknown. I didn't set eyes on marijuana until much later, when I was a police reporter for the *Fort*

Worth Star-Telegram. And I didn't smoke any until several years after that. As I recall, the Arlington city medical examiner, an old man with weak eyes, was addicted to an opium-based tonic used by women for menstrual cramps, but people were polite enough to pretend he was merely senile. Hypocrisy was considered an essential part of daily existence, maybe even a character trait. In retrospect, the tempo was therapeutic. People were permitted to set their own pace and stomp their own snakes. But experimentation and invention were regarded as offenses against nature.

I didn't realize how acutely boring Arlington was until I graduated from high school and went away to college in 1952. The sort of wild, fast life that my later friends who grew up in Dallas or Fort Worth would describe—consorting with black musicians and gangsters, dancing at joints like the Rocket Club on Fort Worth's Jacksboro Highway, reading Henry Miller—sounded almost surreal to a cub from Arlington. Rock and roll hadn't yet been invented: Hank Williams was as crazy as it got in my crowd. None of the kids I grew up with drank, and very few smoked. For all practical purposes, Arlington was dry. There were a couple of beer joints on the edge of town, but the nearest liquor store was five miles out the Fort Worth highway, a place they called Village Creek. One of the highlights of my life was riding out there with my dad—"going to the creek," he called it—every couple of weeks. Daddy would buy a bottle of Jim Beam and a couple of football cards to bet the college games, and the one-armed guy behind the counter would give me a handful of bubble gum. The creek wasn't exactly nirvana, but it was as close as I got.

If Arlingtonites wanted to have a really hot time, I learned later, they drove to the Bagdad Club in Grand Prairie or the Triangle Inn on the Fort Worth highway. Daddy knew a gambler at the Triangle Inn who had once shot a man. For years I pressed him for details, but all Daddy ever told me was, "Tommy has a history, son." That was more than I would ever have, I thought at the time.

Nobody in our family drank to excess, with the exception of my maternal grandfather, who I never knew except for the stories Momma and her sisters told about what a scumbag he was. On holidays Daddy and Uncle Gene would knock down a few, but I never saw them drunk. Daddy worked six and sometimes seven days a week at his job as a senior cost estimator at General Dynamics in Fort Worth: he was proud to be a "candy striper," as members of management (with their candy-striped security badges) were called. Daddy worked long and hard until the position eventually ground him up and then spit him out when he got too sick to work. Momma, who worked in a dress shop and was almost habitually cheerful, might have a couple of eggnogs at Christmas, at which time she and her sisters were likely to serenade the family with numerous verses of "Bye Bye, Blackbird." There was no television back then, so my acquaintance with fast times and high living came mostly from movies. Movies made me ache to get the hell out of Arlington.

Nearly everyone in my family enjoyed good health until my final year of high school, when my dad began to suffer from a series of afflictions, later diagnosed as Addison's disease, a failure of the adrenal glands for which there was no cure at the time. He lived another twenty years, dying by inches, gradually losing his strength and his zest for life. The disease progressed so slowly that it really didn't get my full attention until near the end, when he was forced into early retirement. This meant that after he died Momma would receive about half the pension she had counted on. The main reason I decided to become a journalist—other than the fact that all journalists are rich, famous, and uncommonly handsome—was to write about the way giant corporations treat people like my daddy. After Daddy died, my mom married a longtime family friend, Harold Nelson, who had just endured the death of his own wife. They bought a home in El Paso and then proceeded to travel the world, until Harold died a few years ago. Momma celebrated her eighty-eighth birthday on Valentine's Day 1997, with a couple of margaritas and an order of sea bass at her favorite restaurant in Juárez, Mexico. Momma may outlive God.

Going to college wasn't just exhilarating, it was revolutionary. I discovered a new world filled with infinite possibilities—music, books, art, politics, travel, cheap thrills. What a rush, never knowing what might happen next, what might change your life, who might appear in the booth beside you, drinking coffee all night and talking about the Spanish Civil War or (God help us) the Law and Supply and

Demand, calculating the odds that the evening would end with double orgasms under the ramp at Gate 42 of Memorial Stadium. By the end of my sophomore year I had read all of Hemingway, none of it for credit. This was an entirely new experience for me, reading not because it was required but because it was fun, learning that I didn't have to buy a ticket to spin away to exotic places. I carried a notebook in the back pocket of my jeans, pausing in stairwells to scribble notes or record random passages of poetry, or nursing a beer at Pete's on the Drag while composing descriptions of people and things I had encountered.

I learned to love hanging out at Pete's, a hole-in-the-wall bar across from the University of Texas campus on Guadalupe. The stubby little Greek who ran the joint never asked a chap for his driver's license or inquired why he wasn't back in his room studying for his biology exam. Pete made me believe in myself, acknowledged me as one of the grown-ups, though I doubt he knew my name. Hanging out, playing shuffleboard or watching Jersey Joe Walcott fight some bum on the tiny black-and-white TV above the bar, became a necessary part of existence, a mirror image of the straight life, the price one charged for paying the price. Belonging, I discovered, was the other half of Being. The Fraternal Order of Misfits had tapped me on the shoulder and invited me to be a brother in beer, in sex, and in outrageous opinion.

I never joined a real fraternity. For one thing, my family could barely afford to keep me in school, much less pay fraternity dues. I waited tables at my boardinghouse, and picked up and delivered dry cleaning. I like to think I was not the type to associate with fraternity riffraff, but I did permit myself to go through Rush Week and enjoyed what I remember of the experience. That's because these rich geeks from Houston treated me to an evening at the famous Chicken Ranch in La Grange, east of Austin. The Chicken Ranch was the model for Larry L. King's *Best Little Whorehouse in Texas,* and it was far better to have been there than to have seen the show on Broadway. I fell in love with a girl named Patsy from Highland Park on my first visit, and with someone else nearly every time I made the trip. No matter how much I spent, I always left the Chicken Ranch richer than I came. Throughout my college years in Austin, I continued to take advantage of this cultural phemomeon anytime I could save up five dollars and catch a ride. I tell people that college can be wonderfully educational if you don't let the curriculum get the best of you.

College was also the time I became integrated, or as integrated as one got in Texas in those days. Rhythm and blues was big in the early fifties, and so my after-hours hangouts were black hovels on the wrong side of the tracks. They barely opened before midnight, but at that point a fat, sweaty man named Preacher picked up his alto sax and began blowing the pants off "Lawdy, Lawdy, Lawdy, Miss Claudie!" and then the sparrow named Ellie Mae with the needle marks on her arm started chirping "Fine Brown Frame," and the rafters shook, and white folks and black folks and brown folks blended in blue smoke and went progressively crazy. I loved it. I'd never been a part of anything so exciting. Some of it was the sensual pleasure of sharing an experience with blacks, something I had never done before, a conceit no doubt because we truly weren't sharing anything except the dark corner of a dingy room. These after-hours adventures pierced centuries of bondage, my own if not theirs. But there was something else even more urgent and sensual and satisfying about the black jazz joints. The action was overtly sexual, an erotic promise far more intoxicating than the beer and wine they served in tin cups.

I don't remember having hangovers back then. I'd stumble back to my room a few hours before daylight, sleep the sleep of the very dead, wake with a jolt, and start my race across campus, juggling a cup of coffee and a bag of books, dressing along the way. Once fully awake, I had this unspeakably sublime feeling that I'd spent the evening captured by aliens, that I'd visited a deep blue planet in some undiscovered universe, a place so beautiful and wonderful and far away that words could never describe it. It made me want more. It made me believe that there *was* more, that if I would just let it happen life would take me to places and show me things no kid from Arlington ever saw before or ever would again.

College was interrupted for a couple of years when I got drafted into the Army. That's when I first started smoking, not because I particularly enjoyed it but because there's not much else to do in the

Army. Besides, you got free cigarettes with your C rations. I read many books in the Army and matured some, then I returned to civilian life in 1956 and finished college at Texas Christian University. Even before graduating I got my first newspaper job with the *Star-Telegram.* That's when I first met Bud Shrake and Dan Jenkins, two other journalism graduates of TCU who worked as Fort Worth newspapermen. We became lifelong friends.

All of us wanted to be writers, me and Bud and Dan. We talked about writing all the time, and basically wrote to amuse ourselves and each other. I don't know if I taught them anything, but they taught me that the first thing a writer has to do is live like a writer. Writers figure things out, not by logic but by living. Imagination can take a writer to great places, but only if he's already been there. For a couple of years, Bud and I worked the police beat for rival papers, I for the *Star-Telegram,* he for the *Press,* competing head-to-head but in a way that made sense to us. A writer must pace himself. We developed a system that allowed the two of us to drink beer at the Office Lounge across from the police station while an eager and bright copy boy named Steve Perringer monitored the police radio. If Steve heard a police call that he believed was sufficiently important—we taught him how to run a preliminary check—he trotted over to the Office Lounge and disturbed our afternoon writers' conference. And we took it from there.

In 1958, Blackie Sherrod, the legendary sports editor, left the *Press* and moved to the position of executive sports editor of the much larger *Dallas Times Herald,* taking Shrake with him. Dallas in those days was considered big-time, especially if you came from Fort Worth. When Sherrod departed, Jenkins was promoted to run the sports staff at the *Press,* and I was his first hire. I covered high school sports and wrote a column twice a week. Covering crime had been a good education in journalism, but covering sports was more fun and, from the standpoint of developing a writing style, more important for what I had in mind. The great thing about writing sports at the *Press* was that nobody expected a story to tell who won and who lost. I mean, things ain't that simple, right?

In 1960, Sherrod hired me to join his emerging staff at the *Dallas Times Herald.* It was my big break, and I was determined to make the best of it. A year later, he also hired Jenkins. There was one, brief shining moment in 1961 when the sports staff of the *Times Herald*—Sherrod, Shrake, Jenkins, and Cartwight—was the best ever assembled.

By then, I was running in high gear. Coffee, cigarettes, and antacids got me through the day. Whiskey and the intriguing possibility of sex got me through the night. If the AIDS virus had been around when I was young, I probably wouldn't be available to write this book. Basically, my habits at the time of my heart attack were the same ones that I had been developing since the late fifties and early sixties, my decade as a newspaperman.

Two

I thrived on stress back then. When you are young and fairly sure
you'll live forever, stress can be a powerful stumulant. In those days
a newspaperman in Texas with five years of experience made about
$120 a week. Low pay and high expectations required a stumulant
stronger than ambition. The pressure of deadlines and the Zeuslike
wrath of the formidable Sherrod kept me primed. I was full of confidence that the future would take care of itself—and determined to
live life to its fullest—but I knew that if I ever looked back or even
stopped to think about it, fear would eat me alive.

My first wife, Barbara, and I lived with our two preschool-age
children, Mark and Lea, in an apartment two blocks from the Southern Methodist University campus. The apartment cost more than a
third of our income, but Barbara was tough and had already learned
the basics of surviving as a writer's wife. Shrake and his first wife,
Joyce, and their two sons lived across the courtyard from us and
were our closest friends.

These were mainly happy, carefree times. Newspaper people
work weird hours, under weird circumstances, but I was making a
concerted effort to keep my life as normal as possible. Five mornings
a week I went to my office before six o'clock, worked until our second deadline at noon, had lunch with newspaper pals, covered sporting events in the evening when necessary, and spent what time I
could with my family. Shrake observed much the same routine. We
occasionally slipped away to carouse with colleagues, and we always kept an eye out for opportunity and adventure.

Most of the young families who lived in the apartment complex
had connections at SMU, and many, such as Joyce Shrake, taught at
what was sometimes called the Vanderbilt of Texas. In this intellectually charged atmosphere, games were played. Shrake and I invented a card game that we called Naked Bridge, the object being to
get everyone naked as quickly as possible. Since our wives refused
to participate, we usually played at the apartment of a neighbor.
Naked Bridge started with several rounds of drinks and usually
ended when either the host or hostess slapped the other and accused

him or her of making improper sexual advances to one of the undressed participants. It was good clean fun. But problems started
when neighbors who hadn't been invited began a whisper campaign
that Shrake and Cartwright were masterminding orgies. We denied
this, of course, and after a cooling-down period things returned more
or less to normal.

They might have stayed that way except one morning the wife of
a history professor discovered that a dozen pair of panties she had
left drying on the clothesline had been mutilated. "Oh, dear Lord!"
we heard her cry out. "Some pervert has eaten the crotch out of all
my panties!" On closer inspection, the crotches hadn't been eaten
but rather dissolved with some kind of acid. Shrake and I, being old
police reporters, launched our own investigation. But because of the
vicious orgy rumors with which we had once had to contend, suspi-
cion turned on us. When either of us would walk across the courtyard, children would run home screaming, doors would slam, and
blinds would snap shut. Even our wives weren't altogether convinced
of our innocence (and I'll have to say, in all honesty, that I began to
wonder about Shrake). The mystery was finally resolved when juve-
nile detectives informed us that they had made an arrest. The culprit
turned out to be a teenager in the next block who had some kind of
love-hate deal for his mother.

Newspaper mornings were trips to hell. I'm a chronic slugabed.
Most mornings I would hit the third-floor sports department at the
Times Herald fifteen or twenty minutes late, half dressed, coffee
spilling down my shirtfront, already in full panic. While Blackie
glared, I'd slam my alarm clock to the floor and trample it—Sherrod
loved a good show and would forgive almost any offense if the of-
fender could make him smile—then I would settle behind my typewriter and try to look scholarly. Inside, I was terrified: nothing holds
the promise of disaster so uniquely as a blank sheet of paper. For the
next ninety minutes I would struggle to pull words from the cobwebs
in my brain and stitch them into coherent sentences, knowing always
that the approaching deadline would be followed by another deadline and then another.

Shrake and I sat at adjoining desks, back-to-back when at our
typewriter tables. Every morning we addressed our typewriters like

two legionnaires ready to defend our posts against thundering hordes.
Morning after morning, knocking down eight or ten cups of coffee,
enveloped in the purple haze from unfiltered Chesterfields, glancing
occasionally at the clock and at each other, feeling the strain of
deadline and wondering if this was the morning we'd blow it. One
cold, rainy December a few minutes before deadline, I leaned over
and pulled the sheet of paper from Shrake's typewriter. He had written just one forlorn phrase. It was "Ah, youth!" And that was one line
more than I had written.

Ah youth! A quarter of a century later I still think of that line and
laugh. The youthful presumption of invincibility afflicted almost all
of my newspaper pals in the sixties. It was the decade in which the
placid agenda of the fifties—sock hops, Geritol, and Patti Page—
was replaced by sex, drugs, and rock 'n' roll, at least among young
America. It was the decade when I left Arlington behind once and for
all. As a lifestyle, it had come upon me as suddenly as light follows
darkness.

Nearly everyone I knew had been divorced at least once. Everyone screwed around. Everyone drank to excess. Everyone smoked.
No one exercised or made the slightest attempt to eat a balanced diet.
I don't think cholesterol was even a word. Everyone was insufferably
self-righteous. Civil rights had finally become a movement rather
than an abstraction, and marching in the name of Dr. Martin Luther
King absolved old guilts and promoted feelings that we had sepa-
rated ourselves from the bigotry and the dreary materialism that in-
fected our parents. Every generation feels that it has been liberated,
and our liberation was different only to the degree that we celebrated
it almost to death.

Journalists have always believed that they had a license to indulge. Part of the job. And it was true that sportswriters could hardly
avoid offers of free booze. Nearly every luncheon, press conference,
or sporting event featured an open bar. Professional teams had hos-
pitality suites. Some PR guy was always around to pick up the check.
One did not have to imbibe, but one was encouraged to—and one
risked the scorn of peers if one declined. You drank and you smoked
for the same reason you wore a trench coat and sneered: because

Bogart did. You played hard-boiled reporter as much as you practiced it.

Nobody thought tobacco was harmful, either, much less addictive. Sexually transmitted diseases seemed like something left over from World War I. Amphetamines? Doctors gave them out to people who needed to lose weight or who complained of fatigue. Sports teams handed them out like candy. Just outside the Dallas Cowboys training room, at the entrance to the practice field, hung three five-gallon tins, open to all who happened by. One contained salt tablets, a second lemon-flavored vitamin C, and the third five-milligram Dexedrine. I never passed the can without taking a couple of the heart-shaped orange tablets. Speed made me smart and funny, or so it seemed at the time. It made me feel like one of those perpetual-motion gadgets you see in novelty shops, moving effortlessly as long as its batteries last. Though I was going nowhere at double time, from where I stood it seemed like another great journey into the unknown. Journalists love the illusion that they are above it all. Sure we're ankle-deep in blood, but it's always someone else's blood. Some unknown stiff, age approximated, meaningless address recorded, and brief, unfortunate history imprinted in six-point New Roman type, in time for the first press run.

The late Dick Hitt, one of my pals from Dallas newspaper times, expressed this sentiment exactly when he wrote in his *Times Herald* column a few days after my heart surgery: "Ever since his antic and eloquent days as a *Times Herald* sports columnist, there's been a law on the cosmic books granting immunity and perpetual function to taxes, Volvos and Gary Cartwright. The idea of his being under arrest is not an unprecedented concept among Cartwright buffs, but *cardiac* arrest? How could anything so dreary, calamitous and pompous-sounding as myocardial infarction happen to this droll daredevil, our literary loose cannon who viewed the world from strange and wondrous angles . . . ?"

I traveled with a rowdy, thirsty, irreverent, and very talented crowd of writers back in the sixties. Hitt, Shrake, Sherrod, Jenkins, and I met nearly every day for lunch at Nick's bar near the courthouse or Shanghai Jimmy's, a hovel a few blocks from the newspaper. Shanghai Jimmy served a single dish—chili rice, dispensed in cardboard containers, with lots of onions and extra cayenne pepper for those who felt particularly adventurous. We sometimes drank together in the evenings, plotting revenge on various editors and publishers—funny, when we were together that way, we never thought of Sherrod as an editor or boss—supporting each other's aspirations, closing the bars with original songs composed on the spot, and finishing sometime after midnight at an all-night joint on Cedar Springs, with orders of chili cheeseburgers with extra onions and siders of pecan waffles. The price of excess—and you could count on this—was heartburn and hangover. You dealt with it, that's all. You mocked it. Jenkins once observed that his hangover "won't take yes for an answer." And yet to a man we held the deep conviction that anything worth doing was worth overdoing.

Between rounds, we amused each other by reciting the first line of novels we intended to write, or forming lists of answers to the great questions of Western Civilization. Jenkins, who would later write such best-sellers as *Semi-Tough* and *Baja Oklahoma,* was the first to theorize the Ten Stages of Drunkenness—charming, invisible, outrageous, bulletproof, and so on. Science has been building on that theory ever since.

After our first marriages broke up, Shrake and I shared an apartment on Cole Avenue, not far from downtown Dallas. This was in 1963, shortly before the assassination of President John Kennedy. Our refrigerator was full of beer and half-eaten yellow or green lunch-meat sandwiches. Our apartment became a hangout for entertainers, gangsters, and other creatures of the night. Jack Ruby and some strippers, musicians, and comedians from his Carousel Club were frequent guests. I thought back to my days in Arlington and dearly wished they could see me now.

That was the year that Shrake had an affair with Jada, the Carousel's star stripper, whose specialty was hunching a stuffed Bengal tiger while screaming orgasmic auras almost too high for the human ear to detect. Jada was the most interesting and exotic woman I ever met. She traveled with an entourage of mysterious people who always seemed to have just returned from Ankara or Beirut. When I married for the second time—to an airline stewardess named Mary

Jo—Jada gave us a two-pound cookie tin filled with manicured marijuana as a wedding present.

After the assassination, Jada split from Dallas and we didn't see her again for a few years. In the early seventies, Shrake and I ran into her in San Francisco, where she was the boss of a gang of bank robbers. The driver of the gang's getaway car was Chet Baker, one of the great jazz musicians of the fifties, by that time a shriveled-up junkie. That's how life was back then—totally unreal. Jada was killed in a mysterious car crash in Louisiana a few years later, an event that continues to interest those who see the JFK assassination as a grand and endless conspiracy.

I learned one great lesson during those newspaper years in Fort Worth and Dallas. If you love living, you must be prepared not to take life too seriously. My hero and role model was the actor Robert Mitchum, the first of his Hollywood crowd to be busted for marijuana possession. When they asked him later how he found his stay in prison, Mitchum said deadpan: "Just like Hollywood, but without the riffraff." Mitchum reportedly showed up at a Hollywood costume party dressed as a hamburger—his naked body slathered with ketchup and contained between two buns. On several occasions, I did an imitation of Mitchum's act, though I didn't always wait for a costume party or bother with buns. Old-timers still speak with great reverence about the time I stripped naked at Sherrod's Christmas party and did a spirited lap in the pool.

My friends and I survived the rigors of daily journalism by making fun of the everything, including our profession, always mindful that our greater mission was to expose hypocrisy and deflate pomposity. More than once, Shrake, Jenkins, Hitt, and I composed works of fiction and slipped them into the paper as fact. (As part of management, Sherrod conveniently looked the other way during our hijinks.) Among other notable contributions, we invented a town called Corbett, in some unspecified part of Texas, and gave it a cast of characters who periodically appeared without additional explanation in the news columns of the *Times Herald.*

In 1962, the Corbett Comets went to the state finals in high school football. The exploits of the twin halfbacks Dickie Don and Rickie Ron Yewbet were the stuff of legend. The Comets won every game, 3–0, on a last-second field goal by Dickie Don. Tragically, Dickie Don died of mumps on the eve of the championship game. Rickie Ron, however, picked up the fallen banner and scored eight touchdowns as Corbett prevailed over the fictional East Dozier for the state title. Something was always cooking in Corbett. Parodying the provincial boast, frequently heard in Texas, that the University of Texas band owned the world's largest bass drum, we informed readers that E. O. (Shug) Kempleman, the local Ford dealer, had generously donated the world's largest bass tuba to the Fighting Comet Band. The following spring, Kempleman lost the race for mayor of Corbett to his archrival, F. D. Orr.

Ultimately, our fun and games were frustrated by the fact that nobody ever caught on. What's the fun of being irreverent if the reverent fail to take offense? You want to know how we got caught? Hitt made an anonymous phone call to the managing editor, Hal Lewis. The next day, an unamused Lewis posted a very stern, no-nonsense memo on the newsroom bulletin board, threatening to deal harshly with future lapses of journalistic ethics such as the Corbett invention. The memo was overly long and sloppily written, so Hitt took it down that night and edited it.

Three

By 1968 I had had enough of the daily grind. It had been great fun, and an education that money can't buy, but it was time to move on. By then Shrake and Jenkins had moved to New York to work for *Sports Illustrated.* Shrake had already published his first novel and was about to publish a second. After one final three-month fling as a sports columnist for the *Philadelphia Inquirer,* I packed everything I owned into a U-Haul trailer and headed for Austin, Texas, to pursue a new career writing books, screenplays, and magazine articles.

I knew by then that I could make a living writing. The pressure cooker of a newsroom can fry the brain if you let it, but learning to concentrate amid the clatter and chaos was very good practice for the future despair and indecision that echo in the hollows of a writer's brain. Even today, I find it difficult to write without some distraction or reminder that time marches on.

When I moved to Austin in 1968, the city was already evolving into the pop-culture capital of Texas, and the easiest place to score an unbelievable variety of drugs. Billie Lee Brammer, who had published *The Gay Place* in 1961 and was quickly becoming a legend, lived with his second wife, Dorothy Browne, in the tumbledown Caswell mansion on West Avenue at 15th Street. In the 1890s the Daniel Caswell family had been among the wealthiest and most prominent of Austin, and eventually the Women's League of Austin would restore Caswell House to its original grandeur. But in the sixties when Bill Brammer occupied it, the run-down mansion was to Austin what Gertrude Stein's salon at 27 Rue de Fleurus was to Paris in the twenties. It was a way station for intellectuals, artists, musicians, writers, and politicians and other power-trippers. If anything, the conversation at Brammer's was wittier than it was at Gertrude's, while pot, speed, mescaline, acid, and peyote were served rather than *eau-de-vie.*

Shrake had also moved to Austin by then, having convinced his boss at *Sports Illustrated* that it's as easy to commute between Manhattan and Austin as it is between Manhattan and Connecticut. Austin's original writers' colony consisted of Shrake, Brammer, and

myself. As far as I know, there were no other working writers in
Austin (and very few in Texas) in the late sixties. One does not count
the academicians at the university who authored books with titles
along the lines of *A Definitive History of the Cotton Exchange: Are
Boll Weevils Really the Antichrist?* Today dozens of talented and successful writers live and work in Austin. It's also the home of *Texas
Monthly* and a burgeoning film industry. Jerry Jeff Walker and Willie
Nelson moved here in the late sixties, and were quickly followed by
caravans of musicians. Austin must have more musicians and writers per capita than any other city its size in the world.

Austin was the prettiest and most interesting city in Texas in
1968 and it's the prettiest and most interesting city today. There are
rolling hills, spring-fed rivers and creeks, and a laid-back attitude
that seems immune to change. Power and privilege coexist with privacy and the right to be yourself. The physical dimensions of the city
have changed, of course, changed dramatically: with the arrival of
the computer and high-tech industries, the town has expanded like
a balloon. Meadows have been paved over, hills invaded by roads
and highways, vast areas of virgin timber leveled for home con-
struction. But the central part of Austin where I live has changed
only for the better.

Our neighborhood seems like a small town of grassroots activists
and people who dabble in the arts. The University of Texas campus
and the state capitol are a few blocks east of my house, daily re-
minders of the history and institutional eccentricities of this state. By
day the streets pulse with the schemes of ambition and the hedonistic strivings of the insatiable. At night and on weekends the seren-
ity of well-deserved rest prevails. Wafting through the giant oaks,
pecans, and elms that shade quiet, out-of-the-way streets and stately
nineteenth-century homes one can hear, depending on the day of
the week, Mozart, Bach, Miles, and Coltrane or local bagpipers and
drummers who gather every Friday at the neighborhood pub, the
beloved Dog & Duck.

People in our neighborhood like to walk or bike. There are a series of small parks that converge into a hike-and-bike trail a few
blocks to the west, along the sheltered banks of Shoal Creek. Each
spring for the last thirty-four years, musicians, face painters, jug-

glers, belly dancers, and a donkey named Eeyore flock to the largest
of the parks to celebrate the donkey's birthday. It's a quintessential
Austin event. The hike-and-bike trail runs from the Colorado River
(1st Street) to 51st Street, but the section near our house is one of the
few places in town where dogs can run free without a leash. Two or
three days a week, a couple of hours before sunset, you'll find me and
my Airedales exploring the trail and communing with nature.

There is a ten-year period of my life, from roughly the early seventies to the early eighties, when my Austin memories come in
streaks and blurs. I'm told that others who lived here at the time have
the same problem. I can vaguely recall my second marriage breaking up, because I associate it with the days just before my fortieth
birthday. I remember sitting on the steps of my apartment drinking
beer with Shrake and Jerry Jeff Walker when Mary Jo came down the
stairs carrying all of my earthly possessions bundled in her arms. She
dropped them at my feet and walked away without a word. I remember thinking: Damn, is that pitiful little pile everything that I own?

And I remember the birthday itself because I was in Mexico
City with my two sons, Mark and Shea. Shea was only about five and
was still living with me in Austin, but Mark was seventeen and lived
in Atlanta with my first wife, Barbara, and my daughter, Lea. Mark
and I had always been especially tight, but because of the distances
I saw Mark and Lea only two or three times a year. That was a great
week, the week of August 10, 1974, one of my best. Everywhere I
looked, God had a message and it was always positive and pointing
in my direction. My direction was onward and upward. Turning forty
and on top of the world! Nixon resigned the presidency the day we
arrived in Mexico City from the Pacific Coast town of Mazatlán. With
my two boys at my side, we celebrated with a long dinner on the roof
of the Majestic Hotel, across from the central plaza and the National
Palace. Shea was too young to understand my joy in Nixon's misfor-
tune, but Mark said, "This must have been the way the slaves felt
when Lincoln signed the Emancipation Proclamation." The day after
Gerald Ford was sworn in, I took the boys to the Pyramid of the
Sun. On the way, Mark showed me the day's headline: "Ford Wakes
Early, Makes Own Breakfast." Yeah, it was going to be a good day
all around. The three of us climbed to the top of that magnificent

pyramid and sat there for at least an hour, making up stories that
suited us, looking over the ancient Valley of Mexico, feeling happy,
proud, and right.

A couple of weeks later, I moved to New York to wait out the di-
vorce. The following summer, the summer of '75, I returned to
Austin. I met Phyllis that summer—at the Willie Nelson Fourth of
July Picnic, of course. Meeting Phyllis saved my life, though even
this fortuitous turn of events took almost more time than I had left.

The fuzzy period in my memory coincides, not coincidentally,
with the founding of Mad Dog, Inc. Shrake and I formed this shad-
owy organization for no particular purpose except that the Vietnam
War was going on and it seemed like a good idea. We prided ourselves on living on the edge: some would say that we lived delu-
sionally, but from our perspective reality covered more than a single
dimension. Mad Dog reflected that perspective. We had stationery
and cards printed up defining our motto: "Doing Indefinable Services
to Mankind." Our credo was "Everything that is not a mystery is
guesswork." For several years, we tapped deserving people and inducted them into the Universal Order of the Mad Dog. The initiation
ceremony consisted of passing around a bottle of tequila, after which
the new member was given a Mad Dog card, two pesos, and a kiss on
the cheek. Charter members included David Richards, a prominent
Austin labor lawyer, and his live-wire wife, Ann, a future governor
of Texas. Former Cowboy football player Pete Gent and his wife,
Jodi, were other original Mad Dogs and part of the Mad Dog Talking
Troupe that appeared without warning at concerts and on the sets of
movies. It is difficult today to describe just what Mad Dog was all
about—to think of Mad as having a *purpose* is to comprehend the
perfect oxymoron—but you might think of it as a metaphor of its
time.

One early project was our attempt to buy a town, which we
would rename the Free State of Mad Dog. Richards, our legal ad-
viser, actually made an offer to purchase Shafter in far-west Texas.
An old quicksilver-mining town, Shafter had a railroad track that
connected with the track in Presidio, which in turn was part of the
Chihuahua–to–Los Mochis railroad that crossed the spectacular
Copper Canyon—Mexico's version of the Grand Canyon—on its

way from the desert of Texas to the Pacific. We felt that owning a
town with a railroad would be neat. We had even looked into the fea-
sibility of purchasing an old Pullman and converting it into a private
car. Though our cash offer fell far short, Shafter got on the map anyway as the location for the movie *The Andromeda Strain,* and it
played a role in Mad Dog's future development. After our failed attempt to purchase the town, several of us wrote under the name M.
D. Shafter in the seventies.

The nights and days of Mad Dog were punctured with wrenched
excess disguising itself as art, and vice versa. Shrake and I occasionally pretended to be an Italian acrobatic act called Le Flying
Punzars. Wearing scarlet-and-yellow capes and green tunics with a
backward winged letter P in the center, we spoke broken English and
told stories of how we had represented our country at the 1952
Olympics, only to be disqualified when we failed the gender test. Our
dream was to do the impossible—the death-defying Triple Somer-
sault, without a net, of course. You may recall that the Triple was also
Burt Lancaster's goal in the movie *Trapeze* with Tony Curtis and Gina
Lollobrigida. Phyllis would sometimes put on a skimpy outfit and do
Lollobrigida's part. To this day Phyllis can still break me up by saying in her Lollobrigida accent: "I was always very strong in the
leeeeeegs."

Once or twice the Punzars performed in public. One memorable
evening we were at the Riviera Club in downtown Dallas with Lamar
Hunt, who once owned the Dallas Texans in the American Football
League, which later became the Kansas City Chiefs of the NFL. On
this particular night Shrake and I were both wearing red Texan blaz-
ers, and we began to drop hints to our waitress and to people at
nearby tables that we were some sort of international athletes, tour-
ing the country. *"Non parlo zee En-GLA-sa . . . how you say? . . .
molto buon!"* I told an attractive woman in a lavender off-the-
shoulder gown. As the evening progressed and our Italian accents
became more pronounced—and the drugs began to cut in full throt-
tle—we started to believe we really were the Punzars. Bob Halford,
who was the public relations director of the Texans and a good friend,
played along. During an intermission in the floor show, Halford asked
the master of ceremonies to introduce the world-famous Punzars and

announce that, for the first time ever, we would attempt the death-defying triple—without a net!

A spotlight was trained on center stage. Drums began to roll. The audience was hushed in anticipation or at least confusion. The woman in the lavender gown seemed to tremble as we took our positions, Shrake as the catcher, me as the flier. We had no idea what we were about to do, absolutely none. Shrake, who at six-feet-six is at least eight inches taller than me, crouched slightly to reduce the differences in our sizes, then clasped his fingers, making a foothold for me. I came running at him full speed, leaping at the last second and attempting to engage my right foot in his clasped hands. Instead, my foot landed squarely against his chest, sending Shrake tumbling backward into the drummer. I fell across both of them, knocking over a set of cymbals, which crashed into more cymbals, creating a racket that sounded like the bombing of Dresden.

As was our custom, we sprang to our feet and began to bow profusely and blow kisses to the audience, which sat stunned in an icy silence. You'll just have to take it on faith that it was funny at the time.

Shrake and I first met Dave and Ann Richards in the early sixties in Dallas. Long before she stopped drinking and decided to run for elective office, Ann was a political activist and a famous force of nature among our state's small, gritty band of liberal Democrats. Ann and her friend Betty McKool, wife of state senator Mike McKool, were renowned hostesses who delighted their friends and shocked everyone else with their salty language and iconoclastic humor. Their yearly Christmas cards became collector's items. One card had Ann and Betty dressed as Mary and Joseph looking down at the manger with startled expressions. The caption read: "It's a girl!"

After the Richardses moved to Austin in the early seventies, their hilltop home in Westlake became a sort of Mad Dog sanctuary and the scene of some of our city's most memorable parties. Ann launched one priceless gathering in honor of *New York Times* editor Abe Rosenthal. Shrake met the esteemed editor at the door, dressed as a giant Tampax. Rosenthal, I assure you, has not forgotten that evening. On occasion, Bud and I would put on our Punzar capes and Ann would dress as Dolly Parton—a gigantic blond wig, tight red dress, rolls of cotton stuffed in her bra—and we'd head out to Armadillo World Headquarters for an evening of Austin culture.

Ann took her first oath of office as Travis County Commissioner at the Raw Deal, a downtown greasy spoon run by Eddie Wilson, the Mad Dog who started Armadillo. The attitude at this café–beer joint foreshadowed Austin's eccentric 6th Street entertainment district and was spelled out in a sign over the entrance: "Remember, you came looking for the Raw Deal, the Raw Deal didn't come looking for you!" When Ann started moving up the political ladder toward the Governor's Mansion, Mad Dog discreetly faded from public view.

Another of our Hall of Famers was Marvin Schwarz, a well-known Hollywood producer who fell in with Mad Dog around 1970 while producing a screenplay of Shrake's then titled *Dime Box.* Within a year of casting his lot with Mad Dog, Schwarz had: (1) been banned from the lot of 20th Century–Fox by a studio executive; (2) sold his home in Benedict Canyon and caught the first plane out of town; (3) hitchhiked across Africa; (4) entered a Buddhist monastery, where he spent four years. Later he called himself Brother Jonathan and operated a Buddhist retreat in Boulder Creek, California. I've never been entirely clear if Marvin's *Razor's Edge*–type reaction was a burnout or an epiphany, accountable to his disgust with the shallowness and egoism of the film industry or to his enlightenment by Mad Dog.

Schwarz was never your typical Hollywood dealmaker, but he had a reputation for making intelligent movies and bringing them in on time and on budget. A slender man with graying Buffalo Bill hair, a droopy mustache, and flinty mother-of-pearl eyes, Marvin had an eye for the outrageous. He loved Bud's screenplay about a turn-of-the-century Texas outlaw who moves to the town of Dime Box, Texas, and tries to go straight only to realize that straight is more crooked than his previous occupation. Marvin decided to shoot the film in Durango, Mexico, where he had filmed an earlier success, *The War Wagon,* with John Wayne and Kirk Douglas. Dennis Hopper was signed to play the lead. Dennis was still riding the crest of *Easy Rider;* his subsequent bomb, *The Last Movie,* hadn't yet been released. An all-star supporting cast was assembled, including Peter

Boyle, Warren Oates, Janice Rule, and Ben Johnson. Perhaps the volatile combination of Mexico, Hopper, and Mad Dog foredoomed the production.

The Mad Dog Talking Troupe arrived in Durango several days before production began, in a van driven by Shrake and a Winnebago driven by Peter Gent. On the sides of each vehicle were signs proclaiming "Mad Dog Production Company." Since Marvin had already been inducted into Mad Dog—and since Shrake and I were working on a new screenplay for Schwarz—he authorized the production company to rent us two houses and gave Mad Dog free run of the production office and set. After a while, people got the impression that Mad Dog, not 20th Century–Fox, was the real producer of this film. In short order Mad Dog had presented cards, pesos, and the ceremonial slugs of tequila to Hopper, Boyle, Oates, Howard Hesseman, Ralph Waite, Warren Finnerty, and one or two other members of the cast. Each accepted the honor with gratitude and humility. Peter Boyle was so moved by the gesture that he ruined the next take by flashing his Mad Dog card to the camera.

The juxtaposition of Hopper and Mad Dog at the same site—the actual location or "street" of Dime Box was the village of Chupaderas, an Indian name for the witches who suck blood and brains from deformed and disabled children—brought all sort of strange creatures to town. Among them was Arthur, a crazed chemist from New York, who arrived with a bag of goodies that included a homemade batch of vanilla-flavored LSD. More than two dozen hallucinogenic plants grow wild in the states of Chihuahua and Torreón, and most of them appeared at one time or another in the Mad Dog Winnebago. Warren Oates puréed a bag of magic mushrooms and served them on crackers. Someone else ordered two tanks of nitrous oxide from Mexico City. The production took place during the chill of winter, and the Winnebago became a sort of lounge where actors and chosen hangers-on could warm their hands and get their heads right between takes.

On several occasions, in the interval between the final rehearsal of a scene and the actual filming, Dennis and the Mad Dogs would restage the action—without telling the director or cameraman. "On, man, that's so far out!" Dennis would cackle when we would suggest improvization. "This is straight out of Cocteau, working with the accident." The longer we were in Durango, the crazier it got—until there was virtually no separation between the movie that Schwarz was producing and the one we were living.

To help him get in character, Dennis carried a loaded .38 in his boot. Several others on the set also carried pistols, including a stuntman named Pee Wee whose specialty was the fast draw. Very late one night after many rounds of tequila, Pee Wee and Peter Gent squared off in a fast-draw contest. Peter's gun wasn't loaded, but we found out later that Pee Wee's was. As the days and weeks passed and reality blurred, the chance of someone getting his head blown off increased exponentially. Bobby Hall, an old character actor, smashed a beer bottle against the bar one night at a party at Marvin's house and went after another actor with the jagged end. No doubt Hall had smashed bottles in a dozen barroom fights on camera, but this time the glass was real and he cut off his right thumb.

All of us played extras or small roles in the movie, but on the day that I was to play a congressman's aide in a big production scene we decided to film our own movie-within-the-movie. Warren Oates didn't have to work that day, so he brought his Super 8 camera to the Winnebago. Shrake and Gent also had Super 8s. I joined them fresh from wardrobe, in congressman's-aide costume: spats, derby, vest, and heavy coat. To get ourselves in the proper mood, we crushed up some Dexedrine, flambéed it in brandy, and took it with spoons of vanilla acid.

The first part of our shoot couldn't have gone better. With three cameras, a real Hollywood street, dozens of actors, and hundreds of extras at our disposal, we began to improvise. The real camera crew was at the other end of the street, lighting their own scene. I plucked a carrot from a basket on the set to use as a prop. Between takes of the real movie, I would pull back my coat and flash the carrot for our cameras, making it look like an act of pure depravity. After a while everyone wanted a part in our picture, which was taking on a life of its own: it became known as *The Congressman's Carrot*. Actress Lee Purcell fondled the carrot lecherously. José Torvay, the great

Mexican actor, sniffed it. Hopper dropped it down the front of his overalls and pulled it from his boot. Ben Johnson slapped leather with the carrot in his holster. Then by midmorning the acid started to cut in.

In the real movie, my role was to stand in front of Ben Johnson, Clifton James, and several others while someone made a speech, then walk through the crowd passing out campaign leaflets. This was part of a much longer scene and therefore required that everyone keep his place so that the numerous setups would match: it would take the full day to wrap the entire scene. But as the acid took hold, I forgot for long stretches that this was a movie set and that certain rules of conduct were expected. Once I started walking away just as the camera was ready, only to be guided gently back to my place by our newest Mad Dog member, actor Howard Hesseman, who was helping direct the second unit. "Are you okay?" he asked. I babbled something about needing to catch a train for Cleveland. Howard looked at me, then at Shrake and Gent, who were filming each other from the underside of a wagon, understanding, perhaps for the first time, the true and mean depths of Mad Dog.

By lunch all of us were full-bore crazy. My three cameramen had lost their equipment and I had lost most of my congressman's-aide outfit, dropping it item by item along the street. We climbed a hill to another part of the set known as Preacher Bob's Cabin and drank a few beers, losing track of time and purpose. Things didn't get really tense until *after* the lunch break. While half a dozen actors, hundreds of extras, and one of the most expensive camera crews in the world waited on the set to resume filming, a very tiny but key part of the scene was missing—me! I was hopelessly lost in Preacher Bob's Cabin, reeling under the effects of LSD, sweating like a pig, and under the impression that I was Charles Dickens and this was London during a siege of the black plague.

The director and crew were about to panic. A scene that had already cost the production company hundreds of thousands of dollars was about to go up in smoke because one stinking extra had vanished in the middle of the day. Fortunately, Howard Hesseman had the presence of mind to grasp the situation. Howard, who had been a member of San Francisco's great improv group The Committee, spotted the discarded items of clothing worn by the congressman's aide and guessed what had happened. He carefully gathered the costume, then borrowed Marvin Schwarz's yellow VW and drove to the top of the hill.

"It's time," he said, pulling me from the cabin.

"Yes," I agreed. "It is time." I had no idea what Howard meant, but I didn't resist as he helped me dress and delivered me in a heap back to the middle of the set.

As Howard guided me to my position in front of Ben Johnson and the waiting cast of hundreds, I gave him a puzzled look and asked, "Is somebody having a party?"

"Something like that," he told me, adjusting my derby. "Just stand right there."

"I'll see that he does," Ben Johnson volunteered, placing a gentle but firm hand on my shoulder. Now Ben Johnson did not drink, use profanity, or subscribe to any of the insane and totally hedonistic principles of Mad Dog, but he was a compassionate and good man. He also had a very strong grip, and this helped me get through the longest day of my life.

The Congressman's Carrot, as it turned out, was no more successful than the real movie, though in both cases the producer was on the side of the angels.

As he had so many times before, Marvin Schwarz overcame Hooper, Mad Dog, and a lot worse. After three crazed months in Durango, he delivered the film on time and on budget to 20th Century–Fox. There are various stories about why Schwarz and Fox parted company. Schwarz said it was because the studio in its stupidity changed the name of the film from *Dime Box* to *Kid Blue* and arbitrarily substituted its own cut for Marvin's cut, which was far superior.

In an interview a couple of years ago with *Variety*, Schwarz reviewed his long-dormant Hollywood career and said: "For what reason does someone make a film? Ego is number one, followed by money and fame. I had those things and it wasn't enough." In the twenty-five years after he left L.A. and the movie industry, Marvin was offered many chances to produce new movies, but he turned all of them down. "I don't want to sound smug, but after all I've done and seen, it would be meaningless," he said in the *Variety* interview. "The whole point of Buddhism is getting rid of the 'I' and transcending the ego. There are too many egos there."

One of the strangest things about those Mad Dog days in Durango is that all of us who survived them have remained friends. After the filming, I began a six-month Texas Institute of Letters fellowship on the J. Frank Dobie Ranch west of Austin. Peter Boyle, Howard Hesseman, and Marvin joined me there for extended visits. Pete and Jodi Gent stayed at the ranch nearly as long as I did. Gent started his book *North Dallas 40* at our apartment in Durango and finished it at the Dobie Ranch.

All the original Mad Dogs did well, though not necessarily in the areas planned. Howard went on to star as the drug-inspired disk jockey Johnny Fever in the highly successful television series *WKRP Cincinnati*. When the series went into syndication, he got a check for $30 million and bought an apartment in Paris. Peter Boyle played dozens of great roles in subsequent movies—including *Young Frankenstein* and my all-time favorite, *The Friends of Eddie Coyle*— and bought an apartment on New York's Upper East Side. The screenplay that Shrake and I began writing in Durango was finally produced twenty years later as a made-for-TV movie by CBS. We had called it *Rip* and written it with the notion that Ben Johnson and Warren Oates would play the two lead roles. CBS changed the title to *Pair of Aces* and cast Kris Kristofferson and Willie Nelson. A year later the network filmed a sequel, titled *Another Pair of Aces*. Marvin Schwarz, of course, became Brother Jonathan, a man who found God not at Central Casting but in the mountains of Nepal, and who gave up glamour for serenity and never looked back. He and Bud remained best friends, corresponding and talking on the phone regularly.

Dennis Hopper's career was almost wrecked during the craziness that swallowed Durango. He continued to work, but mostly in small roles that required little attention to detail. When he came through Austin about ten years ago, Dennis was half off the wall, popping pills, drinking tequila, and falling over his own feet. Phyllis and I took him with us to a Jerry Jeff Walker concert, where he got on the stage and babbled nonsense—to a standing ovation, I might add.

When we next heard of him—in a newspaper account maybe a week later—Hopper had been discovered wandering aimlessly through the Chihuahuan desert, naked and incoherent. That's when he went away to Whiskey Tech to take the cure. After that, his career soared to heights none of us had ever imagined.

In the eleven years since he sobered up, Dennis has acted in forty-eight movies and directed six others. "He also considers himself a Republican," Ann said in dismay after having lunch with Hopper in October 1997, at the Heart of Austin Film Festival.

When Dennis comes to town now, it's to play golf with Bud and Willie. At lunch a few years ago at the Raw Deal, we shared tumblers of iced tea and I joked that the drugs we took these days were for hypertension and diabetes. Dennis admitted: "I wasted twenty years of my life drinking and doing drugs. That's twenty years of work I'll never do." Shrake, who hasn't had a drink in more than ten years now, told us: "I wake up at three in the morning revisiting those places and remembering our drunken adventures. Only now they don't seem funny."

I confessed the decade-long deadspot that blighted my memory. "I'm sure I must have been around in the seventies and eighties," I told them, "because I see my name on books, screenplays, and magazine articles. But it's as though someone mailed them to me in a box with no return address."

I didn't have the heart to tell them the rest of it. It's what I don't see that fills me with regret: all the work that was never attempted because my body and brain were pickled in the pursuit of . . . that's the real rub; I can't remember what I was pursuing.

Four

$\mathcal{M}$y first warning that the attrition of the fast life would inevitably take its toll was in 1977 when Billie Lee Brammer died at age forty-eight, from an overdose of several unspecified drugs. Brammer's *Gay Place* had been labeled a classic by Gore Vidal, but Billie Lee never wrote another book or much of anything else.

About a year after Brammer died, I had a brief scare—too brief, as it developed, and not scary enough to make me seriously alter my lifestyle. A routine physical revealed that my blood pressure was a remarkable 235/180. The nurse who recorded this reading ran down the hallway shouting for her colleagues to "come look at this!" Must have been some kind of record.

An hour later I was in the hospital, being pumped full of stuff to bring my blood pressure down to acceptable numbers. My doctor told me to try and recall if I'd taken any drugs the previous day. I'll never forget the look of amazement in his eyes as I began to itemize them. "Let's see, I had a few drinks, maybe ten double scotches, maybe more. And some beer. And some wine. And some tequila. Then . . . oh, right . . . I remember now, we smoked some pot, a lot of pot. Then . . . oh, yeah, about two in the morning somebody passed out some speed." When he was signing my release three days later, the doctor gave me a sharp look, waggled his finger, and warned: "Remember now, no more speed!"

Right, doc! I took the warning literally: to this day I haven't used speed again. But since the doctor had not said specifically that I was to avoid whiskey, pot, cigarettes, or other specific stimulants, I permitted myself to believe that anything except speed was acceptable.

Until then, I'd never worried much about blood pressure. I wasn't even sure how to explain it, though I found out in the days that followed. In the normal course of things, your heart pumps blood through your arteries and to all parts of your body. Arteries are muscular and elastic—or they should be if you are healthy—and they stretch according to how much force the rushing blood exerts. Normally, your heart beats sixty to eighty times a minute, causing your blood pressure to increase on the beat and decrease when the heart relaxes. The increase is called the systolic pressure, and the lower reading when the heart is relaxed is the diastolic pressure. When a doctor or nurse records your bp—say it is a normal reading of 120/80 (120 over 80)—the upper number is the systolic and the lower number the diastolic. The harder it is for blood to flow through your veins, the higher the numbers and the more strain on your heart.

Nobody really knows what causes hypertension, but researchers have discovered some specific factors that increase the chances that a person will develop it. They include heredity, race, sex, age, obesity, and sensitivity to sodium (salt). Drinking too much, using oral contraceptives, and being physically inactive also contribute to the disease.

The experience did cause me to watch my blood pressure. I was careful to take medication to keep it under control, and I increased my daily activity and made some changes in my diet, particularly my intake of salt. I had craved salt all my life, but I started using Lite Salt, which is half sodium and half potassium, or sometimes NoSalt, which is exclusively potassium. Over time, salt substitute tasted almost the same as salt. I even carried it with me when I ate out, in a small plastic vial normally used to carry cocaine. At a restaurant in Taos, New Mexico, one night, I took the vial from my pocket and, without thinking, sprinkled a liberal amount of NoSalt over my steak. "Good Lord!" I heard a biker at the end of the table cry out. "That freak from Austin just put coke on his steak!"

Phyllis and I had moved to Taos for about eighteen months while I worked on a book about the drug-dealing Chagra family of El Paso and the murder of federal judge John Wood. Research put me in constant communication with drug users and dealers, and gradually I went from using cocaine on rare occasions to using it fairly often. To paraphrase what the poet A. E. Housman wrote about the medicinal effects of ale, at times the world seemed not so bad and I myself a sterling lad.

Coke is the great deceiver: under its influence, you believe that you could drink all night without getting drunk. And it's true that some cokeheads can drink enormous quantities of alcohol while still talking and functioning more or less normally. That's one of the qualities that make this drug so insidious. It deludes the user into believing that drug-induced euphoria is a type of super-reality. Even when the evidence is overwhelming in the opposite direction, people believe that coke heightens their sense of awareness and sharpens their insight. What it does is change their personalities. It makes them mean, selfish, stupid, and capable of acts that are totally out of character and frequently self-destructive.

Normally, Phyllis is the best-natured, most cheerful person I know—almost impossible to perturb—and yet we had several vicious arguments during that period of our marriage. Several times we found ourselves yelling and screaming obscenities at each other. Our marriage was about to break up because of my love of coke. Thank God my senses returned in time to spare us.

In 1980 we returned to Austin, where I went on staff at *Texas Monthly*. Over the next three or four years, we moderated our drinking habits, though we both ventured over the line more frequently than we realized. We had good jobs and worked hard at them. Phyllis sold real estate and frequently made more money in a year than I made, which gave me more latitude as a writer. We had become partners in every way, and our marriage was far stronger than it had been.

We celebrated my fiftieth birthday in a complimentary suite at the Fairmont Hotel in San Francisco, arranged by my old friend Debbie Cartwright (no relation), who was head of public relations at the Fairmont in Dallas. Our great drinking buddy Teeta Walker gave us first-class tickets on Delta and traveled with us. Mark showed up unexpectedly on my birthday, as he always did on very special occasions. The kid hadn't lost his touch. He bribed a limousine driver he met at the airport to drive us around town for a few hours while the Houston oilman who was actually paying for it was occupied with a lady of the night. We had dinner at Ernie's and drinks with some of the female impersonators at Finocchio's and still returned the limo before the oilman got wise. The next morning when I looked out the window of our room, the tugs in the bay were firing arches of water, welcoming the majestic U.S.S. *New Jersey* into port. It was a truly magic moment, and my son and I hurried down to the bay and toured the great aircraft carrier. Turning fifty was mellow, but there was a definite sense of aging, of having witnessed—good Lord, could it be half a century?—of debauchery.

Teeta Walker was a Southern belle, right out of Tennessee Williams, a chain-smoker and drinker of straight shots of vodka on the rocks. Like Phyllis and me, she was also a foodie with tastes for the exotic. She dubbed me "Emperor of the Entrails" in tribute to the fact that I could cook liver and onions better than anyone she had ever met. Liver is a food to which no one is indifferent: you either love it or you hate it beyond description. As a prank, we had a liver-and-onions dinner party, without warning our guests of the menu. Mike Sharlot, who is now the dean of the University of Texas School of Law, somehow got through a a few bites before breaking down and confessing that liver was his idea of hell on earth. I told him that liver was good for him. I thought it was, at the time. I had read that liver is rich in iron and various vitamins. Little did I know that it also contains large amounts of fat and cholesterol. Those were not yet familiar statistics, but they were about to be.

We rented a house on 28 1/2 Street, not far from where we live now. I turned the den into an office and worked there on my various projects. By this time I had been promoted to senior editor at *Texas Monthly* and contributed eight or ten stories a year. I wrote a particularly unforgettable article titled "I'm the World's Greatest Cook," informing Texans how to double-dip chicken or steak in buttermilk and flour before frying. This was a secret I learned from a fat black woman who ran a roadside fried chicken stand on the highway outside of Temple. My mission was to collect similar recipes, try them myself, then write about them. Phyllis was famous for her cream gravy and biscuits, and I passed along those recipes to an appreciative public.

At the same time, I was becoming concerned about my weight, which now approached an incredible two hundred pounds. Over the years I had tried almost every diet that came on the market, including the Drinking Man's Diet, which allows a dieter to consume unlimited quantities of alcohol, and the Dr. Atkins Diet, which advises dieters to eat pig skins rather than apples as between-meal snacks. Though I know now that all these diets were worthless and possibly harmful for me, I always managed to lose weight. And of course I also

managed to gain it back, with some to spare. On this particular occasion, I tried the Scarsdale Diet, supplementing it with some of my
own inventions, including a wonderful sugar-free sorbet made from
fresh raspberries and lemons. Phyllis and I both lost ten pounds on
the Scarsdale. And we both gained back twelve. The illusion of
health remained strong, however. I felt good about my marriage, my
career, my friends, my future. Twice a week I walked my Airedales,
Bucky and Abigail, on the Shoal Creek hike-and-bike trial.

Looking back, I see now that there were some deepening shad-
ows. Age was having its way. Time was definitely proving to be unrelenting. One by one, my old pals were hitting the wall, sometimes
not too hard, sometimes permanently. And each time the shock failed
to deter those of us who were still racing, still in the hunt for whatever it was we believed was out there.

I didn't see Bud nearly as often after 1985. That was the year
Bud learned he suffered from diabetes and a distended liver. He
stopped drinking, at which time we discovered we had much less to
talk about. Then Sam Whitten began to fade. A couple of years earlier, Sam had been named Librarian of the Year in the state of Texas
and we had celebrated heavily, but now he was in the hospital, dying
of emphysema. Teeta also suffered from emphysema, and so did my
longtime friend Lopez. Both were in and out of the hospital several
times. Sam finally died in 1993. Lopez died in August 1995. Teeta
died the following winter.

Ann Richards's family persuaded her to take the cure at St.
Mary's Hospital in Minneapolis. She returned home sober, divorced
David, and launched a new career in politics. Ann and Bud became
an item while she was governor, not lovers exactly but two old and
dear friends who enjoy each other's company and find comfort in
AA meetings and good movies. We make what we can out of what's
left of life, old chums.

In the summer of 1996, about the time I was starting this book,
I was jolted to learn that Dick Hitt had died of throat cancer. Apparently he had been dying for more than a year, but had instructed
his wife, Polly, to keep his condition secret. I've heard that he
weighed less than ninety pounds at the end and had long since lost

the ability to speak. He wanted us to remember him as he was—and we do.

Most of us remember what we were, and sometimes that's our problem. In our dream of life we run effortlessly across meadows of yellow wildflowers and leap across deep ravines as easily as we might step over a puddle, mindless of mortality. Nothing bad touches us: we don't tire, we don't want, we don't hurt. Fear may chase us—we *expect* it to—but it never catches up. We remember the high times and bury the low, only they don't stay buried. A man who lost one of his legs in a motorcycle wreck told me that in his dreams he is always whole. But then he wakes in a cold sweat, shaking uncontrollably and feeling the permanent emptiness about him. Eventually we all wake to reality.

I hardly noticed myself breaking apart, but when my friends began to crumble and dissolve before my eyes, I felt myself washing out to sea.

Part Two:

HITTING THE WALL

Five

Letter to My Friends

September 21, 1988

The question I've been asked most often in the past month is: How does it feel to have a heart attack? Not the way you think, I tell people. It's not a sharp, stabbing pain but a dull, tight ache across the chest, as though a bear were sitting on you reading the sports page. It's hard to breathe and the pain is fairly constant. It's something like that 3 A.M. sensation when you wake from a stupor induced by a No. 2 Mexican Special with six beers and extra hot sauce. When I explain it that way, people seem to understand. Just like heartburn, eh? Right, only a little higher up and immune to Alka-Seltzer.

All things considered, the heart attack was a bit of luck. Otherwise, I wouldn't have gone to the hospital and found out that my heart arteries looked like Highway 183 at rush hour—90 percent blockage on one side and 70 percent on the other. The heart attack was fairly mild—no permanent damage. Left unchecked another six or eight months, however, I might have been looking up at ground-hogs. It was necessary to insert five bypasses around the blockage, but they tell me that in a few weeks I'll be better than ever, if you can imagine such a possibility.

I don't remember anything about the operation. One minute I was in the prep room, discussing morphine and other pleasurable drugs that an obliging nurse was pumping into my arm to make surgery go easier, and the next I was waking up in intensive care, hoping that Mark and Phyllis had forgotten that I'd insisted they bring me an order of ribs. Somehow in the intervening eight hours, I'd temporarily lost my taste for barbecue. All that night I swam in and out of consciousness, waking just long enough to cough up some gunk and get another jolt of morphine. By the third day I was walking the hallways and copping feels from nurses. It was downhill after that.

You meet a lot of interesting people in hospitals. While they were prepping me for an arteriogram, I met a young technician who claimed to be pubic barber to the stars. "What stories I could tell!" he murmured, moving his straight-edge razor down my inner thigh. I also met a chubby woman chaplain whose job it is to wake up patients and tell them about her troubles. I never actually met the hospital dietitian at Brackenridge, but what can you say about a person whose idea of supper is two pounds of broccoli and filet of goldfish? All the doctors and nurses I met were hardworking, dedicated, and able to laugh at the macabre procession of institutional craziness.

I've been home for two weeks now and can do all the things normal people do. Yes, that too—only not as fast, or with as much élan. I haven't had a cigarette in twenty-eight days, eight hours, fourteen minutes, and eleven seconds. But who's counting? I can eat or drink anything I want, as long as I lose twenty pounds. There is a catch in every medical prescription. It makes you drowsy or kills your appetite or reminds you of things you can't do anymore anyway.

The rehab therapy has been fun and helped stabilize my sanity. Since the doctor told me to avoid work—stress, don't you see—for the first few weeks, rehab is the only activity that breaks up a chain of catnaps. I've been walking 40–45 minutes two times a day. My favorite route is the University [of Texas] area, along sorority row, where I have observed that a middle-aged man on foot is cause for locking of doors and windows and inspiration for a new round of Bush/Quayle bumper stickers on BMWs.

When I visited the doctor yesterday, he thought I was doing well enough to return to work. I think I will get a second opinion.

The best part of this whole ordeal has been having time to visit with family and old friends. Lord but there are a lot of them out there. You forget how many until, at some critical juncture, the lights flicker for a moment. When things steady up, you take stock and realize they've been there all the time, much farther than the eye can see. In the past year I probably hadn't seen Bud more than half a dozen times, but I saw him about that many times last week. He came by to join my morning review of sorority row. I don't even want to think how the sight of two infirm and permanently corrupted lechers affected the girls on sorority row, but an elderly neighbor woman called Phyllis and asked where I got that tall, cute nurse—meaning Bud, of course.

That's what keeps things in perspective, the tall nurse and all the other old pals from the halcyon days that got us where we are today—at the door of intensive care. The visits, the letters, the cards, phone calls, flowers, plants, books, magazines, teddy bears, balloons, Chinese food, soups and pies smoothed out the jagged edges and filled in the depressions. It's hard to brood when Dorothy Browne is in the same room. It's hard to wallow in self-pity when Fletcher Boone is lurking in the corner, waiting to steal your pain pills. It's hard to know what to say to all those who were there for me—Phyllis, Mark, Helen, Lea, my mom and Harold, my sister Gail and her daughters, Cindy and Debbie—Greg and Tracy, who almost beat me to the hospital, and Mike Levy (I introduced the esteemed publisher of Texas Monthly *to my mom as my editorial assistant and she said I ought to make him shave) and all the TM folks—Lopez, Susan, Larry L., Dan, Teeta, Christy, Sue, Carol, Marge, and many, many others—thanks doesn't quite sum it up. As usual, words fail me. But you know what I mean.*

with love,
Gary Cartwright

When I wrote that communal thank-you note nearly ten years ago, I had an ulterior motive. I wanted to see if I could still write. Writing is not like riding a bicycle, or at least I don't think it is. It comes from some godawful secret place you stumbled across, and if you lose your way there is no guarantee you'll find it again. As weird as this sounds, what worried me most during those strangely out-of-body days after surgery was the fear that I was washed up as a writer.

Later, I learned that other writers had endured a fear as bad or worse. Larry McMurtry, who had a quadruple bypass in December 1991, stopped writing, lecturing, traveling, or even visiting his bookstores. "I couldn't even read—not a book, for two and a half years, and I owned three bookshops and 500,000 books!" he wrote me. "I felt that I had become an outline; then I felt that someone was erasing the outline and that I was simply vanishing—evaporating."

While I went through nothing that crippling, the experience of writing that simple thank-you was, from my perspective, a baptism of fire. It was my way of assessing the physical and emotional damage of having my chest ripped open and my heart in the hands of some strange doctor whose name I barely remembered.

The ordeal of surgery left a hole somewhere in my being, a feeling that I would never be the same, though I couldn't guess what the difference would be. Could I write, for example, without a cigarette in my mouth? I never had before, not in my professional life. Cigarettes were part of the literary process, a continuum in the mathematics of a composition. Whatever the changes ahead, I knew from the start they would be large and maybe ugly.

I have discovered that where aging in general and heart disease in particular are concerned, doctors and writers have one thing in common. We are both masters of denial. We don't mind discussing these dark subjects in the abstract. Indeed, both of our professions depend on it. But we hate to get personal, or admit they could happen to us.

And yet we are reminded daily that the ravages of time spare no one. The mighty fall as dependably as the lowly, and sometimes faster and harder. It all happens in the blink of an eye: generations are born, reproduce, and die while we are still searching the box score for our names.

Dustin Hoffman, who is forever fixed in our memories as the sweet, goony Benjamin Braddock in *The Graduate,* turned sixty in 1997. The eternal nymphet Brigitte Bardot was sixty-two in September 1996. The musician who introduced many of us to rock and roll, Buddy Holly, would have been sixty in 1996 if he had lived. Willie Nelson will turn sixty-five in April 1998. Mickey Mantle, the greatest baseball player of my generation, and my partner in the long-defunct Boozers' Out-to-Lunch Bowling League at the Cotton Bowling Palace in Dallas, died at age sixty-five in 1996, his liver petrified by years of drinking and carrying-on.

In one of Dan Jenkins's books, a character comments on the three most salient pieces of advice for the aging male:

1. *Don't trust that erection you wake up with.*
2. *Never pass up an opportunity to take a piss.*
3. *Never,* never *trust a fart.*

Anyone over the age of fifty-five can appreciate the humor and wisdom of these observations. Whether we are talking about the structural designs of Frank Lloyd Wright or of God, the plumbing usually goes first. Yet we do not dwell on such warnings until we ourselves hit the wall, normally at ninety miles an hour. Now that I think about it, Dan didn't dwell on them either. It wasn't Jenkins who pointed out these inevitabilities of life, it was a character in one of his books. The difference is significant.

Dan was almost sixty-five when he hit the wall, but he had been on a collision course for most of his life. I've known him for nearly forty years and I cannot visualize Dan without (1) a cigarette, (2) a cup of heavily creamed and sugared coffee, and (3) "a young scotch," as Jenkins referred to the most recent glass of J&B and water in his grasp. For years Dan ate nothing except "browns and whites," meaning meat, potatoes, cream gravy, white bread, chocolate cake. No greens, yellows, red, or oranges were permitted in his company.

In the early seventies, Dan, Bud, and I took our families on a month-long vacation in Acapulco. We rented a villa perched on the

top of a cliff overlooking the ocean. The villa, once owned by the
Mexican movie star Dolores Del Rio and later by John Wayne, reportedly came equipped with the best cook in Acapulco, an old
woman who woke very early each morning, attended mass, shopped
at the local market for the freshest meat and produce, then spent the
remainder of the day preparing gastronomic masterpieces for our
pleasure.

Each afternoon Dan sent his children—Sally, Marty, and
Danny—down to the kitchen to spy on the old woman and tell him
what was on the menu for our dinner. "We don't know what it is,"
they would report, "but it has a lot of arms and legs." Dan, June, and
most of the kids ate most of their evening meals at Denny's.

Dan is the coolest guy I ever met, debonair, polished, and self-
confident almost to the point of absurdity. Back when we were working at the *Fort Worth Press*, we assumed that sooner or later New York
would call us to the Big Time, and most of us wondered if we could
cut it. Not Dan. To Jenkins, Manhattan was just Fort Worth with sub-
way trains and rude people who talked funny.

On arriving in New York to work for *Sports Illustrated*, Dan
looked around for the hottest spot in town and was informed that it
was the back room at P. J. Clark's. You had to be somebody to get in
the back room. That first week, Dan introduced himself to Jimmy,
who guarded the door to Clark's back room. As soon as Dan had
slipped Jimmy a twenty, Dan became somebody and got a table near
Ed Sullivan. After that, it only got better. Dan and June's first apartment was at Lexington and 86th, on the classy Upper East Side, one
floor below Robert Redford and around the corner from Blooming-
dale's. A few years later they moved to Park Avenue. Park *Street*, Dan
called it.

Dan got his first wake-up call in 1988, sitting with television
sportscaster Pat Summerall at the bar at Juanita's, the Fort Worth
branch of the Mexican restaurant chain that June and her sisters
founded. Dan had been under considerable pressure. A Hollywood
production company was filming a movie of his book *Dead Solid
Perfect* and Dan was wrangling with the Professional Golfers Association over some problem dealing with the production of the film. He
was sitting at the bar, bitching about this and about life its ownself,

when his eyes began to blink like a projector film that has slipped a cog. Without a word, he slid off the bar stool and onto the floor.

Friends thought at first that he had had a heart attack. Someone called an ambulance. After a few seconds, Dan's eyes popped open as suddenly as they had snapped shut. Told that he had passed out, Dan protested: "That can't be right. I've never passed out in my life!" They took him to Fort Worth's All Saints Hospital anyway and ran a battery of tests. It wasn't a heart attack, as it turned out. Dan was merely suffering from acute anemia. A normal blood count is 14. They clocked Dan at 5.4, about one point above dead solid dead.

They advised Dan to slow down, and for a few days he did, then he resumed life as he had always known it—cigarettes, coffee, young scotches by the carload. Jenkins had a burglar's talent for finding an escape clause in the most closely worded edict. Advised to take iron tablets and eat lots of meat, Dan informed us, "Everyone ought to be anemic. It means you get to eat lots of steak."

That entire experience did nothing to diminish Dan's conviction that he was bulletproof. But behind his back, time was creeping closer. Five years after the episode at Juanita's, Dan was reading in his living room when a jolt of pain shot across his chest. This time he was pretty sure it was a heart attack. Again they rushed him to the hospital, and again there was no indication of a coronary. The diagnosis was pericarditis, an inflamation of the membrane (pericardium) covering the heart. "Athletes have it," he bragged, as if pericarditis were the thing to have this season.

This brush with mortality was not so easily dismissed. After that, Dan regularly reported to the Mayo Clinic for stress tests—the Mayo Marathon, he dubbed these exercises. During a stress test, doctors hook you up to an EKG machine and a blood pressure cuff while you exercise on a treadmill. It's the best method available to determine if you have blockages in your coronary arteries. Dan flunked his first test.

His doctor ordered an angiogram, a procedure in which a plastic catheter is inserted into the heart and an opaque dye is injected. Using an X ray, doctors study the path of blood through the system of arteries supplying the heart muscle with blood and pinpoint obstructed areas. An arteriogram takes about an hour and is mostly painless. Happily sedated, the patient feels only a warm sensation when the dye is first flushed through the arteries. The patient is awake the whole time, more or less. The doctor may ask him to take a deep breath and hold it. He may ask him to cough. A technician will ask him to breath through a mouthpiece so that the exhaled air can be analyzed. The patient can even watch part of the procedure on the TV monitor, though it is not as intellectually stimulating as *Oprah*.

Dan's angiogram revealed—no surprise—clogged arteries.

This resulted in the first of two angioplasties, also called balloon surgery. This is a procedure not unlike the angiogram, except this time the plastic catheter that is inserted carries a tiny balloon at its end. Upon reaching the obstructed area, doctors inflate the balloon, hoping to force the obstructing materials to spread out so that the artery regains some of its former internal dimensions.

After his first angioplasty, Dan made some effort to modify his diet. He disdained his daily lumberjack breakfast of eggs, sausage, biscuits, and gravy, settling instead for cornflakes or oatmeal. Sundays he splurged, eating two eggs over easy. No sausage, no gravy. The stunningly beautiful and resourceful June persuaded him to eat an occasional green and yellow, and substituted reduced-fat ice cream for his customary dessert. He even cut back on the smokes, from four down to two packs of Winstons a day.

At June's insistence, Dan eventually stopped smoking altogether, at least in front of her. He still stashed smokes in his golf bag and travel kit and bummed them from friends at golf tournaments and football games. Nine months later, after another failed stress test and another angioplasty, doctors told Dan the bad news: Angioplasty wouldn't cut it in his case. It was time to have a bypass.

Bypass surgery is considerably more complex and risky than angioplasty. Instead of running a small tube into the coronary arteries, surgeons cut a large opening down the center of the chest and pry open the breastbone with a jack. Using drugs, they stop the heart, keeping the patient alive with a heart-lung machine. Surgeons then open the heart muscle and sew replacement arteries above and below the clogged places in the original arteries, using veins borrowed from the patient's chest or legs. (Bypass veterans can spot another merely by noting the arching, scarlet-red scar running for five or six inches above the inside of the knee and down the calf.) A bypass is nothing more than a detour, a way for the blood to flow around the obstruction and keep the heart alive. Nevertheless, a bypass is to angioplasty what a pipe bomb is to a Fourth of July sparkler.

"I couldn't believe it when he said I needed a bypass," Dan told me later. "I was still feeling good. I still hadn't had a heart attack. But they told me that if I did have one, it would be my last. I said, 'Okay, but I want the top guy.' "

The surgeon who did Jenkins's triple bypass is Harold Snyder, one of the best in Florida, a six-handicap golfer known to his colleagues as the Bald Ego. Dan recalls, "He was cocky and arrogant, which was exactly what I wanted in a heart surgeon." Snyder told Jenkins that by the morning after, he would be walking the hospital corridors, and that within five weeks doctor and patient would be playing golf together—which of course they were.

Dan recovered from bypass surgery quicker than anyone I've ever heard of. Nursed back to health by his wife—June, "the Angel of Dien Bien Boulevard in Ponte Verde, Florida"—he experienced no postsurgery depression and had no regrets. Two months after the operation he was back at work, bitching of course that he could have finished a book in the time that he'd lost. But the experience definitely got his attention.

When I talked to Dan in the fall of 1996, shortly before his sixty-sixth birthday, he was recovering from a second abdominal surgery for hernia, but was otherwise clean and healthy. "After the bypass," he told me, "the changes in my life were huge. They were immense. I walk three miles a day and watch my diet. I started having one or two J&Bs and water instead of thirty and gave up the three or four packs of Winstons a day that I had smoked for forty-five years. The hardest part was trying to write without a cigarette. That's the hardest thing I've ever tried to do. I still cheat now and then."

Bud Shrake hit the wall in 1984, at age fifty-two. At the time, he had just finished writing a play, *Pancho Villa's Wedding Day*, which was being produced in Austin. Simultaneously, his screenplay *Songwriter*, starring Willie Nelson and Kris Kristofferson, was also being filmed in Austin. Bud had started playing golf again, usually in the mornings with Willie and former University of Texas football coach Darrell Royal, at Willie's Pedernales Country Club in the hills outside Austin. By early afternoon Bud would be at the bar at the Quorum, a downtown club owned by our old friend Nick Kralj. Fourteen hours later, he would still be there.

Day after day, night after night, Bud played golf in the morning and drank all afternoon and all night at the Quorum. It was the only place he felt at home. If Dan was in Austin, he'd stop by the Quorum, knowing that's where he could find Bud. I would stop by from time to time, usually late in the afternoon and never for more than an hour or two. This was the time just after Phyllis and I had returned from Taos and were struggling to right our lives and make peace with the world and with each other.

In some way I couldn't explain at the time, the Quorum seemed a disaster waiting to happen. Not that it wasn't a fascinating hangout, probably the most interesting in Texas. Nick himself is something of a legend, a gambler and dealmaker who grew up on Galveston Island when it was still known as the Free State of Galveston and a prudent man carried a gun at all times: Nick still packs a .38 and was an ardent opponent of the state's right-to-carry law on the grounds that "when I walk into a place, I like to know I'm the only one packing."

The Quorum was filled daily with politicians and power brokers, the men (and an occasional woman) who ran the state. Ethics, morality, and character were jokes to these guys, as were concerns about liquor curfews, drug laws, and any other rule that applied to normal mortals. These men seemed to have mutated into a new species. It was assumed, not without reason, that when the time was right they would control the world. Any problem, any inconvenience, someone at the Quorum had the answer. You got the feeling that the fix was always in.

One of the regulars was the irrepressible Frank Erwin, at that time the chairman of the University of Texas board of regents, and the gentleman for whom the present Erwin Center at UT is named. A close friend of former governor John Connally, Erwin had a reserved table in the corner and held court daily. The Chairman, as he was always called, analyzed the geopolitics of the Arab world and predicted the rise and fall of oil prices as casually as he might discuss how the Longhorns would do on Saturday against the TCU Horned Frogs. "You know George Washington was born in Texas, don't you?" the Chairman would say. "That's right. He moved to Virginia at an early age 'cause his daddy told him, 'Boy, if you can't tell a lie, you'll never make it in Texas!' " During the Quorum years, the Chairman was cited on more than one occasion for driving while intoxicated. He was always able to convince prosecutors that it wasn't the whiskey that caused his burnt-orange Cadillac to weave from curb to curb, it was the medication required to treat his allergies. Erwin died a few years later, in 1980, the same year Ann Richards went for treatment.

Disaster was narrowly avoided one night when Bud insisted on driving Dan back to his hotel—in a pounding rainstorm, as fate would have it. I had left the Quorum hours earlier, and when the next morning I heard what had happened I broke out in hives. A couple of cops in a patrol car had spotted Bud's maroon Mercedes doing a Frank Erwin along San Jacinto Boulevard and pulled him over. They had our boys cold. Bud spent the night in jail, and Dan spent the night on a bench just outside, waiting for Bud, who was charged with a DWI. Thanks to friends at the Quorum, he escaped with a $500 fine and a two-year probated sentence.

Life continued more or less uninterrupted, except that Bud began to notice that his hangovers were getting more severe, harder to deal with. "I've had hangovers for years," he told me, "but nothing like these. I feel incredibly bad. I'm so tired when I wake up that I can barely get out of bed. Out at Willie's the other morning, I was so bushed I had to stop playing and sit down by the tee."

Finally, Nick persuaded Bud to see a doctor. Shrake didn't trust doctors and hadn't been to one in years, but Nick's friend Dr. Jerald Senter had a reputation that impressed even Bud. According to Nick, Doc Senter had done some hard living in his own day and was still on call, saving a younger generation from perils he knew only too well. In the fifties Senter gave weekly checkups to the girls at Hattie's, a legendary whorehouse on South Congress. Long before the theatrical world decided that the best little whorehouse was the Chicken Ranch in La Grange, the best little whorehouse in Texas was Hattie's. According to folklore, when the legislature needed a quorum for a key vote, Texas Rangers were dispatched to Hattie's to round up the necessary number of senators and house members.

Doc Senter gave Bud a complete physical and told him that he suffered from diabetes and a distended liver. "Let me put it this way," the doctor said. "You can go back to the Quorum and be dead by Christmas, or you stop drugging, drinking, and smoking. It's all up to you, but if you follow my advice, you'll come back in a year and say, 'Doc, I don't know why I used to drink so much!' "

As I say, these things are trickier than they first appear. Shrake stopped smoking and drinking that same day, though he started smoking again—then quit again—several years later. He also put himself on a diet, in a manner of speaking. Shrake has always had the most curious eating habits. When we lived together on Cole Avenue in Dallas years ago, the only food he kept in the house was Velveeta cheese, mayonnaise, and sliced bread. Following that logic after his visit with Doc Senter, Bud decided that the best way to lose weight was eat quarts of "I Can't Believe It's Yogurt" heavily sprinkled with trail mix. "I thought that was diet food," he told me.

He didn't lose weight, of course, and what's more he felt even worse than before. *Pancho Villa's Wedding Day* was in its second production at the Austin Opera House, and Bud would stand in the lobby and greet people before every show, shaking hands and faking conversation as well as he was able. By the end of Act One, he would feel so rotten he'd go home, so sick he could barely drive.

One night it was especially bad. He felt clammy, dizzy, incoherent. He believed he was about to faint. One of the actors, a middle-aged Mexican-American, asked Bud if he had diabetes. The actor knew the signs because he had it, too—the insulin-dependent kind. He took Bud to the dressing room, where he kept a meter that registered blood sugar level. Pricking Bud's finger, he took a reading of the blood sample. "It's four twenty!" he announced, in the voice one would use to shout "Fire!" At 180, sugar starts draining straight into a diabetic's bloodstream. At about 425, the diabetic goes into a hypoglycemic coma, which is almost always fatal. If a diabetic's blood sugar is too *low*, he can jack it up by drinking a glass of fruit juice. If it is too high, on the other hand, there is nothing to do except pray, and hope to ride it out. Someone drove Bud home, and somehow he was able to ride it out.

The next morning Bud went to see Doc Senter, then did what he should have done after his first visit—he bought a blood testing kit at the drugstore. Now he uses it at least once a day. He tries to keep his blood sugar level between 80 and 150. "The meter is sort of like a thermostat," he says. He also educated himself on some basics of nutrition. Frozen yogurt and trail mix can be loaded with fat and calories and glucose, and are definitely not health foods. If you are a diabetic, you might as well eat poison. With the help of Marty Leonard, a nutritionist, Shrake put himself on a true diet. Marty cooks and freezes meals especially tailored to Bud's demands, and Bud simply pops them in a microwave. Taped to the door of his refrigerator is a sign that warns: "Everything You Put in Your Mouth Counts!" He has lost fifty pounds and has had no more serious problems with diabetes.

He made a point to stop by Doc Senter's office and tell him, "Doc, I don't know why I used to drink so much—or how I got so much work done!"

Six

I hit the wall in 1988, shortly after my fifty-fourth birthday. We had celebrated with Dorothy Browne and Jan Reid, who were married by then and had become our constant dinner and travel companions after Teeta Walker got sick. I'll never forget my birthday dinner. It was a hot August night and we dined at Jeffrey's, on pâté, snails, oysters, chicken livers, steak, duck, many bottles of wine, and finally espresso and chocolate decadence. A few weeks later, as I was whistling a happy tune on the hike-and-bike trail with Abby and Bucky yapping at my heals, I felt the pain in my chest. Nothing alarming, not at first. I had been suffering heartburn for years, but it always went away. This time it stayed for dinner and spent the night.

I didn't sleep at all. I propped several pillows under my head to make breathing easier, but that heavier-than-life feeling only intensified. I drank four Alka-Selzers without results. I listened to the clock, changing positions every few minutes. I walked out to the backyard and breathed deeply of the moist summer air. Bucky nuzzled me from behind and I sat on the back steps for a time, stroking and brushing him. No moon at all, I told Bucky, my voice trembling, more certain by the minute that this was something far worse than heartburn. I had gone through a whole bottle of Rolaids but the pain kept on and maybe even intensified. By the early hours of the morning, I was exhausted but still unable to sleep.

Without waking Phyllis, I went quietly to the kitchen and telephoned the doctor who had been treating me for high blood pressure. When I told him about the chest pains, he told me to get to the nearest emergency room, fast.

Phyllis drove, glancing at me from time to time, worried not only about what might be happening but how I would deal with it. I don't do well with pain. I sat sulking, smoking a cigarette, angry to be inconvenienced. When I don't sleep well, it ruins my whole day. That's as far as I had thought it through. The words "heart attack" may have crossed my mind—I don't remember—but if they did they were summarily dismissed.

Within minutes I was flat on my back in the ER at Brackenridge

Hospital, wires and tubes running from my arms and chest, doctors, nurses, and technicians moving about in no particular hurry. Blood tests showed abnormal levels of enzymes. I watched a technician read something from my electrocardiogram chart and speak to a doctor, who nodded. I was slipping in and out of consciousness, aware that Phyllis was holding my hand, but too zonked on the medication running up my arm to make sense of what was happening. I do remember someone telling Phyllis, "He's had a heart attack," and still nothing registered. I can't remember feeling afraid, or apprehensive, or even particularly curious. It was all so unreal, like something happening in a bad movie.

Sometime that same day a doctor I'd never met wheeled me to the lab and did an angiogram. I learned later that the doctor was my cardiologist, Chuck Wilkins. A few hours later he came by my room with a diagram of the heart and its arteries. Using a ballpoint pen, he shaded in five areas that were at least partially blocked. One section of relatively small arteries on the right side was completely blocked. The others were in the 50–75 percent range.

Wilkins told me that there were so many blockages that an angioplasty was out of the question. He recommended bypass surgery. "What's that?" I asked. He told me, avoiding clinical terms when possible. I must have nodded that I understood, but I didn't. How could I possibly imagine being cut open from the bottom of my neck to just above the navel? How could anyone understand having his heart stopped while someone fiddled with the plumbing? These are not things that real people are capable of comprehending.

I must have been in shock, because for the next several hours I just lay there, hearing the steady tick of the clock on the wall, trying to puzzle out the situation, groping to calculate the options, my mouth dry and my naked feet alternately too hot or too cold. It was the loneliest time of my life. Finally it came to me—there were no options. Bypass surgery or a second heart attack, this one probably fatal. I do not read the Bible regularly, but I remembered listening to Tom Landry, who coached the Cowboys when I covered the team, hearing the absolute conviction in his voice as he read a passage from the Book of Joshua. "Be strong and of good courage, fear not nor be afraid, for the Lord thy God will not fail thee nor forsake thee." I kept saying those words, over and over to myself. *The Lord will not fail thee.* You gotta believe.

That night I talked it over with my family—with Phyllis, my mom, my stepfather, Harold Nelson, and my son, Mark, who had driven down from Dallas as soon as he heard the bad news. Having Mark there was almost as important as having Phyllis. They were the two people I couldn't do without. Whatever was to happen, I knew now, it was out of my hands.

Later, Dr. Stephen Dewan, the surgeon who would perform the bypass, stopped by the room to introduce himself and answer questions. Dewan looked hardly old enough to have graduated from Boy Scouts, much less medical school. My mom asked to see his driver's license. I asked to see his hands. Apparently this is a fairly common request of heart surgeons. Dewan smiled and brought his hands up chest high, rotating them slowly so that I could see from all angles. His hands seemed sure and steady—and unusually clean and well manicured. I liked that. I liked him, knowing it was better that way.

I can barely recall the details of those few days. It all happened so fast and was so unexpected. No time to dwell, no time to be afraid. On Thursday, I first noticed the chest pains out on the hike-and-bike trail. Early Friday, Phyllis drove me to the ER. I met Dr. Wilkins that same day and heard the curious phrase "bypass surgery." On Saturday I met Dr. Dewan. Sunday was a holiday for all except emergencies, so surgery was scheduled for first thing Monday morning.

Phyllis walked beside the gurney, holding my hand all the way to the operating room. At the door she kissed me and told me not to worry. "I'll see you in a while," I said. "I'll probably be hungry, so get some barbecued ribs." Phyllis assured me that she and Mark would have the ribs waiting.

Inside, the ER was cold as a meat locker. They keep it that way so the surgical team won't sweat on your open heart. A technician asked me what music I preferred. "Mozart," I said. He looked through the stack of CDs and informed me there was no Mozart. "How about Bach?" he asked. Okay, Bach was fine. The last thing I remember before awaking in recovery ten or twelve hours later is the life-sustaining drive of Bach's Suite in G Minor.

I have intentionally saved telling you about the moment of truth, that inescapable hour when I pondered my own mortality. It happened the night before surgery. My room had been crowded with friends and family much of the evening, but by ten o'clock Phyllis herded them out and shut the door. It was the first time all day we had been alone. This could be our last night together, though I tried to not think about it. But that was the truth. Tomorrow, who knows, a great love affair might end. I had done a lot of praying. I had asked God to spare me, to spare Phyllis, to spare our family, if He was so inclined. Either way, I asked the Lord to give me courage. Make me strong. Make me able to do what I have to do. "Thy will be done," I said, knowing that God knew that this was the best I could do to prove my faith. I was trying to act unafraid, not at all sure that I was getting away with it.

"Try to not think about it," Phyllis said, sitting on the side of the bed and holding my hand. I pulled her close and we kissed. I could feel her breasts brushing against my arm.

"I'm trying," I said. "There's just one thing."

"And that is?" she asked, smiling to let me know she was reading my mind.

"What if I get down there . . . and they start to cut me open . . . and suddenly . . . suddenly I realize . . ."

"That you're horny?" she prompted.

"Yes. What if that happens?"

"That would be a shame," she admitted.

"Exactly!"

Phyllis excused herself and disappeared into the bathroom. I closed my eyes and tried to picture us together. One of my arms was wrapped in a blood pressure cuff and the other was hooked to an intravenous tube that was connected to a support system above the bed. Another wire ran from my chest to the EKG. Not especially romantic, I thought, but then I've seen worse. I felt at peace and said another prayer. "Thank you for Phyllis, for the love and the passion and the friendship that we share, and for the goodness and completeness of our lives." I felt myself drifting, being carried God knew where by the tide of life. I think that I knew then I was going to be okay.

I felt her at the foot of the bed. Propping myself up as best I could, I looked her over, taking my time, enjoying the moment. She was wearing a lacy black slip, one shoulder strap hanging loose, ready to fall away. She cocked one hip, and in that saucy way she has thrust her breasts forward until the slip strained at its seams. She had that pouty, sultry, Lollobrigida look that drives me mad. "I was always very strong in the leeeegs," she said in her Italian accent.

In the deep throes of foreplay we did not hear the beeper when it went off. But an orderly down the hall did. The orderly and one of the floor nurses burst through the door like federal agents raiding a nest of terrorists. A few steps behind was the head nurse of my floor, a tall, pleasant woman with a faintly Swedish accent. Then I heard the incessant beep-beep-beeping of the life-support system by my bed. It was the signal that my intravenous solution was about to run dry and needed to be replaced.

While the orderly and the other nurse fumbled with the equipment, the head nurse looked at me. I can't recall her name—Kathy? Karen? something like that—but I can see her clearly in my memory. She put a finger to her lips, telling us to wait until the others had gone. When we were alone, she stood with her back to the door, barring anyone else from entering. "There is no way to lock it," she said. "But when I leave, you put a chair in front of it. I'll watch from the nursing station and keep them away."

That was a great night for love. I had already drifted off to sleep when Phyllis left. I dreamed of angels. I will happily concede that June Jenkins is the Angel of Dien Bien Boulevard, but on that August night in 1988, the Angel of the Cardiac Ward at Brackenridge Hospital was a nurse with a faintly Swedish accent. Wherever she is, I want her to know that two of us remember her.

Seven

$\mathcal{T}$he most lame-brain commercial on television is a scenario in which we hear Woman No. 1 confiding to Woman No. 2: "Heartburn is just nature's way of reminding me to take my Tums!" Woman No. 2 asks the obvious: "Why would nature want you to take Tums?" Why indeed. Yet Woman No. 1 flashes her friend a smile usually reserved for the terminally clueless and replies in a word: "Calcium!"

Yes, it is true that women need extra calcium, especially as they begin to age and the risk of osteoporosis is great. For that matter, so do men. Though it has not been widely discussed in medical literature, men also are at risk of osteoporosis, a metabolic bone disease that causes its victims to lose bone mass. But there are dozens of more effective and less expensive ways to take calcium than by chewing a couple of antacid tablets. Also, people with chronic heartburn might mistake an attack of angina—a frequent precursor to a heart attack—for just another episode of acid indigestion. I have lost count of how many people have told me they misidentified heart attack as heartburn.

"The trouble is that some people can mistake acute heartburn for angina," Dr. Charles Wilkins, my cardiologist, told me. "Indigestion is an acid burning starting in the stomach and working its way up. Angina is a dull, heavy pressure that can't be localized. It comes on gradually and there's no acid feeling.

"People who have had heartburn in the past may feel a different, dull pressure and ignore it. They deny it is anything worse than heartburn. Ninety percent of my patients who deny it before a heart attack feel every little twinge *after* and call me to report it."

Dr. Wilkins also told me about an emergency room doctor at Sheppard Air Force Base in Wichita Falls, Texas, where Wilkins was stationed after completing his residency. This doctor complained constantly about heartburn and slugged down bottles of Mylanta while attending to patients in the ER at the base hospital. One day Wilkins telephoned the doctor's home only to learn that he had just dropped dead from a myocardial infarction—aka a heart attack. This doctor was in his mid-forties, worked out regularly at the base YMCA, and had treated dozens of cases of angina and myocardial infarction in his medical career. Yet he failed to recognize his own symptoms.

A heart attack can drop you anytime, anywhere, with or without warning. You can have a myocardial infarction while running a hundred-meter dash or walking a leisurely pace along a hike-and-bike trail. You can have one playing tennis or bridge, driving a car or taking a nap. You can have one before dinner or on a full stomach. Not long ago Bud Shrake was examined by a doctor who advised Bud that he would need surgery in three weeks. Three days later, while attending a medical seminar, the doctor dropped dead of a massive heart attack. Chuck Wilkins estimates that one-third of heart attack victims die immediately or within a few days.

Heart attacks are the result of a disease called atherosclerosis. Though the heart attack may come suddenly and without warning, the disease has been years in development and might have been detected and prevented with proper medical care. Atherosclerosis adversely effects the arteries that carry blood to the heart. Over the years, even as the arteries harden and become less flexible, deposits of a fat called cholesterol begin to accumulate along their inner walls, much as rust and mineral deposits build up on the inside of water pipes. Forming into pockets of plaque, the fatty yellow stuff bulges and grows and gradually restricts the flow of blood to the heart. This causes the heart to have to work extra hard to distribute blood to the body. If a blood clot forms in the narrowed artery, the passageway is blocked and the flow of blood to the heart muscle is shut off entirely. At this point the person suffers coronary thrombosis or coronary occlusion—technically a myocardial infarction (or MI) is the actual injury to the heart muscle, but physicians use MI synonymously for heart attack.

A person experiencing a chest pain is not necessarily having a heart attack. On the contrary, most people who go to a doctor or an emergency room complaining of chest pains have something else wrong with them. Angina pectoris, a condition less serious than an

MI, causes a similar aching in the chest. It is a symptom caused by blockage, but the blockage does not cut off the flow of blood through the artery entirely, as in the case of heart attack. Unlike a heart attack, an angina usually doesn't do permanent damage, but it may be a warning sign that a real heart attack is on its way. Occasionally a person with an underlying heart disease or a thyroid disorder may experience heart palpitations—a sudden pounding, fluttering, or racing sensation in the chest, sometimes accompanied by dizziness or light-headedness. These may be symptoms of atrial fibrillation (or AF), an irregular or rapid contraction of the atria (two of the four chambers of the heart), which causes this part of the heart to beat out of rhythm with the rest of the heart. Angina and atrial fibrillation are dangerous, but they can be treated before they become life-threatening.

Most cardiologists admit that even they can't tell if a chest pain is really a heart attack until they have seen results from an EKG and blood test. The pain receptors inside our bodies are not nearly as discrete as those on the surface of our skin, which means that pain inside the body doesn't localize the afflicted area. Chest pains could mean trouble with the gallbladder or the stomach, or some type of arthritis, or too many enchiladas. Each person's perception of pain differs, sometimes widely. (Even if the pain is a heart attack, the amount of pain is not a measure of the amount of damage.) "The very best cardiologists are right [about chest pains] maybe seventy percent of the time," Dr. Wilkins told me. "Which means the rest of us are right maybe half the time."

The heart is a tough and amazingly resilent little muscle, roughly the size of a human fist. Wrapped like a small Christmas ham by a network of arteries that surround its exterior, the heart is essentially a pump that causes blood to circulate through the body and back again to the heart. As it passes through our muscles and tissues, blood drops off molecules of oxygen, the blood returns to the heart and then to the lungs, where the carbon dioxide is extracted for expulsion from the body and the blood is reoxygenated.

The heart is divided into two cavities, which are in turn divided into two chambers. The upper chambers are the atria and the lower ones the ventricles. Oxygen-depleted blood returns to the heart through the right atrium and moves down to the right ventricle, which contracts and pumps it through the pulmonary artery to the lungs. The lungs replace the carbon dioxide with fresh oxygen, which is then pumped up to the left atrium and thereafter to the left ventricle. The left ventricle contracts, forcing the new blood through the aorta, a main truck artery of the heart, and from there it is again distributed to the body.

What an absolutely astonishing machine, the human heart. If you have no other reason to believe in the existence of God, consider the design of this one incredible organ. The heart works twenty-four hours a day, seven days a week, and hardly ever complains. No other muscle serves us so well or so faithfully. The heart can even arrange its own detours around blockages, by a process called collateral circulation. What happens in collateral circulation is that nearby arteries sense the distress signal from the blocked artery and force open small branches through which blood can bypass the affected area. If the detour works well enough, a heart attack can be prevented, but don't count on it.

In one of the examining rooms at Dr. Wilkins's office is a clear plastic model of a section of heart artery, ten times actual size. The poor soul who posed for this model had obviously been eating too many cheeseburgers: jagged ridges of plaque protrude from the lining of the artery like volcanic mountain ranges. Over these rough and menacing surfaces flows a red-tinted fluid representing blood. Floating in the fluid are colorless disks about the size of lentils. These are platelets, good cells that aid in blood clotting. When the heart rate and blood pressure increase—as they do when we experience stress or anger—the platelets become sticky and cling together. This is how clots are formed. The primary function of blood clots is to heal wounds, but they can also block arteries.

When the model artery is sitting on a shelf, it appears fairly benign. Though the plaque somewhat restricts the flow of blood, it seems stable, in no danger of being dislodged from its mooring along the artery wall. If this were the artery of a rabbit or another lab animal, there would indeed be no danger: in the case of animals who have been fed a high-fat diet, something traumatic must occur before the plaque can break free. But human beings, alas, are not so fortunate. When we turn the model upside down we simulate what happens in our own arteries when the plaque has built up to a critical point: it erupts like a volcano. A thick stream of plaque pours forth, sweeping up the sticky platelets, swallowing them into its mass, and pushing the entire glob forward like debris in a flood tide. The glob is now a clot, about to block the flow of blood to the heart.

The model doesn't show what happens next, but I promise you it is terrifying. Deprived of oxygen and nutrients, the heart muscle quivers and starts to convulse. Pressure within the heart and lungs increases dramatically. Breathing becomes labored. Within seconds those parts of the heart muscle that depended on the clogged artery begin to die. If 20 percent of the heart is damaged, the patient is a candidate for congestive heart failure, which means that while he is still alive, his quality of life is greatly diminished; in any case, the damaged area is layered with scar tissue that could interfere with the heart's normal work in the future. If 40 percent of the heart is damaged, say good-bye to the cruel world. As I'll explain in more detail later, none of this *has* to happen. Cholesterol level can be checked with a simple and inexpensive blood test, and medication can be prescribed to control it.

Heart disease is an equal-opportunity killer—and may be even harder to detect in women. Nobody is sure why this is true, though part of the reason may be that women are protected in their younger years by the female hormone estrogen. After menopause, when a woman's estrogen level tumbles, she is very much at risk of heart attack and has a lower chance of surviving than a man. Studies published by the American Heart Association show that 39 percent of women who suffer a heart attack die within a year, compared to 31 percent of the men. A woman's chances of having a second heart attack within four years are 20 percent, a man's 16. Heart disease among women shows up almost a decade later than among men. Between ages forty-five and sixty-four, for example, one in nine women has some form of cardiovascular disease. By age sixty-five, the ratio is one in three. Three-quarters of the women who suffer heart attacks each year are sixty-five or older, and nearly half of them die within a year. Among black women the situation is even worse. The heart attack rate for black women is 28 percent higher than it is for white women.

Eight

Until the decade of the eighties, when I had my bypass, the procedure was not universally accepted by surgeons and was only dimly understood by the public. Luckily, I missed reading an article in a 1987 issue of *Texas Monthly* in which Steve Harrigan described a heart bypass operation. I say "luckily" because if I had read Steve's graphic, even morbid, explanation, I might have decided to take my chances on a second heart attack instead.

". . . [as] the surgeons rip into [the patient's] breastbone with a stainless steel power tool, [the patient's] body lurches but his conscious mind stays in hiding [under anesthesia]," Harrigan wrote. "They slice into his leg and remove a long section of saphenous vein, tying off its branches as they go. The breastbone is pried open with a kind of jack—a Cooley retractor—and they cut through the heart, pulling back the shroud of the pericardium to reveal the great ugly muscle itself. Denton Cooley [surgeon-in-chief at the Texas Heart Institute in Houston, and the man for whom the retractor is named] appears at this point and takes over, happily snipping and sewing without a trace of hesitation, inserting the cannulas that channel blood away from the heart so that it can rest as its function is taken over by a heart-lung machine. The patient's blood is cooled by the machine, and Cooley pours a pitcher of cold water into the open chest to further quiet the heart, until finally it is still and the surgical field is clear of blood. The heart, covered with fat, lies as shapeless as an oyster inside the smooth pink shell of the pericardium.

"Cooley makes an incision in one of the arteries and sees, as all the tests have promised, that it is completely blocked. He trims the end off a length of saphenous vein and begins to attach it downstream of the blockage. All the while our patient is so still and distant it seems hardly possible that he could ever come back to consciousness again."

Later, Harrigan visits the recovery room at the Texas Heart Institute and looks across the ward of bypass patients, again still and distant, lying like lumps of sand covered by identically patterned sheets.

"Though most of them are still deep in their anesthetic haze," he continues, "their faces hint at some troubled awareness. Their skin is gray, like the skin of newborn babies, and like newborns they look thunderstruck, grasping for some revelation that will be slow to dawn."

The most critical part of any bypass operation is the time that the patient's own heart is stopped and his life is sustained by the heart-lung machine—"the pump," as it's called in the trade. In the 1970s when the procedure was new, surgeons sometimes needed six to eight hours to complete the operation, literally working against time. More than an hour on the pump can do permanent damage to the patient. At worst, it can cause stroke and kill the patient; at best, it can lower the IQ a few points. Until the last decade, most patients did not do well after bypass surgery, though in most cases it was the last option.

Bypass surgery does not always work, and even when it does work there is no long-term guarantee it will continue to work. Peter Barthelme, a Houston writer, had five angioplasties and then quadruple bypass surgery. A few months later, three of the four replacement arteries had clogged up again. We think of the bypass as a cure-all, but between 2 and 10 percent of patients with transplanted arteries clog up within a few years. Barthelme was told that replacement arteries sometimes clog up because they were clogged to begin with. "I suggested," Barthelme says, "that maybe somebody shoulda run a straightened coat hanger through the arteries before going to all the trouble of sewing them inside my heart."

Doctors now speculate that Barthelme's problem is puny arteries, and they have recommended a "stent," a coil of plastic designed to fit inside the artery and hold its walls open.

The first coronary artery bypass graft surgery—as the procedure is formally called—was recorded at Cleveland Clinic in Ohio in 1973, though a case can be made that the first one actually took place in Houston nine years earlier. During open-heart surgery at Texas Medical Center, H. Edwards Garrett improvised an emergency bypass, attaching an obstructed vessel to another channel through which blood could flow around a blockage. Garrett's heroics were not reported, however, until after the officially recorded bypass in Ohio. (Texas, by the way, is the world capital of the coronary bypass, proving that this state has either the most clogged arteries or the most persuasive heart surgeons.)

Indeed, only in this century have physicians treated heart disease as a serious problem—even though coronary atherosclerosis is in fact a disease of antiquity. Evidence of heart disease can be found in ancient Egyptian papyruses, mortuary inscriptions, and tomb reliefs. The thickening and calcification of the coronary arteries of a mummy from the 21st Dynasty clearly indicate that this fifty-year-old citizen from 1000 B.C. was a candidate for a massive myocardial infarction. It was not until the seventeenth century A.D., however, that coronary circulation was identified.

Although angina pectoris was first described in medical texts as early as 1768, a textbook published in 1866 said that the condition was so rare that a doctor might go five years without treating a single case. The pathologic concept of coronary artery disease and MI wasn't fully developed until the start of the nineteenth century—in James Herrick's landmark paper first published in the *Journal of the American Medical Association* in 1912.

Even then, heart disease remained extremely difficult to diagnose, partly because the term was used to describe a miscellany of conditions. Until fairly recently, many doctors believed that blockages in coronary arteries were not curable, that the only result possible was death. Dr. George Burch, chairman of the Department of Medicine at Tulane University from 1945 to 1975 and a major player in the field of cardiology, was notoriously skeptical of the coronary bypass. Chuck Wilkins, who was a med student at Tulane when Burch was there, remembers him as a confirmed fatalist who discouraged his students from practicing the procedure. "Die fast and alone," Burch famously advised, emphasizing his distrust both of hospitals and of medical science's ability to prolong life. In 1984, at age seventy-four, Burch developed angina pectoris. He treated himself with nitroglycerin, but would not discuss his periodic chest pains with colleagues. "One day in his office in 1986," Wilkins told me, "Dr. Burch informed his secretary he felt weak and was leaving for the day. He drove himself home and gave himself an electrocardiogram, which confirmed his suspicions that he was having an acute MI. He took some glycerin, went to bed, and died." When you are wrong in the cardiology business, you are dead wrong.

The first electrocardiographs were installed about 1914 but were of little use because medical science had not yet identified specific patterns of coronary disease. Only after 1920 was it possible to get a definite diagnosis of heart disease. That's when doctors began to understand that when the muscular tissue of the heart is diseased, the heart's contractions will cause abnormal variations in the electrical currents recorded by the electrocardiogram. At that point it began to dawn on medical science that heart disease was neither rare nor necessarily fatal.

The coronary bypass, of course, was a great leap for both doctors and patients. By the 1990s it was almost as common as an appendectomy. Surgeons discovered that they could save time—and patients—by grafting the damaged artery to one or both of the mammary arteries, located on either side of the chest. Grafts that utilize mammary arteries are not only easier and safer to preform, they stay open longer than grafts that use other arteries or veins.

I am happy to report that there is a new type of bypass surgery available that greatly reduces pain, trauma, chance for infection, length of time in the hospital, and the medical bill. It is called minimally invasive direct coronary artery bypass (MIDCAB).

MIDCAB begins with a simple three-inch horizontal incision from nipple to breastbone, rather than the traditional power-tool approach, which splits a twelve-inch gap in the chest and leaves the patient's chest for the remainer of his life looking like an aerial photo of the Rangoon Railroad after an air strike. While the heart continues to beat, surgeons bypass the diseased part of the artery by grafting one end of a nearby healthy artery (usually a mammary) to an area downstream of the blockage.

In the past, surgeons were reluctant to preform the very delicate stitching on the beating heart, but a technique is now available that significantly reduces heart movement during grafting. Physicians administer drugs that slow or even momentarily stop the heart, then use special instruments to apply pressure to either side of the artery and stabilize it. In the meantime, the patient uses a temporary pacemaker to ensure that the heart does not stop for prolonged periods. Because surgeons are working on a beating heart, the risk of stroke and death while on the pump is removed completely.

MIDCAB costs about one-third less than conventional bypass surgery, and patients go home in thirty-six hours, rather than five to eight days. Until now, the new procedure has been limited in the number of grafts it could accomplish. There have been successful double and even triple bypasses, and recently a doctor in El Paso successfully completed a quadruple bypass using MIDCAB. Presumably, in a year or two, they'll be able to do a quintuple, such as the one I had.

From where I sit, the bypass looks like a miracle at least as great as Lourdes. It evolved exactly in time to save a lot of people I care about. At least a dozen of my friends have had bypasses, including Jim Lehrer, who worked at the *Dallas Times Herald* when Jenkins and I were there. Lehrer, the illustrious anchor of PBS's *The News Hour with Jim Lehrer*, went to the ER twelve years ago complaining of tightness in his chest and a tingling in his left arm. An electrocardiogram failed to find any abnormalities in or injuries to his heart, but he was nevertheless hospitalized for observation in the intensive care unit. This precaution saved Jim's life. He woke about five the next morning feeling as though a truck had rolled over his chest.

A nurse told him: "Mr. Lehrer, you've just had a massive heart attack. It's lucky you were here!"

Not everyone agrees that the bypass is miraculous and wonderful. Three years after his quadruple, the Pulitzer Prize–winning novelist Larry McMurtry was sucked under by what shrinks call an "anniversary reaction"—a psychic devastation that hit several months after the successful bypass and that left him feeling as though he no longer existed. "I think the few hours that you're dead [i.e., on the heart-lung machine] opens a gap that's nearly impossible to close," he wrote me. "At least, I can't close it." Larry mailed his friends a copy of an essay he wrote describing the emotional deficit that the operation left, but he didn't publish it because his cardiologist warned him it would scare too many people.

In his essay, Larry writes that a month after surgery he went to Tucson, where he walked, rested, and read Proust and all three volumes of Virginia Woolf's *Diaries*. But a few weeks later all content seemed to drain from his life. He stopped reading, writing, operating his bookshops, lecturing, writing screenplays, even traveling—except for regular trips to see his grandson. Until that time, he wrote, "I had been reading three newspapers a day and leading a type-A East Coast life; I had just finished being president of an international writers' organization for two years. All that soon came to feel as if it belonged in another person's biography: the biography, for instance, of the person I had been before the operation. But I had ceased to be that person; I acted him or impersonated him as best as I could, for the benefit of loved ones; I managed to retain certain of his abilities, but not all. When I began to write again . . . the book I wrote arrived as if by fax from my former self, ten pages a day, typed about as fast as a fax machine can deliver."

He slept an average of three hours a night, waking each morning at exactly three-fifteen, feeling "as if I were holding up the ceiling, or holding at bay a beast, by an act of unrelenting will. I felt that to sleep in darkness would be to die. . . ."

A few months later, in March 1992, Larry realized he could no longer stand to be alone. He moved in with two friends, writer Diana Ossana and her daughter, and scarcely left their house for a year and a half. Eventually, Ossana became his writing partner. Larry was able to call back the substance of his art—"gather enough of the fragments to make a fair showing"—but his emotional intensity had disappeared. Ossana continues to be his partner and his emotional prop.

Anyone who has gone through a bypass is bound to have mixed and confused feelings, though the intensity of these feelings obviously varies from patient to patient. You're glad to be alive, but you feel a separation, an aging that can't be explained by the calendar. Something is gone from your life, something that cannot be retrieved.

Perhaps, as McMurtry says, you are doomed to live in fragments. If so, that's just something else you have to deal with. If Lehrer, Jenkins, McMurtry or myself had been born twenty-five years earlier—before the advent of the heart bypass—we wouldn't be here to amuse you with our tales. I'd rather live in fragments than not at all.

Nine

I make no claim to be an expert on the medical problems of the aging, but having witnessed in myself and my rowdy friends an ungodly number of them—heart disease, hypertension, diabetes, kidney disease, sexual dysfunction, enlarged prostate gland, stress—I am prepared to tell you about my Domino Theory: If you fall victim to one, you'll probably be flattened by another. They seem to work in concert, I'm sorry to report.

Hypertension (high blood pressure), for example, precipitates heart disease, stroke, kidney disease, and diabetes. Diabetes can cause damage to both large and small blood vessels and result in complications affecting the kidneys, eyes, nerves, heart, and gums. Better than 40 percent of those who suffer from diabetes also have hypertension. Stress can bring on hypertension, heart disease, and stroke. All of the above work to create sexual dysfunction or impotence. Conversely, bringing one of them under control can sometimes corral others.

What follows is a sum total of my medical research on the afflictions that have brought me and my friends to our knees, what they are, how you can spot the symptoms, and what I did about them. I'm also including some timely tips on how I improved my sex life, a concern to almost everyone over fifty, though not limited to that age category by any means.

HYPERTENSION

Blood pressure is the force of blood pushing against the walls of our arteries. On the heartbeat, the pressure rises; when the heart is relaxed, it falls back. The systolic (or top) number in a blood pressure reading indicates the maximum amount of pressure on the artery. The diastolic (or lower) number indicates the minimum pressure. The higher the numbers, the harder it is for blood to flow through the arteries. There is no normal blood pressure reading, but adults registering 140/90 are marginally high and in danger of getting worse.

Blood pressure is regulated by arterioles, small vessels that branch off from the arteries. Arterioles work something like a nozzle on a garden hose, which regulates the flow of water through the hose according to how wide the nozzle is opened. When arterioles are narrowed for some reason, they restrict the flow of blood and cause blood pressure to get higher. When that happens, the heart is forced to work harder.

There are no symptoms of high blood pressure, which is why some call it "the silent disease." In most cases there is no known cause, nor can high blood pressure be cured. It can be *controlled*, however, with medication, exercise, and diet. I use three different hypertension medications daily, four if you include the diuretic Lasix. The diuretic causes me to urinate more times a day than I care to reveal, thereby eliminating excessive salt from my system. Doctors always recommend that people with high blood pressure reduce their consumption of salt.

Salt is sodium chloride, an essential element for health when it is properly balanced. Our bodies require only about half a gram of salt daily, but most of us average eighteen grams, or about three teaspoonfuls. Some of us naturally crave salt. Researchers at the department of psychology at the University of Washington believe the mothers of those who crave salt suffered from morning sickness while pregnant with them. According to this theory, Mom's vomiting altered her fluid balance, triggering her offspring's desire to seek extra sodium.

Those with hypertension should replace table salt with a low-sodium substitute, or better yet with herbs and spices. But that's not enough. Salt shows up in almost all canned and processed foods, in amounts that vary widely. For example, three-quarters of a cup of wheat flakes contains 231 milligrams of salt. The same amount of puffed rice or wheat without salt contains only a trace of sodium. A four-ounce glass of tomato juice has 243 milligrams of salt, while the same size glass of grapefruit juice has just 1 milligram. Learn to read the salt contents on labels or consult tables giving sodium amounts.

Most of the low-sodium substitutes use potassium instead of salt, but potassium can be a problem, too. It is important for heart patients to keep a good balance between the sodium and the potassium in their bodies. Sodium and potassium have opposite electrical charges. For your heart's electrical system to work correctly, there must be an adequate amount of sodium outside a cell and an ample supply of potassium inside. When I was first diagnosed with high blood pressure, my doctor was constantly admonishing me to cut back on sodium and make sure I got enough potassium. For a time I even took potassium pills. In recent years the problem appears to have reversed. Now the problem is keeping my potassium level down. This is because one of the medications that control my blood pressure, Capoten, also inhibits the passage of potassium through urination.

One more caveat concerning hypertension. Some people suffer "white-coat hypertension," meaning that their blood pressure is normal most of the time but suddenly rises when they visit their doctor. This is fairly common among men, but rare among women. There is, however, a reverse condition called "white-coat normotension" that causes other people's blood pressure to *drop* when standing face-to-face with a physician. Researchers suspect that normotensives' deceptively low blood pressure in a medical setting may be a by-product of life in the fast lane. These people are so stressed out that visiting the doctor's office is a way to kick back and cool out. Weird, eh?

DIABETES

Diabetes is a group of conditions in which glucose (simple sugar) levels are abnormally high. About sixteen million people in this country have some form of this disease, but only half of them know it.

There are major two types of diabetes, Type I and Type II. Type I, which usually appears in childhood, requires the use of insulin to maintain normal blood sugar levels—and in fact even to survive. Type II, which usually appears in people who are fat and over forty, accounts for 90 to 95 percent of the cases of diabetes. Type IIs do not require insulin to survive, but some people need it nonetheless to keep sugar levels down. Both require constant monitoring of blood sugar.

The proteins, fats, and carbohydrates that make up our diet break down inside our digestive system into simpler, easily absorbed chemicals, one of which is glucose. Glucose circulates through the bloodstream to the cells, where it is used for energy. In order for cells to absorb glucose, however, the hormone insulin must be present. Insulin is produced by the pancreas. In people with diabetes, the pancreas either fails to produce insulin or doesn't churn out enough of it to allow glucose to enter the cells. As a result, sugar builds up in the blood, overflows into the urine, and passes out of the body unused. The body loses its most important source of fuel, even though the blood contains large amounts of glucose.

Until very recently, high blood sugar was defined as any reading measuring above 139. Doctors now believe that anything above 125 is cause for immediate concern. Symptoms of high blood sugar include extreme thirst, frequent urination, fatigue, blurred vision, and vomiting. Low blood sugar (hypoglycemia) can also cause a person to lose consciousness or have a seizure. People with low blood sugar can become cranky, tired, sweaty, hungry, confused, and shaky. Hypoglycemia is more easily addressed than hyperglycemia. A glass of fruit juice usually fixes the problem.

Among the many dangerous side effects of diabetes are an eye disease called diabetic retinopathy, which causes changes in the tiny vessels that supply the retina and could cause the retina to detach from its normal position, and a nerve disease called diabetic neuropathy, which can affect arms, legs, feet, internal organs, and specific nerves in the torso, back, or head.

Type II diabetes can often be controlled with weight loss, exercise, and diet. When first diagnosed, almost all diabetics are overweight and out of shape, and most have little knowledge of nutrition. Different foods have different effects on blood sugar levels. It is more important for diabetics than for others to have consistent eating habits and times. Doctors can often spot candidates for the disease by observing the way a patient is built, particularly the ratio between hip and waist. "Better a pear than an apple," the saying goes—"Better a big butt than a big gut." For reasons unknown,

Mexican-Americans are genetically at high risk for diabetes. One theory is that during times of famine centuries ago in the Southwest, the bodies of their Indian ancestors adapted to store extra energy. Today, under the handicap of our Western diet, that same mechanism causes them to be overweight.

IRREGULAR HEARTBEAT

Just as medical science has discovered recently that depression is fairly common among the elderly, we are now learning that many older people may suffer a slow or irregular heartbeat without anyone suspecting that there's a problem. The symptoms can be as subtle as occasional light-headedness or even lethargy. What that elderly person needs to get him or her up and dancing may be a pacemaker.

One doesn't have to have a heart attack or even heart disease to need a pacemaker. The heart's natural pacemaker, which sends electrical impulses down the walls of the heart and causes it to contract and pump blood, can for no apparent reason develop a partial or complete short circuit. Mine developed a partial short circuit in 1990, two years after my bypass surgery. My symptoms were in no way subtle: I blacked out a couple of times. This was because my heartbeat dropped below fifty beats per minute.

The fix was simple. A surgeon installed in the left side of my chest a battery-powered artificial pacemaker about the size of a book of matches. It works the same way my natural pacemaker did before short-circuiting. When my heartbeat drops below a certain level, a sensing devise in the pacemaker activates and sends impulses down tiny wires attached to the walls of my heart. For the first few years, when my pacemaker was set at sixty beats per minute, I felt an unpleasant tingling in my chest when the gadget activated. Eventually, Corinne Wise, director of Heartwise Monitoring Service, determined that I could tolerate a lower level and reset it at fifty. Since then I almost never feel the thing going off, which indicates that most of the time my heart is contracting and pumping without help from the artificial pacemaker.

Newer models than mine have computerized "memories" that

tell exactly how many heartbeats are natural and how many are artificial. These memories tell technicians precisely when a pacemaker is worn out and a new one is required. In my case, Corinne has to make some educated guesses based on my track record and the amount of energy required to make my heart muscle respond. Normally, a pacemaker will last from four to eight years, which means I'll need a new one soon. "The newer ones are engineered not only with memory but with quite a few creature comforts," Corinne tells me. "These are options, like power windows and power seats on your car, but keep in mind that the more bells and whistles you order, the sooner you'll need new batteries."

Artificial pacemakers have gotten some bad press, mostly because of urban myths. For example, it was assumed for years that people with pacemakers couldn't go near microwaves. This assumption apparently started in the early seventies in Minneapolis, where waves from a transmission tower confused a pacemaker worn by a print shop employee. If microwaves were ever a consideration for pacemaker wearers, that day ended long ago. More recently, portable digital telephones were regarded as a problem. Again, the problem was greatly exaggerated. If certain models of the phone were extremely close to a pacemaker—for example, if the phone was carried in a left shirt pocket, directly over the pacemaker—it could interfere with the pacemaker's on-off switch. "There is a soup of signals in the air," Corinne Wise says. "It is possible that all the digital technology we have today could affect a pacemaker, but it would have to be very close to the pacemaker to make a connection." On the other hand, people with pacemakers should use caution when having an MRI or taking up arc welding or being around anything that throws off a strong electrical field.

Most pacemaker wearers go quietly about their normal lives, nobody the wiser. This is as it should be, because if they had to walk around with a scarlet P on their foreheads, Boy Scouts would be trying to help them cross the street. It is absurd to think of these otherwise healthy citizens as crippled, yet families and friends are frequently overprotective and discourage new patients from perfectly harmless hobbies such as gardening and golf. The Federal Aviation Administration has made it extremely difficult for anyone with a pacemaker to get a pilot's license. "A person with a pacemaker is safer at the controls of an airplane than a pilot who doesn't wear a pacemaker," Wise points out. "But the FAA's attitude shows how pervasive that mind-set is." A pacemaker is the exact opposite of a handicap. One of her clients is a ninety-one-year-old woman who has worn the same pacemaker since 1978. Another is eighty-four-year-old Beverly Sheffield, Austin's longtime parks director and the guy who dreamed up our famous Zilker Park Christmas Tree. Two or three times a week, year-round, you can find Sheffield swimming laps in the frigid waters of the Barton Springs pool. But only his close friends know he has a pacemaker.

KIDNEY DISEASE

Kidneys are the filtering systems that clean waste products from our blood, maintain fluid balance, and help control nutrient levels. If kidneys are not working properly—if wastes, fluids, and nutrients are building up in our bodies—we are in danger of ailments such as high blood pressure and diabetes. Diabetic nephropathy, a kidney disease that develops among nearly half of those who have had diabetes for twenty years or more, can cause the kidneys to fail, a condition called end-stage kidney disease. People whose kidneys fail must either have their blood cleaned by a dialysis machine or get a kidney transplant.

The kidney disease that I have is called nephrotic syndrome. Not to be confused with diabetic nephropathy, nephrotic syndrome shows up when protein accumulates in my urine. There is no cure for this particular type of kidney disease, though the disease has been been known to reverse itself in rare cases. My doctor tells me that there is a 50 percent chance that my kidneys will fail in another five years. I have high hopes that I will prove to be one of the rare cases of reversal. So far, so good.

In the meantime, I do a twenty-four-hour urine test every three or four months, meaning that I collect urine for a twenty-four-hour period and have it tested for protein loss. The good news is that I'm losing less protein than I was a few years ago. I try to restrict the protein in my diet. The function of protein is to build and repair tissue, but if this is to happen the right type of protein—so called high-biological-value protein—must be eaten. High-quality protein comes from eggs, meat, fish, milk, and poultry. Protein from vegetables and grain, primarily dried beans, peas, nuts, and peanut butter, is considered of low biological value.

You can see the problem that kidney disease poses in terms of diet. Since I have to limit both fat and protein, carbohydrates must take on most of the load. I love dried beans and could eat them three times a day, but because they are low-value proteins I have to use restraint; sometimes, I admit, I fail. Eggs, a high-value protein, must be restricted because of their high cholesterol content—though some nutritionists now believe that eggs or any other foods high in dietary cholesterol are of no consequence to heart patients, that only serum cholesterol derived from saturated fat causes arteries to clog. Phyllis has devised a way to prepare an excellent green chili omelet using egg white, but while the whites of eggs are free of cholesterol they are high in protein and, again, restrictions must be made.

Diseased kidneys also lose some or all of their ability to control the sodium level in the body, making it even more important to avoid foods with high salt content such as olives, soy sauce, luncheon meats, and processed foods. People with kidney disease are also advised to avoid using salt substitutes, which are nothing but potassium, a problem in itself.

Everything in life in a trade-off. I really believe that and practice it in all phases of life, but especially in dietary matters. Whether we are talking about egg yolks vs. egg whites, salt vs. salt substitute, or hamburger vs. soyburger, decisions have to be made using common sense. We can't be perfect, so we have to be smart and accept the trade-offs and use them well. The more medical problems I encounter, the more I understand the wisdom of this.

PROSTATE DISEASES

The prostate is a chestnut-sized male gland, located just below the bladder and encircling the urethra. The ducts that control ejaculation pass through the back part of the prostate gland, whose purpose is to produce seminal fluid, which joins with sperm to produce semen at the moment of ejaculation.

The prostate is located in front of the rectum, through which it can be felt when it is enlarged. More than half of the male population over the age of fifty suffer from an enlarged prostate, called benign prostatic hypertrophy or BPH. This condition commonly causes an obstruction of the urethra and makes urination difficult. Though BPH is not life-threatening, it is frustrating, embarrassing, and sometimes painful. Treatment consists of regular sexual releases, hot baths, and massage of the prostate. It also helps to avoid alcohol.

BPH can be treated by medication. One good drug is Cardura, an alpha blocker used to control high blood pressure; it relaxes the "smooth muscle" of the prostate and allows urine to flow more freely. Hytrin works equally well, but Proscar works in less than half of the cases.

When the swelling of the prostate is caused by infection, the condition is called prostatitis. Patients suffering from prostatitis need to urinate frequently and usually experience a burning sensation during urination. Prostatitis can usually be treated with antibiotics.

The real danger of the prostate is prostate cancer, the second leading cause of cancer death in men and a problem of growing concern to health care specialists. If detected early, many of these cancers do not result in death. Some prostate tumors, however, are fast-growing and aggressive and can metastasize to the bone or to distant parts of the body very quickly. This type of cancer is far more difficult to treat.

Physicians can detect the presence of prostate cancer with a simple blood test called a PSA or prostate specific antigen test, which measures the protein antigen in the prostate. If production of the protein is greatly elevated, cancer is suspected. When a tumor is present in the prostate, doctors can usually feel a lump or nodule. In this case, they will order a prostate ultrasound examination and a biopsy—two parts of the same procedure.

Some cases of prostate cancer respond to medication, others require surgery. Surgery for prostate cancer, while not minor, isn't major either, though the operation is far from pleasant. The procedure consists of running an instrument through the penis and coring open the prostate. Dr. Paul Kaufman, a urologist at Austin Diagnostic Clinic, explains, "If you think of the prostate as an orange, surgery removes the fruit and leaves the rind."

Kaufman recommends that men undergo both PSA blood tests and rectal exams once a year. The two tests can detect trouble before it becomes life-threatening. Incidentally, men should abstain from sex for at least forty-eight hours before having a PSA test. A roll in the sack can mess up your PSA levels, sending them up by about 40 percent. That means that a normally healthy guy could be mistakenly sent for a biopsy when in fact all he really needs is a nap.

STRESS

Stress is the booger in the closet when the lights are off. You can't see it, but you feel the menace deep in your bones. Stress not only affects you mentally and emotionally, it also causes profound physical changes that prepare your body for "fight or flight." This built-in survival response occurs involuntarily whether you are involved in a real life-threatening situation, stuck in a traffic jam, or just trying to balance your checkbook.

Stress begins with anger or fear, either of which signals the adrenal and thyroid glands that trouble is afoot. These two glands combine to release the stress hormone adrenaline, which jump-starts your body and increases your strength and speed. It also causes rapid changes in body chemistry. Your blood pressure, heart rate, respiration rate, and blood sugar level all increase, and your respiratory passageways dilate. These stress hormones may also disrupt the plaque clinging to your artery walls and increase the stickiness of platelets that form clots, pushing you closer to a stroke or heart attack.

This complex stress adaption system involves virtually every organ, gland, and chemical in your body. Continued exposure to these hormones can cause steroid poisoning, leading to osteoporosis, diabetes, hypertension, redistribution of body fat, premature aging, and many other problems. Most of all, stress rolls out the red carpet for heart attacks.

There is no way to avoid stress, not the way things are today. You see it everywhere—in the increased incidents of violence on the highway, in episodes of domestic abuse, in the thousand-mile stares of pedestrians in large cities. Living in New York back in the mid-seventies, I couldn't help notice that people hurrying along the streets actually leaned forward, their heads a good six inches in advance of their feet, their minds already working at some task their bodies would not reach for a while. Hardly anyone seemed able—or willing—to relax and enjoy the moment. When society has reached the point where some people find that the only place they can really relax is at their doctor's office, we have a problem, folks.

Researchers have discovered that stress related to discrimination is as much a health risk for African-Americans as smoking or a high-fat diet. We have known for a long time that blacks were victims of hypertension and heart disease in far higher percentages than whites, but have blamed diet and genetic factors. To most blacks, I imagine, it comes as no surprise that stress kills as many of them as too much of Mama's fried chicken. Until recently, complaints of stress building up because of pervasive workaday racism were widely dismissed by whites as exaggerated. But occurrences such as the videotaped beating of Rodney King, the cross-examination of Los Angeles police detective Mark Fuhrman, and the exposure of bigotry among Texaco executives have exposed a climate of discrimination that is caustic and habitual. Researchers have also learned that blood pressure is higher for working-class blacks who accept unfair treatment as "a fact of life" than for blacks who challenge it.

There are some techniques that can help all of us manage stress.

Be aware of negative thoughts. Every time you allow anger and frustration to take control, they drain away good energy and sidetrack things that are important. The next time you are in a traffic jam or are the target of an insult, take an inventory of the situation and ask yourself: Is this worth a heart attack? Can I do anything to modify this situation without making it worse? What harm has this situation caused me? What's my hurry? Put on your favorite CD, and sit back and listen. There is a great line from one of Willie Nelson's songs that advises, "Time will take care of itself, if you'll just leave time alone."

Make time to relax. Don't take it, *make* it. I make time three days a week to exercise, which I regard as a priority, not a luxury or a hobby. The way I figure, I don't have time to *not* exercise. Nothing relieves my stress better, faster, or more surely than a long workout at Big Steve's. Physical fitness gives me a feeling of well-being and brings out the positive. You can relieve stress by playing tennis or any sport, or with aerobics, jogging, or even walking. People who meditate or practice yoga tell me those are great techniques for neutralizing stress and restoring balance. Praying helps, I know that.

Get a sense of humor. Hell, if you can't laugh at a traffic jam, what can you laugh at? People who wallow in negativity, who brood and resist change, who refuse to make decisions, are people who have forgotten how to laugh. Once you deal with a problem, good humor just naturally flows back into the vaccum.

OSTEOPOROSIS

The first time I heard of osteoporosis was when my granny fell and broke her hip not long after her seventy-sixth birthday. It wasn't the force of the fall that caused her hip to fracture, the doctor told me, but rather that the hipbone had been weakened by a metabolic bone disease called osteoporosis, which causes bones to lose density and strength.

Granny wasn't one of those stooped, frail old women you see at the mall, bent over their canes and unable to stand straight—women who are obviously suffering from osteoporosis. Part Comanche, this scrawny little woman who helped raise me was strong as an ox and had the constitution of a slab of granite. She dipped snuff, drank half a pint of whiskey a day, and fried nearly everything that she ate. She loved to walk—I think Granny could have walked all day—and she could work in her garden for six or eight hours at a stretch without tiring. As far as I know, Granny had never been sick a day in her life. But after breaking her hip, she began to wither away. She never got back on her feet and some months later died in a nursing home.

You hear of similar cases nearly every day, old women and occasionally old men, breaking their hips or spines. One day they seem relatively healthy, then the next day they trip and fall—and in the days that follow, almost without fail, they began sinking like rocks. We think of our bones as a permanent structure over which our skin and muscle are hung, but in fact they are changing constantly, losing masses of calcium and gaining new ones. As we age, unfortunately, we tend to lose more than we gain, and there lies the problem.

The reasons why women develop osteoporosis far more often than men are instructive in terms of what causes the disease and how it can be prevented. Women tend to build less bone than men when they are young, and they tend to be less physically active, meaning that their bones are not as strong. Most of us reach our maximum bone density by age twenty-five to thirty and decline after that. Girls in their early teens typically become deficient in calcium, a mineral that is not produced naturally by our bodies but is absolutely essential for the formation and health of bones.

At about age fifty, when women reach menopause, their ovaries stop producing the female sex hormone estrogen. With the loss of estrogen, a rapid acceleration of bone loss occurs, particularly from the spine. Physicians originally believed that this was just part of the aging process. Since women no longer needed to reproduce, they no longer needed estrogen. But in 1985—more than a decade after Granny died—medical science documented that elderly women who took estrogen replacement had 50 percent fewer fractures than women who didn't take estrogen.

Today we recognize the three most important reasons why women develop osteoporosis 80 percent more often than men: calcium deficiencies, lack of exercise, and the effects of menopause.

IMPOTENCE

This is the affliction that hardly anybody talks about, even among friends—*especially* among friends. A few years ago I probably couldn't have defined the word. Impotence simply means that a man can't get an erection or can't keep one long enough to complete sexual intercourse. In our macho culture, however, impotence has come to be equated with a lack of manliness. Real men can get it up, anytime, anyplace.

Sorry, but that is a big lie. Among the population in general, 10 to 15 percent of all men experience some degree of impotence. But above age sixty, *one in every three* suffers impotence. Almost every case can be treated and overcome if the sufferer would admit his problem and seek medical help. It has been estimated that thirty million American men are impotent, and yet fewer than two million have ever been treated. "Most men know more about the workings of the combustion engine than about the dynamics of their own sex lives," writes Dr. Erwin Goldstein, a urologist at the Boston University School of Medicine.

Most of us grew up believing that men older than sixty-five weren't interested in sex, let alone capable of having it. As we approach that age ourselves, however, we learn how wrong we were. The interest is usually there, and if it's not, injections of the male hormone testosterone can rekindle it. More often, it's not the desire but the capabilities that cause sexual dysfunction. This is particularly true of men who have suffered from heart disease or any kind of vascular problem. The arteries that supply blood to the heart are not much different from the arteries than supply blood to the penis: when they are clogged by cholesterol, the damn organ stops working. Fortunately, improving blood supply to the penis does not require bypass surgery. Penile injections, penile inserts, and hand-operated vacuum erection devices can all stiffen the ol' resolve, if you follow my meaning.

"If you want it, you can have a satisfactory sexual relationship into your nineties," Dr. James Barada, a prominent Albany, New York, urologist told *New York Times* reporter Sandra Blakeslee. A man in his nineties won't respond to sex the same as a man in his sixties, just as a man in his sixties won't respond the same as a man in his forties, who in turn won't respond the same as a man in his twenties. With the passing of years, more direct stimulation and more fantasy (and of course more time) are required to raise the curtain on the sex act. But no matter what the age, the emotional, physical, and psychological needs are there, and so is the ability to enjoy the simple pleasures of a good roll in the sack. Believe me when I tell you that it's better than ever at sixty.

Doctors used to think that all impotence was psychological. "That was before we knew much about the physiology of erections," says Paul Kaufman, my Austin urologist. Kaufman told me that only 5 to 10 percent of cases of impotence are caused by psychological factors: depression, stress, or performance anxiety, which is the fear of failure leading to more fears of failure. An even smaller percentage are caused by neurogenic problems: nerves to the penis that age and wear out, for example, or spinal cord, pelvis, or back injuries. The vast majority of cases of impotence—about 85 percent—have physical causes and can be corrected.

Though researchers have not paid much attention to women's sexual problems, they have discovered that a variety of vascular problems can cause a lack of orgasm in women. Anything that deprives either the penis or the clitoris of oxygen—vascular problems, sexual abstinence, lack of exercise, sleep deprivation, drinking, smoking, diabetes, injuries—contributes to sexual problems in both men and women.

The relaxed penis has less oxygen than any other organ, with serious consequences for some men. Without oxygen, tissue inside the penis becomes less elastic and less able to expand, causing muscle cells to atrophy. When this happens, the cells lose their elasticity and their ability to relax. On the other hand, nature provides men a sort of sexual therapy during the erotic stimulations of dreams. Most men get an erection sometime during the night as they sleep, which fills the penis with oxygen-rich blood and breaks down the low-oxygen tissue that accumulated when the penis was soft.

My impotency, I discovered, was caused both by low levels of testosterone and vascular obstructions. For a while I took testosterone injections biweekly, but more recently I was introduced to Androderm, a medicated skin patch, which I change daily. The patch maintains a steadier level of the hormone than biweekly injections, so you don't experience peaks and valleys. The most popular drug to increase the flow of blood to the penis is Prostin, which you can either inject in the side of the penis or insert in the urethra. MUSE, the brand name of the insert, is by far the favored method. I can tell you that the combination of the patch and the Prostin worked wonders in my case. The first time I used the drug in the privacy of my closet, Phyllis called out from the bedroom and asked me if it was working. "Does the term 'Louisville Slugger' ring a bell?" I replied. Phyllis howled with delight. This spontaneous bit of levity shattered what might otherwise have been a tense and awkward moment in our love life. After that the Louisville Sluggers became our little joke, our way of agreeing that while penile injections or inserts are not the sort of foreplay one would prefer, they invariably lead to great and memorable moments. The Slugger, bless his heart, is like the child we never had.

In the 1970s, penile implants were regarded as the gold standard of treatment for sexual dysfunction, but today most urologists consider them a last resort. Implants require very expensive, potentially dangerous surgery and do not always work as advertised. A friend in Houston had a penile implant with disastrous results. His story is instructive.

He got the implant on the advice of a golf acquaintance who assured him that his own implant made airline stewardesses faint with pleasure. But my friend's urologist failed to warn him that because he was a diabetic, his risk of infection from the implant was greater than normal. (The doctor also neglected to mention the easier, safer options of injections, inserts, and vacuum pumps.) The implant model that my friend selected consisted of an inflatable cylinder planted in his corpora (the spongy tissue of the penis), a fluid reservoir in the abdomen, and a pump in the scrotum. By squeezing the pump, he could force fluid to the cylinders, causing the penis to go rigid. A squeeze of the pump's release value reversed the process. He referred to his new member as "Robodick."

He wore his Robodick for nearly a year, but it never worked as advertised. It hurt all the time and hurt worse when it was pumped up. "When I had an erection," he told me, "it felt like a pair of pliers." Then one morning, sitting in his office, he looked down and saw that the seat of his chair was covered with blood. The operation had caused an infection in his scrotum, which had ruptured the skin and begun to hemorrhage. The condition was additionally complicated by his diabetes. His only recourse was to have Robodick surgically removed, again at considerable expense.

After the infection had healed, my friend went back to his regular doctor (not the urologist) for advice. By this time he had learned about injections, inserts, and vacuum devices and thought he'd try one or all of them. To his absolute horror, he was told that the implant had destroyed the erectile tissue inside his penis. It was gone and could not be replaced.

"My God!" my friend said to the doctor. "Are you telling me I'll never have another erection?"

The doctor shrugged and said, "You're nearly seventy—you've screwed enough."

"In a sick way, that reminded me of the old joke about a guy who goes to his doctor complaining that he can't piss," my friend told me. "The doctor reminds the guy that he is ninety-three years old and tells him, 'Don't worry about it—you've pissed enough.' "

Part Three:

PICKING UP THE PIECES

Ten

*W*hen they warned Phyllis that my recovery would be punctuated by wild mood swings, she thought to herself: What else is new? Wild mood swings were the least she expected, having lived with me for a dozen years now. Women who marry writers, or at least those who stay married, develop a special kind of detachment. They chill out from the center until they achieve a state of grace in which time and events free-float at the margins of perception. They view every crisis and turning point with the deep assurance that nothing is ever as bad (or as good) as it seems at the moment. Tantrums, sulks, snits— they all hit like summer thunderstorms and pass just as quickly.

Thinking back, I probably wasn't as bad as she had expected. Having my chest ripped open encouraged in me two virtues that have never been my strong suits—patience and humility.

I began learning them the moment I awakened in intensive care. Pop! I was back among the living, and the pain was something to behold. Indeed it was! My whole upper body felt as if I had been blindsided by Dick Butkus. I felt like a newborn baby, helpless and beyond vanity or pride. I couldn't swallow or even clear my throat without a new slash of pain throttling my senses. I got patience and humility the way some get religion, on the road to Damascus, as it were.

After the first shock, I learned quickly to move very slowly, if at all. The quiet inner voice of survival spoke so that only I could hear. It told me.

Deliberate every act carefully, calculate and weigh it against alternatives. Say, for example, that you need to pee in your bedside pitcher. Rehearse exactly how you will manage it, well in advance of the act itself. Okay? There is no shame in peeing in a pitcher, not anymore, but rather deep gratitude that you are able to accomplish so great a task. Even after they take you from intensive care and move you to the far more comfortable ambience of a private room, *think* before you act. Make every movement a priority of the will and a marshaling of the sum of your knowledge and experience. You'll get the hang of it presently. You'd better.

One of the things they encourage a bypass patient in post-op to do is cough. Coughing clears the lungs and reduces the chance of pneumonia and fever. Every cough feels like you've been hit in the sternum by a .45 slug. There is the additional raw pain from where they dug a vein out of your leg, and the stab of countless needles and the irritation of countless catheters leading off to God knows where, but these are nothing, trifles compared with the exquisite pain in your chest.

By the second day I was sitting up in my room. The breathing tube that had run to my windpipe had been removed, permitting me at last to yell at anyone I pleased. Still, it did not please me to yell. Yelling was an activity that some former me indulged in from time to time. It no longer served my purpose or suited my personality, which seemed to have been surgically removed and replaced with a more timid, reluctant, and hopefully graceful personna.

Some sister of mercy was kind enough to provide me with a heart-shaped red pillow, a sort of surrogate teddy bear that I could hug to my bosom to absorb the shock of coughing and clearing my throat. I was grateful beyond words. I still have that little heart-shaped pillow, on the chaise longue next to my bed.

A pimply-faced orderly dropped by my room at regular intervals to make certain that I practiced my deep-breathing exercises. For this he provided a cylindrical vacuum tube with a mouthpiece and a Ping-Pong ball seated at the cylinder's bottom. Around the circumference of the cylinder were marked the numbers from one to ten, which measured progress. The object is to take a deep breath, then exhale enough air to raise the ball. You are supposed to raise it a little higher on each attempt. Years ago at the Dallas Cowboys training camp in Thousand Oaks, California, I had tried a similar exercise, breathing into a device called a Vital Capacity Register, and had achieved excellent results—far better, for example, than quarterback Eddie LeBaron. But the first time I tried it after surgery, the Ping-Pong ball might as well have been a sixteen-pound shot.

Like everything else after surgery, breathing exercises get a little better, a little easier, a little more comfortable, with each effort.

The worst part of those first few days was the pain. It was almost constant, and I spent my time watching the clock on the wall across from my bed, calculating the minutes and seconds until my next shot of morphine. Nearly as bad was the feeling of immobility. I was wrapped like a rodeo calf in a tangle of tubes and wires. I couldn't even get out of bed to go to the bathroom. Both arms were black-and-blue from the constant need to relocate the catheter through which nurses administered drugs and took blood samples. A tube ran from my chest, draining fluids that accumulate during and after the operation. Snaking off in another direction were wires connecting the electrodes glued to my chest to an oscilloscope, a device that allowed the nursing staff to monitor my heart rate and rhythm. I was instructed to lie on my side as much as possible—lying on your back is bad for your lungs—but the ordeal of trying to turn over broke new ground in this marathon of pain.

Constipation is fairly common after surgery, and when I finally felt the need for a bowel movement on the second day, I was allowed to step from my bed for the first time and told to squat on what looked like a child's training potty. A beefy, humorless nurse stood watch, arms folded tightly across her enormous breasts, one foot tapping the floor impatiently. Just as I thought I was about to achieve success, I was startled to hear her bark, "Don't *strain!*" In an instant my anal sphincter snapped tighter than a turtle's jaws. I told her that I'd changed my mind, that I'd try again some other time.

By the third day, I was allowed to get out of bed and walk to the bathroom without assistance. I was overwhelmed with a feeling of freedom and relief. I'll tell you something, sir or madam, if there comes a time in your life when the simple act of being permitted to take a dump in private lifts you to a state of unqualified joy, you will have discovered humility.

The entire experience of open-heart surgery changes your life as surely as the loss of an arm or leg. Part of your heart has died, and there is nothing you can do to alter that situation. Face it, you are beginning the last chapter of your life. Grafts don't always last, so maybe you'll be in the operating room again, maybe soon. You are no longer in control of your life, not that you ever were, but small pleasures such as smoking, drinking milk shakes, and eating bacon-and-tomato sandwiches are history. Your lifestyle is about to get drastically rearranged, and you are ready—or so you tell yourself.

"Everyone gets religion in post-op," Dr. Chuck Wilkins reminded me, "but not many keep it."

I had never thought much about death before, but I thought about it a lot during those first few days after surgery. I had brushed against death, felt its clammy texture and its hot breath. That was a hard fact and I couldn't change it. But thinking about death started me rethinking life. From this point forward, I realized, life was a new kind of risk requiring new attitudes and procedures. If I let it, every twinge and unexplained chest pain could throw me into a blue panic. I could allow myself to be psychologically devastated by the heart attack and become a full-time patient, constantly monitoring my heart and planning my next trip to the emergency room. Or I could remember that life up to this point had been a series of unexplained physical phenomena and events. What I had just experienced was merely another one, admittedly worse than usual, but nothing to dwell on. As Nietzsche observed, that which doesn't kill us makes us stronger. I made a conscious decision to treat the ordeal as though it were a very nasty cut requiring an extraordinary number of stitches, not something that would change the focus of my life. I was convinced that this attitude was necessary for survival, and I believe it even more strongly ten years later.

I am not going to sugarcoat it, however—bypass survivors face major attitude adjustments. The fear, anger, and depression that are common in post-op may very well follow you home. You can almost count on it. But you can also count on these emotions lessening and then vanishing fairly soon. Helen Thorpe, a senior editor at *Texas Monthly,* told me about her uncle, a duck farmer in Ireland, who was depressed for weeks after his bypass surgery. Then, as if by magic, he seemed to change his entire outlook on life. "He became whimsical," Helen recalled. "He started spending more time with his nieces, slowing and measuring his pace, savoring each day of his life." In other words, he stopped feeling sorry for himself.

Almost all bypass patients experience bouts of depression after being released from the hospital, though I can't remember being anything except damn happy to be going home. Jenkins and I have in common the belief that if bad luck tumbles down from the sky, then your odds of its happening again are astronomical. That's not scientifically proven, granted, but some people are just that way. Some people get depressed, others don't. The "anniversary reaction" that Larry McMurtry experienced can be devastating to the extreme, which is one reason that surgeons are pulling away from the radically invasive form of bypass and using instead the minimally invasive procedure with its simple three-inch horizontal incision. If doctors can eliminate the heart-lung machine and use in its place drugs and a temporary pacemaker, bypass surgery won't be much worse than an appendectomy.

Normally, postsurgical depression hangs around one or two weeks, though it can last much longer unless you recognize it and do something about it. The warning signs of depression include difficulty sleeping, poor appetite, fatigue and low energy levels, trouble concentrating, feelings of listlessness or irritability, apathy, low self-esteem, despair, and slovenliness. Remember, these symptoms are normal—though not necessarily inevitable. But if any of them persist more than a few days, tell your doctor. They could be a sign that you are falling into depression and need a medication to kick it.

You are bound to feel weak at first. This is not because of your damaged heart but because you've been in bed for a week or ten days. Without activity, muscles lose 15 percent of their strength in just one week. The only way to regain strength is to exercise. Walking is the easiest and best exercise, especially for the first few weeks. Don't push it. Though I had been used to walking about four miles two or three times a week, I discovered on my first postsurgical outing that I couldn't make it to the end of my block. Phyllis had to help me back to the front steps, where I sat for about ten minutes, frustrated to the point of tears, wondering if I'd ever be whole again. The next day I got all the way to the stop sign on the corner and back again. I felt much better then. Within a couple of days I could make it around four blocks, and after six weeks I was back on the hike-and-bike trail with my dogs, doing my old four-mile routine.

Regular exercise is only one of the lifestyle changes your doctor will suggest. The doctor will also tell you to stop smoking and to avoid exposure to tobacco smoke, and to establish a diet low in fat and cholesterol and high in dietary fiber and antioxidant vitamins. Some patients may also be advised to take one or two aspirins a day to help prevent blood clots. If you are overweight, you will need to lose some pounds. If you have high blood pressure, the doctor may put you on medication or adjust the medication you are already taking. There are a number of nonpharmacological ways to reduce blood pressure and prevent or avoid stress. Stress is your worse enemy.

Doctors can prescribe medication for some of the major risk factors, namely high blood pressure, high cholesterol, and diabetes. But coronary artery disease (CAD) is your problem, and you are the only one who can deal with it. The other major risk factors—smoking, lack of exercise, obesity, and stress—all require major lifestyle modifications on your part. And even conditions like high blood pressure, high cholesterol, and diabetes require that you change your habits. One purpose of this book is to convince readers that modifying one's lifestyle is not the same as stupefying it. With common sense and patience, I promise that these changes can make life richer and sweeter than you ever imagined.

Cutting your risk of heart attack to zero sounds impossible, but most of us can do just that. Decades of research have identified the problems and risks, and almost all of them are in our power to control. Smoking, high cholesterol, and high blood pressure account for 85 percent of all heart attacks. The one risk we can't control—family history—can be minimized by controlling the others. Dr. William Castelli, one of America's foremost cardiologists and director of the famed Framingham Heart Study, says that the secret is *knowing, monitoring, and controlling* risk factors. "If all Americas did this," he claims, "heart disease would be eradicated, as polio was."

Eleven

Almost every doctor I talked to and every paper I read on the subject of heart disease fingers blood cholesterol as the Public Enemy No. 1 to the human heart. Smoking is a distant second.

Those who grew up in the 1950s never heard the word "cholesterol," but in the 1990s it's the most used word in the fields of health and nutrition. Almost every can or package in our pantry or refrigerator has the cholesterol content printed on its label. Thanks largely to research on cholesterol, the death rate for heart disease in America began to fall in 1964, and the trend continues. As a general rule, a 1 percent reduction in total cholesterol causes a 2 percent reduction in heart attack. If a man lowers his blood cholesterol from, say, 250 to 200 milligrams per deciliter (mg/dl), he reduces his risk 40 percent.

Cholesterol is a waxy molecule present in blood plasma and all animal tissue. It is essential for producing hormones and is produced naturally by the liver, its rate of production depending on how much of the foul yellow stuff we absorb from animal products. Some cholesterol-reducing medications work by tricking the liver so that it slackens off its own production and sucks more cholesterol from the blood.

There are two types of cholesterol—low-density lipoprotein (LDL), a blood substance that contains large amounts of fat and that tends to stay in the body and build up into mounds of plaque on artery walls; and high-density lipoprotein (HDL), a protein that carries cholesterol and other fats away from the arteries and delivers them to the liver for safe disposal. LDL is "bad cholesterol" and HDL is "good cholesterol."

Dr. Thomas Blevins, an endocrinologist at Austin Diagnostic Clinic, explains it this way: "Think of LDL as a transportation system that carries fatty particles to the cells, and think of HDL as a reverse transportation system that picks up cholesterol from your arteries and returns it in the liver, which breaks it down or recycles it. An excess of bad cholesterol and an inadequate supply of good cholesterol are both risk factors for heart attack or stroke. What you need is a balance of LDL and HDL."

One of the great dangers of high blood cholesterol—as in the case of high blood pressure—is that you don't feel it or see it. But just as blood pressure can be easily measured, so can levels of cholesterol, with a simple, inexpensive blood test. Any doctor or clinic can run the blood test and calculate your cholesterol in a few hours.

The American Heart Association calculates that a total cholesterol number of 200 or less erases it as a major risk factor. Between 200 and 240 is borderline high, and above 240 is heart-attack country. By one estimate, 40 percent of the people in this country top 240. While the total cholesterol number is important, it's not the only number you need to know. Normal or safe amounts of HDL or good cholesterol are 35 or higher. Your level of LDL or bad cholesterol should be less than 130. It is extremely important for anyone who has had a heart attack—or, for that matter, anyone over the age of fifty—to know his or her cholesterol numbers. People who have tested normal should continue to be tested every five years. If your numbers are not in the normal range, test every four months, even after you've reached your target.

The battle against cholesterol starts later for women than it does for men, but it is no less important. Whereas women in their midtwenties have lower cholesterol levels than men, the reverse is true once they reach forty-five. Between the ages of forty-five and fifty-five the average woman's cholesterol rises to between 223 and 246. The gap widens further beyond age fifty-five. Though research has yet to pinpoint the healthiest cholesterol levels for women, there is no question that the problems of the sexes are similar. In 1989 about 61 percent of white women and 54 percent of black women had levels of 200 or more, suggesting that they were at risk. As I have said, the chances of a man having a heart attack decrease 2 percent for every 1 percent drop in cholesterol. If the same holds true for women, it follows that reducing cholesterol offers great advantages to both younger and older women.

No matter what the age or sex, lowering high cholesterol levels should be everyone's priority. Cardiologists once believed that most heart attacks were the result of very large blockages, those in the 90 to 95 percent range. More recently they have learned that the vast majority of heart attacks are from arteries that are clogged less than 50 percent—because of the plaque-rupturing process described earlier. People with elevated cholesterol should immediately reduce fat and saturated fat in their diet and stop smoking—smoking inhibits good cholesterol. Cholesterol in the diet is found only in animal products such as meat, poultry, fish, eggs, and dairy foods. Saturated fat is found mostly in animal fat and coconut, palm, and palm kernel oils. The true enemy isn't cholesterol, it's saturated fat. Many researchers now believe that foods high in dietary cholesterol—eggs, for example—do no harm as far as raising cholesterol levels in the blood.

Some medical practitioners believe that you can *reverse* coronary artery blockage through lifestyle changes. Dr. Dean Ornish, a Texas-born cardiologist, is the guru of the reversal movement, which has made his San Francisco–based clinic the model for this school of thought. Ornish preaches an "intense lifestyle modification," which includes a strict vegetarian diet that is virtually cholesterol-free, in addition to light exercise, yoga, and meditation.

Unlike other programs, Ornish's addresses the psychosocial aspects—anxiety, anger, depression, social isolation—with what he calls "stress management." Ornish treats heart disease as a "behavioral illness." Those who are wealthy enough and dedicated enough to follow the program have in fact lowered their cholesterol impressively and reversed blockage in the coronary arteries.

Some of my doctors mistrusted Ornish's research, and even those who believed his data weren't so sure that Ornish was for everyone. One obvious drawback is the necessity that enrollees travel to San Francisco or one of the other locations where Ornish has established franchise clinics. "It's a very expensive approach for very few people," the endocrinologist Tom Blevins says. "It does lower cholesterol twenty-nine percent and does it without medication. But it doesn't tell us how to get the most bang for the buck. Is it a low-cholesterol diet? Exercise? Reduced stress? You can't tell with Ornish's approach." A lot of researchers are backing away from trying to regress high blockages, Blevins added. Instead, they are trying to stablize small ones.

An additional problem with the Ornish approach is the severely restricted diet that it demands. Most doctors know from experience how hard it is to convince patients of the need to cut back on certain foods. Imagine how much harder it is to get them to flat out *stop* eating meat, poultry, fish, cheese, eggs, and milk. "To do this, you need patients who are extremely well motivated in the first place," my cardiologist, Chuck Wilkins, told me. "But with a group *that* motivated, you can demonstrate almost anything." The bottom line for regression, Wilkins said, is how low you can get the LDL. It has to get very low before plaque begins to regress. "You can do it with a very-low-cholesterol diet, or you can do it with medication," Wilkins reminded me. "Medication is much easier. Life is too short not to have a chicken-fried steak from time to time."

The landmark study on the dangers of cholesterol was conducted in 1952 by Ancel Keys, a giant in the field of dietary research. Keys studied the dietary habits of seven countries and demonstrated clearly that the populations that ate the most saturated fat had the highest blood cholesterol and the greatest number of heart attacks. Though the famous Mediterranean diet didn't come in vogue until the 1990s, Ancel and his wife, Margaret, actually pioneered it with a cookbook they published in 1959, *How to Eat Well and Stay Well the Mediterranean Way.* Keys also made clear that there is absolutely no connection between cholesterol in food and cholesterol in the blood—*none!* The notion that dietary cholesterol mattered originated from a study on rabbits and chickens, both highly sensitive to dietary cholesterol. Humans and other carnivores, however, are not sensitive. "It doesn't make any difference how much cholesterol is in the diet," Keys said recently in an interview with *Eating Well* magazine. "What matters is saturated fat, which we've proven raises serum cholesterol."

Several more-recent studies drive home the basic lesson that Keys gave us years ago—*that it isn't dietary cholesterol but serum cholesterol that kills us!* We accumulate serum cholesterol from one place—animal fat. Foods that are merely high in dietary cholesterol—eggs are the most famous example—are in most cases among the least fattening and most heart-healthy things we can eat. In a study of the rate of heart attacks in various European countries, researchers learned that the country with the lowest incidence was the island of Crete, which in the ten years covered by the study had zero deaths related to heart attacks. This seems amazing, considering that many of the residents had dangerously high cholesterol levels. The reason was the diet of the Mediterranean. In another study using six hundred heart patients, half the group ate the Mediterranean diet and the other half ate the diet of the American Heart Association (AHA). Though both groups got about 30 percent of their total calories from fat, the Mediterranean group showed a remarkable 76 percent reduction in heart attacks compared to the AHA dieters.

The difference was that the Mediterranean group ate more monounsaturated fatty acids while the AHA group ate more polyunsaturated fatty acids. Monounsaturated fats are more stable and resistant to oxidation than polyunsaturated fats. Oxidation is a known contributor to heart attacks. (Researchers also theorized that low dietary levels of oxidation-prone fats might explain why cancer rates were lower in Greece, southern Italy, and other places where olive oil, which is rich in monunsaturated fat, was part of the daily menu.)

Human nutrition is apparently genetically programmed, which poses this curious paradox: Our game-hunter ancestors consumed far more fat than we do today, but heart disease, hypertension, diabetes, and certain types of cancer were virtually unknown. Researchers have learned that the proportion of proteins to total calories in the diet of ancient populations was three to five times higher than ours. They ate far more meat—ensuring high iron and folic acid levels but also high cholesterol levels. Conversely, their protein-rich diet had less total fat, more essential fatty acids, more fiber, less salt, more vitamins, and a much higher ratio of polyunsaturated to saturated fats than ours.

Although we can help lower cholesterol by changing our diets, giving up smoking, and starting to exercise, some people still need outside help. One research study using a low-fat diet and a tough exercise program proved that patients would need at least one hour of endurance exercise seven days a week to regress coronary blockage. So unless you are a dedicated aerobics practitioner, you probably need help in the form of medication.

Some people need help because they inherited a tendency to

high blood cholesterol. If you are one of them—I am, apparently—
you will be happy to learn that researchers and pharmaceutical companies have come up with a number of excellent medications that do
the job. It's a multibillion-dollar business, in fact, and for this reason research is sure to continue.

The most effective drugs for reducing cholesterol are the so-
called statins—simvastatin, pravastatin, lovastatin, fluvastatin—
better known by trade names like Zocor, Pravachol, and Mevacor,
and Lescol. A very potent new cholesterol drug that just became
available is atorvastatin, trade name Lipitor.

Do not make the mistake of believing that just because you have
never had a heart attack, you are not at risk. There are one and a half
million new heart attack victims each year, and a third of them die.
By one estimate, there are fourteen million Americans in need of
cholesterol treatment, but only about one-fourth of them are actually
getting it. Drugs like Zocor are expensive—my bill for a month's
supply is nearly $180—but it's nothing compared to the expense of
a heart attack, which can run to $100,000 in the first year alone.
Some people who have been on medication stop after a few years.
This is a mistake. If they keep taking it six or seven years, statistics
suggest, the medication can make a major difference. We're talking
life and death.

Even people who do not have high cholesterol levels but do have
some form of heart disease can be helped greatly by cholesterol-
lowering medications. A study of patients who had suffered heart attacks but had moderate cholesterol levels of 200 for total cholesterol
and 139 for LDL showed that with Pravachol the threat of new heart
attacks was reduced 28 percent.

Research has shown that 214 of every 1,000 cardiac "events"
can be prevented with cholesterol-lowering medication. An event
can be a fatal heart attack, a bypass, a stroke, or even a blockage to
arteries in the arms or legs. The same soft plaque that clogs coronary
arteries can also block the supply of blood to the arms, legs, and
penis, and cause nonfatal but painful and embarrassing problems.

My own experience with diet, exercise, and cholesterol-lowering
drugs illustrates the point that I am trying to make. The changes in
my well-being started shortly after I had switched physicians, going

from Wilkins to Blevins—at Wilkins's suggestion. Chuck Wilkins
and I had become friends. It's a mistake, I think, to have a friend as
a primary physician. It is tough for friends to tell friends the hard
facts—tougher still for friends on the receiving end to accept them.
Tom Blevins is more detached, a research scientist as much a physician. On my first visit to his office, Blevins asked me if I had an occasional drink. Yes, I told him with a straight face, *occasionally.*

"How many drinks a day?" he asked.

"Oh, maybe two or three," I lied.

He multiplied the number of calories in three drinks (450) by
365. The sum, 164,250, was how many extra calories I would have
consumed in one year—if I had told the truth about my drinking
habits, which I hadn't. That figure, 164,250, got my attention in a big
way. That same day I visited a nutritionist, who put me on a diet, and
joined Big Steve's Gym. Blevins also began treating me with Mevacor and several other drugs, and later with Zocor.

In six months I reduced my weight from 215 to 175. I reached
the target weight of 175 five years ago, and it hasn't varied more
than a few pounds since then. Total cholesterol eventually dropped
from 309 to 171, HDL improved from 24 to 46, and LDL was cut in
half, falling from 200 to 100. Thanks to the combination of dieting,
exercise, and medication, cholesterol isn't currently a risk factor for
me. Doesn't mean it won't be.

Later I talk about other lifestyle changes, and the problems in
general of aging, but first I have to tell you this great little secret I've
discovered.

No doctor is likely to volunteer this, but there is another drug,
readily available and inexpensive, that reduces the risk of heart disease. No, not aspirin, though it is a potent drug in the treatment of
heart disease, stroke, and even cancer. No, I'm talking about alcohol. Numerous studies demonstrate that low to moderate alcohol
consumption reduces the risk of coronary artery disease (CAD). This
was documented some time ago, but because alcohol was also associated with higher mortality from cancer, strokes, and cirrhosis
among heavy drinkers, the U-shaped mortality curve obscured alcohol's benefits to heart patients. Alcohol is beneficial even to those
who are genetically inclined to heart disease.

Researchers at Harvard Medical School encourage doctors to *prescribe* small doses of booze as another lifestyle modification. "Indeed, the reduction in CAD risk that is associated with light to moderate drinking (25 to 45 percent) compares favorably with the risk reduction of exercise (45 percent), low-dose aspirin (33 percent), maintenance of ideal body weight (35 to 55 percent), and even smoking cessation (50 to 70 percent)," writes a Harvard doctor, Harvey B. Simon. He cautions that he is talking about one or two drinks only. Heavy drinking can damage the heart, liver, kidneys, and other organs. Also, women should be cautioned that even low doses of alcohol may increase the risk of breast cancer. Oh, and by the way, Simon felt the need to add, patients should avoid driving or using dangerous machinery after drinking.

Okay, I know what you are thinking. I know the temptation and know it well. You are thinking that if one or two drinks will reduce CAD 35 percent, six drinks will make you bulletproof. But it doesn't work that way. Heavy drinking is *bad,* no way around it. On the other hand, we all know that doctors tend to err on the conservative side. It's my guess that three or four drinks won't harm you. More than that, you're on your own.

Twelve

$\mathcal{D}$espite the overwhelming evidence that cholesterol is Public Enemy No. 1, the bad habit most of us kick first after bypass surgery is smoking. There is clearly a reason this is so. When your chest feels as though Albert Belle used it for batting practice, the very idea of sucking down hot smoke is abhorent. Little did I realize when Phyllis drove me to the emergency room that early August morning in 1988 that the cigarette I was smoking would be my last. But it was. Having bypass surgery is, in one sense, an easy way to quit smoking, though not one that I recommend.

During my first few weeks out of the hospital, my mind challenged my body on the subject of smoking, conjuring up memories of the pleasures while automatically rejecting the process. I didn't particularly *want* a cigarette, but my mind couldn't avoid the memory of what it had been like, that stumulating rush of nicotine, the calming and reassuring effect. Every time the telephone rang, my hand involuntarily reached for a cigarette pack that wasn't there. Smoking had become second nature. Fortunately, my body won these challenges.

Later, after the pain in my chest had gone away, my mind came to grips with the stupidity and foulness of the habit. By then I had fairly well conquered nicotine withdrawal. Still, the memory remained. It stayed with me for months after I stopped smoking, especially when I saw someone smoking on a movie screen or when I was sitting across the table from Dorothy Browne, who inhaled her king-sized filters with such ecstasy that it bordered on the orgasmic. But with each passing week, the urgency to smoke became less pressing, and eventually smoking passed completely from my mind.

As I mentioned earlier, two of my oldest friends, the incomparably exotic Teeta Walker and the elegant *boulevardier* Lopez, died in 1996 of chronic lung diseases. Both of them were roughly my age and had smoked heavily most of their adult lives.

Teeta's final few months were spent in a long-term-care hospital near Houston, hooked to a respirator. No Russian vodka over the rocks, no cigarettes, no entrails with wine sauce, no silly games that we once played—just a drab room where she must have known she was going to die. Phyllis visited her several times and told me that toward the end Teeta became terrified of having the doors to her room closed—even the door to the bathroom. Teeta's fear and anxiety of being shut up, even for a moment, made her hyperventilate and caused her condition to worsen. She suffered two heart attacks while confined to that room, and the second one killed her.

Lopez also had the choice of continuing to breathe with the assistance of a respirator, how long no one could say. He was clearly dying, but he could have chosen to prolong the end.

We sat for several weeks in his hospital room—Bud, Phyllis, Dorothy, Jan Reed, Jodi Gent, and a few others—waiting for him to die or, in the alternative, make a decision to live the remainer of his days with a tube in his mouth and a tank of oxygen at his side. His spirits were surprisingly high, probably because there was plenty of morphine to help him along. Three days passed, then four. Making the decision to die or live miserably was something we could not imagine, but that was exactly the situation in which our old pal found himself.

We tried to amuse him with our gallows humor, grim-reaper jokes, that sort of crap. We'd been practicing it for years, under less dire circumstances. But after a while it got to be too much. After that, we sat quietly, watching his labored breathing and listening to Lopez's favorite album, a CD of Chet Baker singing love songs, recorded in the 1950s when all of us were still in college. With the assistance of another friend, Travis County probate judge Guy Herman, Lopez dictated his will. Then he told us to call the doctor. He was ready to pull the plug on himself. Even then he lived another forty-eight hours, and we just sat there, watching him grasp desperately for one more breath.

Finally, in true Lopez style, he pulled himself together and delivered one final *bon mot.* "Somebody call a cab!" he gasped. Then he died.

You want to know how smoking destroys the body? Visit a friend dying of chronic lung disease. Or better yet, close your eyes and pretend you are watching your own heart and lungs. I'm serious. Try this exercise:

Pretend you are somewhere deep inside your body, watching an old horror film in exaggerated shades of red and black. Your mouth takes a puff from a Camel and that old demon nicotine rears out of some primal slime. You watch in stunned fascination as it slithers through your body and invades your system, increasing blood pressure, heart rate, amount of blood pumped by the heart, and the blood flow in the heart's arteries. What a rush! While it performs all these tricks, it simultaneously causes the blood vessels to clamp down and constrict. The background music of this mental horror film approaches a crescendo at this point, elevating in pitch until it's as shrill as an air raid siren. Eventually it begins to subside—the increase in heart rate and blood flow is only temporary—and finally it is no louder than the hum of a computer at rest.

But even as the mouth is sucking down another jolt of nicotine—and the process is being repeated—*another* monster appears on the scene, this one even more horrible than nicotine. Picture a deadly cloud of carbon monoxide, rolling down your throat like a disembodied creature from outer space, mixing with your blood, reducing the oxygen available to the heart and to all other parts of the body. The smoke also invades the platelets (clotting agents) in your blood, causing them to mutate into sticky clusters of glop. This is the first and sometimes last movement in the blood clot's ballet of death. If you also have high blood pressure and high blood cholesterol, the film begins its second reel, in which smoking interacts with these two afflictions to markedly increase the risk of heart attack. In other words, the nicotine and smoke acting in concert with high blood pressure and an elevated level of cholesterol become more than the sum of their parts. Like watching Boris Karloff, Bela Lugosi, and Lon Chaney, Jr., in the same flick.

Back in the fifties when Dan, Bud, and I first got the habit, nearly half of the adults in America smoked; today it's about 29 percent. Today everyone knows about the evils of tobacco, but those who have smoked for years doubt that they have the will to stop. It does take some willpower, along with a genuine desire. But contrary to media reports, smoking isn't all that addictive.

There is no agony or serious physical withdrawal as in the case of hard drugs. Nicotine patches and gum help many people: Phyllis quit in the spring of 1996—after watching Teeta and Lopez die— and her method was patches, followed by nicotine gum. She was still chewing nicotine gum ten months later, but let's take it one step at a time. Smoking is like drugs or alcohol in that it is something we do by free choice. Antismoking and antidrug hysterics try to present a picture of children being lured into addiction by cartoon characters or role models, but children have always experimented with forbidden pleasures. I believe that the initial attraction is the very fact they are forbidden. There is nothing intrinsically evil about booze, tobacco, or various substances we classify as narcotics, but that doesn't mean we shouldn't try to discourage their use or give personal testimonials to the harm they can do.

The good news is, if you quit smoking—no matter how long you smoked—within three years your risk of heart attack or chronic lung disease is the same as that of a person who never took up the habit in the first place.

People who smoked for years and then quit are always amazed at how much better they feel, and how much better they can smell— and *do* smell. Heavy smokers aren't aware of smells, including their own, which is considerable. People who have quit soon discover that the stench of stale cigarette smoke is everywhere. You can't avoid it. You notice it in places you never noticed it before—on the breath and clothing of old friends who are still smokers, in the lobbies of public buildings, at airports, and even on the sidewalks outside theaters. Or maybe you walk into a room where someone has smoked recently—the smell nearly knocks you over. The putrid odor of tobacco smoke, you now discover, can linger for days.

Like two old-time sinners who had recently been saved, Bud and I were talking about this phenomenon not long ago.

"Imagine all those mornings at the *Times Herald*," Bud said. "God, we must have smelled like grease traps."

"Worse than that," I told him. "Remember how we used to make fun of people who *didn't* smoke?"

"We'd blow smoke in their direction," Bud recalled.

"We thought we were so damn cool."

Nothing makes you feel as cool as knowing how uncool you used to be.

Part Four:

EATING WELL'S THE BEST REVENGE

Thirteen

7he first thing you need to know about losing weight is that diets don't work without exercise. You can starve off ten or twenty pounds on most any diet if you stick it out long enough—and if it doesn't kill you—but the pounds will come back in spades. Or, at the other extreme, you can become a body builder and turn your 200 pounds of fat into 250 pounds of glistening muscle. But if you need to lose weight, forget the word "diet." What we're talking about here is here is a new way of thinking.

You get fat by eating too much and exercising too little. Your body takes in more fuel than it burns up. The excess is stored as fat. To lose weight, you have to eat fewer calories, but you also have to change your metabolism, the rate at which your body uses and distributes those calories.

Your body requires a certain number of calories a day for energy, the number depending on your age, gender, activity level, and body composition. If your body requires, say, 2,400 calories and you are on a 1,200-calorie diet, your body is only getting half of what it requires. From primitive times, our bodies have been programmed to be alert to the fear of starvation and to act on that fear. So while you will lose weight for a while on your 1,200-calorie diet, the body will soon interpret the weight loss as a life-threatening situation and automatically slow its metabolic rate in its attempt to adjust to the newly restricted caloric intake. One way it does this is by hoarding body fat.

This fat-hoarding process starts you on a vicious circle. As the stores of fat increase, the body resorts to using muscle tissue for energy, thereby decreasing muscle mass. You get tired, irritable, and depressed. You also crave sweets and fat, and more than likely will begin to eat for emotional stability. Because your metabolism has slowed to compensate for the previous lack of calories, the new binge of calories causes rapid weight gain. In order to protect itself from future nutritional trauma, the body tends to gain back more than it lost.

Our bodies prefer a certain weight—researchers call it our

weight setpoint. If you eat more than normal and gain weight, your metabolism increases. This causes your weight to drop until it reaches your setpoint. By the same process, if you diet and lose weight, your metabolism slows down until you gain weight and return to your setpoint. This is the sort of yo-yo effect most of us have experienced on our various diets, losing a little, gaining back a little more, never reaching a goal we only vaguely define.

The amount of muscle a person has determines that person's rate of metabolism. While it is not possible to lose weight permanently merely by dieting, it is possible through exercise and increased muscle to change your setpoint. Exercise and fitness are subjects for later, but for the moment it is important to understand that neither dieting nor exercise alone will help you lose weight. Start thinking of them as part of the same program.

How do you calculate if you really need to lose weight? Many doctors use a formula called the Body Mass Index (BMI) to determine if a patient is at risk for heart disease, high blood pressure, and diabetes. To get your BMI, multiply your weight by 700, divide that number by your height in inches, then divide that number by your height again. If you weigh 180 and are seventy inches tall (five feet ten), your BMI is 26.6. From 25 to 30 is considered low to moderate risk. Over 30 is moderate to high risk.

I have tried just about every diet that came down over the last three decades—the Drinking Man's Diet, the Dr. Atkins Diet, the Pritikin Diet, the Scarsdale Diet, the Air Force Diet, the Grapefruit Diet, the Water Diet. None of them worked for me. Bud Shrake did lose some weight on the Drinking Man's Diet, but only because he didn't eat anything for months except nuts, olives, and orange slices. The Cabbage Soup Diet, like all the one-food-item diets, is not merely useless, it is dangerous to your health, not to mention your social status.

Several years before my heart attack, Phyllis and I both lost between ten and fifteen pounds by following the Scarsdale Diet menus for the recommended two weeks. The determining factor in our weight loss was not that we followed the planned daily menus, which we did, but that we adhered to the additional requirement to abstain

from alcohol. Once the two weeks had passed, we celebrated our
new svelte bodies with multiple rounds of cocktails and quickly regained every ounce. Alcohol not only carries abundant calories—
150 for a glass of wine—but it metabolizes as fat.

My favorite book, at least at the time, was *Dr. Atkins' Diet Revolution: The High Calorie Way to Stay Thin Forever*, which triggered
a storm of protest when it was published in 1972. A cardiologist
turned diet doctor, Robert Atkins went against all prevailing views
of weight loss. Instead of recommending caloric reduction, as almost all diets do, Atkins suggested a diet that was high in protein,
high in fat, and low in carbohydrates. With fewer carbohydrates to
burn, Atkins theorized, the body would instead burn fat. On Dr.
Atkins's regime you could eat anything you wanted, as often as you
wanted, so long as you avoided the deadly carbohydrate. It sounded
too good to be true.

I tried the Dr. Atkins Diet in 1972, shortly after the book was
published, but without noticeable results. One of the things that at-
tracted me to this diet was Atkins's suggestion for between-meal
snacks. Instead of eating a piece of fruit, he counseled, eat a bag of
fried pork skins. That's right, *pork skins*. I loved fried pork skins, and
at that time in my life I was mostly indifferent to apples and oranges.
One night a pork skin accidentally fell from the kitchen counter and
into a sink of dishwater, where it remained overnight. What I discovered the following morning in my kitchen sink made my blood curdle:
instead of the brown, crispy, crunchy morsels I had been devouring
so freely, I looked down on a miserable, deadly-white slab of pig fat.

Even then I didn't question Dr. Atkins's wisdom. Why? Like
most people, I was conditioned to believe that doctors always knew
best, but there is also something in our nature that makes us trust
that which we devoutly desire—a way to lose weight without giving
up burgers and Mexican food. "When you take away carbohydrates
(such as fruit and vegetables), you take away hunger," Atkins assured us. Sounded good to me, very good indeed. But after five or six
days of snacking on pig skins, I realized that I was uncomfortable.
It wasn't exactly hunger that I was experiencing, but it couldn't be
called satisfaction either. I had a terrible, nearly irresistible craving

for—I know now—carbohydrates. After five or six days on the diet I would have traded everything I owned for an apple. Instead, I traded Atkins's diet.

Nevertheless, I decided to give Atkins another try a few years later. This was after I was married to Phyllis, when we were living in Taos. One of the steps that I had skipped when I tried this diet the first time was the urine test stick for ketosis. When you cut your carb intake to zero, tiny fragments of unburned fat called ketones can be detected in your urine. Atkins recommends that you test your urine for the presence of ketones. If the urine test stick turns purple, it is a sign for great rejoicing.

I bought a ketone-testing kit at the pharmacy on the Plaza in Taos, but when I presented one of the slender testing filaments to Phyllis she looked at me as if I'd asked her to stab herself in the eye with a screwdriver.

"Do you seriously expect me to pee on that little stick?" she asked.

"It's the only way you can tell if you've reached a state of ketosis," I told her.

"And why, pray tell, would I care if I had reached a state of . . . what is it again?"

"Ketosis," I told her. "Let me demonstrate."

I led her to the bathroom and let her watch while I passed the filament through my stream of urine. Gradually, it turned rose-colored, then sort of bled out into something that looked like a wine stain. I held it up to the light so that she could see more clearly.

"You see that?" I said, making no attempt to stifle my pride of accomplishment. "That purple color means that my body is excreting ketones and that I am now burning fat as fuel."

She looked at the urine test stick with new interest.

"I think I've seen one of those before," she said. "Aren't these what diabetics use to see if they're about to lapse into a coma?"

I told her that I didn't think so, but just to be on the safe side I would look it up. At the offices of a urologist I had met, I got a pamphlet titled "Insulin-Dependent Diabetes," published by the U.S. Department of Health and Human Services. Thumbing through it, I discovered this passage:

"If your blood sugar levels are above 250 mg/dl before meals, you should test your urine for ketones. Ketones are chemicals that the body makes when insulin levels are very low and excessive amounts of fat are being burned. Ketone buildup over several hours can lead to serious illness or coma, a condition called ketoacidosis."

So much for Dr. Atkins's diet revolution.

Since then, Robert Atkins has published several additional books. The most recent, which I bought in the fall of 1996, no longer advises eating pig skins instead of apples, but is the same unrelenting attack on carbohydrates as his previous works. In 1972, Atkins made a transformation from conventional cardiologist to diet doctor, and now he has made a second transformation from diet doctor to persecuted holistic guru. He believes that the real reason that he is controversial is behind-the-scene pressure from corporations with economic interests in promoting junk food. Heart disease is "a disease of the twentieth century," which Atkins lays at the feet of our changing eating habits coupled with the big money of medicine. "Before economic motives took hold," he writes, "the best thing a cardiologist could do was sit on his hands. When you have economic-driven medicine, people stay up all night long thinking of ways to make money."

Indeed!

Some of what Atkins says makes sense, I must admit. He believes, correctly, that "oxidized" low-density lipoprotein (LDL, or bad cholesterol) is the most significant risk factor in heart disease. This oxidation, which turns cholesterol "rancid," is caused by damaged molecules called free radicals. If you lower LDL, Atkins points out, there is less to oxidize. Atkins has put away his conventional prescription pad and is now advising patients to fight off free radicals with vitamins E and C, as well as beta-carotene, selenium, and other antioxidants.

Another recent best-seller, *Enter the Zone,* by Barry Sears, M.D., is doing great business in Hollywood and in other places where abs of iron and buns of steel are standard residency requirements. Sears's remedy for overweight is the same as Atkins's—attack the noble carbohydrate. According to Sears, "the key to losing fat isn't a matter of cutting calories, it's a matter of reaching the Zone." You can see why his advice goes unquestioned in Hollywood. The Zone, he tells us, "is a real metabolic state (in which the body works at peak efficiency) that can be reached by everyone and maintained indefinitely on a lifelong basis." The Zone is beyond wellness, he continues: it is about optimal health. The problem with all this theorizing is that Sears never makes clear—at least it wasn't clear to me—exactly what he means by the Zone or how it can be measured and quantified.

Some of what Sears writes is absolute nonsense, or so it appears to me. For example, he tells us that eating fat doesn't make you fat. On the contrary, he writes, "You have to eat fat to lose fat." That's just crazy. Fat is fat. Numerous studies have demonstrated that diets with a greater percentage of fats result in greater fat accumulation. Being overweight is a matter of overeating, and it is much easier to overeat in fat calories than in carb calories simply because fat calories are less filling.

Eating highly concentrated *refined* carbohydrates such as Snack-Well does in fact make you fat. Sears is right about that. When the high-carbohydrate, low-fat concept became popular in the 1980s, food processors responded by marketing "fat-free" products created largely from sugars and refined white flour: whole cakes, cartons of cookies, mounds of pasta, and pretzels replaced balanced meals and truly healthy snacks. None of these products contained significant amounts of fiber. As a rule, the more refined and concentrated the carbohydrate, the lower its caloric density and the faster it is absorbed in your bloodstream. This rapid absorption elevates levels of insulin, which in turn makes you even more hungry and encourages your body to store fat. Soon a vicious circle has declared war on your system: you gain weight, which increases insulin resistance—a complication of diabetes marked by need of a high dose of insulin to control high blood sugar and ketone levels—which causes more weight gain, which prompts more insulin resistance. Constant high levels of glucose and insulin quickly elevate risks for diabetes and heart disease.

But not all carbs impact insulin the same way. Studies show that diets as high as 75 percent carbohydrates can drop insulin by 35 percent. Those who claim that all carbohydrates cause increased insulin are misinformed. Carbs that are *unrefined*—such as tubers, fruits, and leaf and seed vegetables—are extremely dense. No matter how hungry you might think you are, you can't eat more than a few hundred calories of these unrefined, slowly absorbed carbs without getting stuffed.

Not all calories are created equal. The thermic effects—the energy required to metabolize calories—are far greater for protein (20 percent) than for carbohydrates (8 percent). Fat barely has a thermic effect (2 percent), which explains why fat slides so easily into fat cell tissue. It is true that if you overeat carbohydrates they can be converted to fat, but it is much easier for the body to deposit fat as fat than is to convert carbohydrates to fat. Fat deposits are clearly influenced by the composition of calories.

There are two basic problems with almost all diets. First, it is hard to get people to stay with them. High-carbohydrate diets, such as those advanced by Pritikin and Dean Ornish, do produce results, but only when they are followed to the letter. This is extremely difficult unless you are prepared to substitute scrambled tofu and vegetables for meat. Instead of worrying what percentage of their calories come from fat, people should pay attention to the kind of fat they are consuming. The villain is saturated fat.

The second basic problem with diets is that they tend to deny us the very foods we crave. Food cravings are a mixture of cultural and economic influences, agitated by the primal fear that somebody is trying to starve us. That's why there is a selective pleasure in chosing the richest, fattest foods. In times of stress, I'll wager, our frontier ancestors got a compulsion for platters of biscuits, steak, and gravy. I know that I do. More's the pity for our overweight society, but I don't personally know anyone who craves broccoli. There is a great line from the short-lived television series *Pearl*— the professor, upon being offered trail mix, says, "Did you know the Donner party had bags of trail mix and yet chose to eat each other?"

I wished now that I had known about the Mediterranean diet in

1989. It's really quite simple: more bread, more vegetables and legumes, more fish and less meat, fruit at least once a day, no butter or cream. The only fat allowed is olive oil, which is rich in monounsaturated fat, which has a proven cardioprotective effect. Fruits and vegetables protect the heart as well as olive oil and are also rich in antioxidants. Legumes, the "poor man's meat" of the Mediterranean, are rich in fiber and plant protein. Grain foods such as bread, pasta, couscous, polenta, and risotto are all high in complex carbohydrates, vitamins, and minerals—with virtually no saturated fat. Avocados and asparagus, both common in the Mediterranean, are high in L-glutathione, an amino acid that can scavenge harmful free radicals that damage the cells of our hearts and other organs.

The underlying success of the Mediterranean diet is the biochemical principle mentioned by Atkins and other low-carbohydrate advocates—insulin resistance or hyperinsulinism. Everything in the Mediterranean diet helps prevent excess insulin release. It also minimizes the consumption of high glycemic carbohydrates—flour pastas, white potatoes, and white rice, for example—whose carb portions enter the bloodstream quickly and pump out insulin in order to handle the sudden glucose surge. The Mediterranean diet, on the other hand, pushes low-glycemic carbs such as grapefruit, cherries, peaches, plums, and kiwi, which are slowly absorbed by the blood.

If I had it to do over again, I'd start on the Mediterranean diet. It's basically the diet that I use today to maintain my target weight.

The diet that finally worked for me, however—and one that I would still recommend to people who need to lose large amounts of weight—was essentially the same one that is suggested by the famous Food Guide Pyramid, published by the United States Department of Agriculture. It is simple, is easy to follow, and is aimed at our optimal health requirements. Best of all, there is little sacrifice of things we crave, and no hunger at all. The pyramid isn't a weight-loss diet in the sense that you can eat all the recommended things and shed pounds. But if you follow the guidelines with some restraint and moderation, you will learn a new habit of eating—and eating well— that will control your weight and make you feel good.

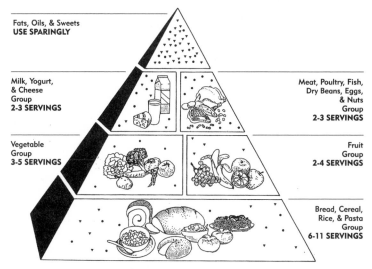

Fats, Oils, & Sweets
USE SPARINGLY

Milk, Yogurt,
& Cheese
Group
2-3 SERVINGS

Meat, Poultry, Fish,
Dry Beans, Eggs,
& Nuts
Group
2-3 SERVINGS

Vegetable
Group
3-5 SERVINGS

Fruit
Group
2-4 SERVINGS

Bread, Cereal,
Rice, & Pasta
Group
6-11 SERVINGS

Food Guide Pyramid

Notice that at the base of the pyramid are the carbohydrates—bread, cereal, rice, pasta. The USDA advises that you eat six to eleven servings from the category, though I can't imagine eating eleven or even ten helpings of pasta or rice. The pyramid exposes one of the primary myths associated with dieting: that pasta is bad for you. Pasta is good for you. What's bad is the cream, butter, and cheese we often mix with it.

The two groups in the level just above the base are also carbohydrates—the vegetables (three to five servings) and the fruits (two to four servings). In the third level are proteins and fats such as milk, yogurt, and cheese (two to three servings), and meat, poultry, fish, dry beans, eggs, and nuts (two to three servings). Long before you get to the top of the pyramid, where fats and sugars (to be used sparingly) are listed, you are stuffed. I don't know if it's possible to eat all the recommended allowables on the Food Guide Pyramid.

The specific diet that my dietitian, Shelley Veltrop, worked out took into consideration that I needed a limited protein intake because of my kidney disease. Also, since it was primarily for weight loss, the diet was more restrictive than the food pyramid, but it followed the pyramid's concept of tapering from a large base of carbs to smaller amounts of proteins and fats. Her diet allowed me ten servings from the bread group, four vegetables, four fruits, three servings from the fat group, one-half to one cup from the milk group, and five ounces a day from the meat group.

That was more than enough to keep me from being hungry and to supply all the energy I needed. For the first time in my life I began to realize that diet is not synonymous with sacrifice. For example, I was surprised how much meat is compressed in just three ounces—a half of a chicken breast, a chicken leg and thigh, two slices of roast beef (three inches in diameter and a quarter of an inch thick), one medium loin pork chop (three quarters of an inch thick), or one hamburger patty (half an inch thick, three inches across). When you consider that one-fourth cup of drained canned tuna or salmon is only one ounce, you get an idea of the volume of meat you can have in a day. The trick, however, is to fill up on vegetables, fruits, and grains.

My diet was formulated to take off about two pounds per week, the recommended amount for healthy and lasting weight loss. That doesn't sound like much but looms large if you stay with it for any time. After four months I had dropped nearly forty pounds. Try to image what forty founds of fat looks like—like carrying around a small pig inside your body! With no suffering and not much inconvenience, I went from a very portly 215 to my target weight of 175.

In the six years since I reached this target, my weight has never varied more than a few points. Today I eat pretty much what I want, though I no longer crave some of the things that used to be problems—bacon and sausage, for example, or whole milk. I didn't know it at the time, but what I had done was not just lost weight—I had changed my setpoint from 215 to 175.

You will quickly learn that for every food you need to avoid there are a spectacular number of foods remaining for your pleasure and enjoyment, and that there are many ways to make them interesting and every bit as tasty as the fattening stuff you used to crave. One of the keys to a successful diet is to eat small amounts fairly often: many nutritionists advise people to eat six or eight times a day. It is important that you do not allow yourself to get hungry. Hunger is your worst enemy. Hunger will drive you straight to Burger King. Instead, carry with you pieces of fruit, bags of carrot sticks and celery, or bagels—just in case the hungers come creeping. By the way, I didn't drink at all for the first six weeks of my diet, but after that I allowed myself four glasses of wine on weekends. I still follow the no-drinking-on-weekdays routine.

Here are the guidelines for losing weight and lowering cholesterol and triglycerides. I still follow them, most of them anyway:

Avoid marbled beef, pork, bacon, sausage, fatty fowl such as duck or goose, processed meats, luncheon meats such as salami and bologna, frankfurters and fast-food hamburgers, and organ meats such as kidneys and liver. Choose, instead, nonfatty cuts of beef with the fat trimmed, veal, chicken, or turkey. When you are making gravy from meat drippings, remember to refrigerate the drippings first so that fat can be removed while preserving the flavor from the meat. Always remove the skin from poultry before cooking: nearly half of a chicken's fat vanishes once it is skinned. You can leave the skin on when you roast a chicken, but remove it before eating.

There is also available a healthy selection of fresh fish and canned fish packed in water. Shellfish such as lobster, crabs, shrimp, and oysters are high in cholesterol but very low in saturated fat, meaning the good stuff more or less cancels the bad stuff.

Meat shrinks when cooked, so for each three-ounce serving of cooked meat, fish, or poultry, buy an extra ounce or two to allow for shrinkage and waste. Allow two extra ounces for meat with bone. Remember, always bake or broil your meat, don't fry it.

Most doctors and dietitians still advise heart patients to limit egg yolks to two per week. Egg whites are fine, as are egg substitutes such as Egg Beaters. Monique's famous green chili omelets are made with Egg Beaters, onions sautéed in vegetable spray, and green chilis— and served with beans that have been refried using only vegetable spray. Sometimes I sneak in some grated Parmesan cheese. I now believe that dietary cholesterol does no harm—that it's okay to eat eggs. But Dr. Blevins continues to caution against all types of cholesterol, and I continue to follow doctor's orders.

The only fruit you need to avoid is coconut, which is rich in saturated fats. In most large- or medium-sized cities, there are great greengrocers or produce markets that feature huge varieties of fruit all year round. Whole Food Store, the Austin-based chain that will soon reach more than a hundred cities a cross America, and the fabulous and peerless Central Market of Austin import exotic vegetables and fruits all year. Nothing is better than a peach, plum, or apricot from South America on a cold winter day. You can spend hours at Central Market sampling fruits you never knew existed—for example, plumcots, which are part plum and part apricots, and melons of all shapes and colors.

One-half cup of fruit is considered a serving, and you should eat at least one citrus fruit daily. Once you've reached your target weight, a diet high in fruit will keep the weight off. Fresh fruit, by the way, is superior to fruit juice. Juice is higher in calories and less filling and has little or no fiber. People who drink a lot of juice to quench their thirst may be adding hundreds of calories a day.

Except for avocados, which contain a high percentage of vegetable fat, most vegetables are not limited. Dietitians recommend one dark green vegetable such as string beans or one deep-yellow vegetable such as squash. Cauliflower, broccoli, celery, and potato skins are great sources of fiber, which is filling and helps cut down cholesterol. Starchy vegetables such as potatoes, corn, lima beans, and dried peas or beans should be considered not as vegetables but as substitutes for a serving of bread or cereal. One-half cup of dried beans is the same as one-half cup of pasta on the food pyramid. Avoid canned beans with sugar or pork added.

Avoid nuts. A lot of people believe that peanuts, walnuts, and almonds are high in protein, but in fact they are mostly fat. Two of those little packages of peanuts they hand out on airplanes pack 169 calories—75 percent or 14.6 grams of which are fat. It is okay, however, to eat pumpkin, sesame, or sunflower seeds.

Grains are a dieter's best friend. Bread, pasta, brown rice, anything made from whole grain will fill you up and slim you down at the same time. People who think they can lose weight by throwing away the bread and eating the meat from a sandwich are fooling themselves. Better to throw away the meat. Rye bread is particularly healthy for the heart. The Finns, who eat a lot of dense, dark rye bread, have 30 percent less risk of dying from heart disease than Americans or other nationalities with lower fiber intakes. Don't depend on the light-colored fluffy bread that passes for rye in American supermarkets, though. You need the dense fibery rye prepared by European-style bakeries.

Watch out for breads or any baked goods with shortening and/or sugar, or commercial mixes with dried eggs and whole milk. Sweet rolls, doughnuts, and pastries of all kinds are out, period. Also, read the nutritional information on boxes of cereal. Most of them contain sugar, which converts readily to triglycerides. Sugar comes in many guises. Look carefully at the label. Dextrose, fruit juice concentrate, high-fructose corn syrup, molasses, crystallized cane juice, and white grape juice concentrate are all just fancy names for sugar.

Choose high-fiber grains such as oats and whole wheat. One roll is one serving. So is a slice of bread, three soda crackers, four pieces of melba toast, or one-half cup of spaghetti, rice, or noodles.

Use only 99-percent-fat-free or skim milk. It will taste watery at first, but you will get used to it. After a few months a glass of whole milk will seem as rich as heavy cream. Cheese should be avoided— I fail this rule several times a week. I hate low-fat cheese, except ricotta. On the other hand, no-fat yogurt and no-fat sour cream—and especially no-fat frozen yogurt, which most major ice cream manufacturers now offer—seem preferable to the real thing. Any recipe that calls for heavy cream tastes almost the same with no-fat yogurt. You can also buy canned evaporated skim milk, which can taste as rich as cream when used in cooking.

When selecting fats and oils, avoid butter, lard, animal fats (such as bacon drippings), cream sauces, palm and coconut oils, and anything else that is high in saturated fats. Examine labels of "cholesterol-free" products for "hydrogenated fats," which are oils that have been hardened into solids and in the process become saturated. Instead, use soft (not stick) margarine and vegetable oils that are high in polyunsaturated fat such as safflower, sunflower, soybean, corn, and cottonseed.

I am particularly fond of olive oil, which has been touted as a heart-smart food. The best olive oil is extra virgin, which means it's the first pressing or extraction of oil from olives fresh off the tree. Nothing has been added except maybe a little warm water to flush away the water-soluble bitterness of raw olives. A spin in the centrifuge removes the waste water. Though whole olives are prohibited in some diets, they are even better for the heart than olive oil, because waste water also functions as an antioxidant and because they are high in fiber.

Avoid any snack food that is fried. And stay away from peanut butter. Even when it is nonhydrogenated, peanut butter is loaded with calories.

Omega-3 fatty acid, a type of polyunsaturated fatty acid abundant in salmon and some other varieties of fattier fish like herring and pollack, is a dietary parodox: a fat that is good for you. Salmon is a high-fat fish, with 46 percent of its calories in fat—that's one reason it tastes so good—yet salmon is a smart choice for dieters because 70 percent of its fat is the kind that doesn't raise blood cholesterol levels. Omega-3 fatty acids also guard against heart attacks and are potent anticlotting agents. Researchers have noted that populations that consume large amounts of fish such as Japan and Nordic countries experience significantly less diabetes, heart disease, and hypertension than other parts of the world, particularly the United States.

All varieties of salmon (except smoked) contain huge amounts of omega-3 fatty acid, as do Pacific and jack mackerel and whitefish (except smoked). Rainbow trout, Atlantic and Pacific oysters, swordfish, bluefin tuna, rainbow smelt, and canned white tuna (albacore) are also high in this amazing fat, though not as high as salmon. If you eat one three-ounce serving of salmon once a week, reports the *Journal of the American Medical Association,* you cut your cardiac risk in half.

The American Heart Association used to recommend that your daily caloric intake be no more than 30 percent fat. More recently it has lowered its recommendation to no more than 20 percent fat. For most people, a good diet would be 60 percent carbohydrate, 20 percent protein, and 20 percent fat.

My particular diet was calculated at 1,650 calories a day, but I never bothered to count them. Counting calories will drive you nuts and send you screaming to the nearest House of Pancakes for refuge. You do need to be *aware* of calories—in particular what percentage of the calories is fat. Nutritional tables and labels supply this information.

Learn to read nutritional tables. They will tell you all you need to know about a food: the serving size, calories, total carbohydrates, dietary fiber, protein, vitamins and minerals, total fat, saturated fat, cholesterol, and sodium. They also list the "daily value" of each of these, based on a diet of 2,000 to 2,500 calories. Pay particular attention to the daily-value percentages of fat, saturated fat, cholesterol, and sodium and try to keep the percentages low. For total carbohydrates, dietary fiber, and vitamins and minerals, your daily value goal is to reach 100 percent of each.

Take caution when buying food items labeled "light" and "reduced fat." These product descriptions are regulated by the Food and Drug Administration of the Department of Agriculture and need some interpretation. "Light" means the food has one-third fewer calories or 50 percent less fat than a standard serving of the traditional food. "Reduced" fat indicates that it has at least 25 percent less fat than the traditional food. If it is labeled "low fat," a serving has three grams or less of fat. And if it carries the "fat-free" label, a serving has less than 0.05 gram of fat. Note that these descriptions do not relate to the number of calories the food contains. Nonfat food can make you fat, too, if you overeat.

A food that is "sugar-free" must contain less than 0.5 gram of sugar per serving. A "reduced-sugar" food, on the other hand, contains only 25 percent less sugar than the regular product.

Many food items do not have labels, of course, and for that reason you need a general awareness of where calories are coming from and what part of them is fat. One baked potato with skin, for example, has 145 calories but only 0.2 gram of fat. You could eat baked potatoes all day and all night and still not gain weight. If you put one pat of butter on that potato, however, you've added another 36 calories and, more important, 4.1 grams of fat, of which 2.5 grams is saturated fat. Whole milk gets 49 percent of its calories from fat, and even 2 percent milk gets 35 percent from fat—saturated fat, at that. On the other hand, skim milk gets only 0.04 percent from fat. Cheese is mistakenly accepted as a high-protein substitute for meat, and yet 60 to 70 percent of the calories in cheese are from saturated fat.

It's smart to cultivate an interest in foods that are high in soluble fibers, such as oat bran or any grain, vegetables, beans, and fruit. Fiber helps reduce cholesterol and is bulky and filling without calories. It is also essential for stabilizing blood sugar levels and appetite. Most Americans get only eleven grams of fiber a day, about one-third what is recommended. There are a lot of easy ways to add fiber to your diet. Mix broccoli and carrots into your salad, for example, or toss in garbanzos or other beans. Thicken soups by adding puréed vegetables. Instead of using oil for baking, substitute applesauce, baby-food prunes, or even mashed pumpkin. Eat the highest-fiber vegetables (brussels sprouts, green peas, sweet potatoes) and fruits (pears, berries). Fiber is essentially a carbohydrate, another argument for not shorting carbs from your daily diet.

Not all carbohydrates, however, work to your benefit. Simple carbohydrates such as sugar break down into glucose in our intestines very quickly and can cause blood sugar levels to fluctuate wildly. Complex carbs such as fruits, vegetables, and whole grains break down slowly and help us maintain proper levels of blood glucose. Complex carbs are also rich in vitamins, minerals, and fiber. Message: Eat more complex carbs and fewer simple carbs.

Regardless of your daily dietary composition, if you eat more calories than you burn, you will gain weight. So-called unlimited foods should still be eaten in moderation. Bud Shrake keeps two signs on his refrigerator. One says: "Everything You Put in Your Mouth Counts!" The other sign is a formula that he uses to calculate how many calories he needs. Bud multiples his target weight, 210, by 14.3. So he needs 2,982 calories a day to maintain that weight. Instead of 14.3, I use 15, the multiple recommended by the American Heart Association. I need 2,625 calories to maintain my setpoint of 175 pounds.

To lose one pound, you need to burn 3,500 calories more than you take in. In other words, you need to run a calorie deficit. In order to lose one pound a week, you need to reduce your daily caloric intake by 500 calories. (Seven days times 500 calories equals 3,500 calories or one pound.) Your diet, therefore, needs plenty of foods with long-burning energy or staying power.

Here are some tips on how to get results from your diet while avoiding hunger and unpleasantness:

1. Balance your food intake throughout the day. Familiarize yourself with the USDA-recommended serving sizes in each group. A standard serving size of cooked, lean poultry, fish, or meat, for example, is two to three ounces. The USDA suggests you have two or three servings each day. So if you plan to eat half a roasted chicken for dinner, skip this food group at lunch. You can eat pretty much what you want as long as you plan your day.

2. Get your serving sizes correct from the start. If the food doesn't have a label, measure it. If the diet calls for one four-ounce glass of orange juice, measure it exactly. After a time you'll be able to recognize what a serving size looks like. Three ounces of meat or fish, for example, is about the size of a deck of cards. More comparisons:

A half cup of pasta is the size of a tulip.
One ounce of cheese is equal to a pair of dice.
Three-fourths of a cup of rice is the size of a tennis ball.
One cup of cooked vegetables is the size of a baseball.
A one-ounce slice of bread is the size of a CD case.
Two tablespoons of salad dressing is the size of an ice cube.
One serving of raw leafy greens is the size of two tennis balls.

3. Listen to your body, not your clock. Eat when you are hungry, no matter how often. Stop eating when you're full, no matter how much remains on your plate. All of us tend

to use the amount of food on our plates as the standard for how much we should eat. Remember to carry with you a bag of snacks—carrots, celery, fruit, and bagels work nicely—to take the edge off hunger. Depriving yourself of food slows your metabolism. The secret is to keep your body moderately stoked up all day.

4. Eat slowly. It takes about twenty minutes for your brain to signal that you are full. You might eat enough to supply your needs in ten minutes but you won't feel full for another ten minutes. Slowing your eating pace lets your brain catch up with your mouth.

5. Learn to deal with restaurants. We all tend to overorder, and then to overeat. Usually, a fiber-rich salad and an appetizer or a bowl of vegetable soup with crackers is about the right amount of food. Fiber is nature's appetite suppressant, taking the edge off hunger with its bulk. Since it takes a while to eat, you'll start to feel full before you finish your first course. A glass of tomato juice works similiarly.

Serving sizes vary widely in restaurants. According to a 1996 *Self* magazine survey, a Palermo Pasta Primavera at T.G.I. Friday's measures more than four cups, easily enough for two people. Ironically, the cheapest meals usually come in the biggest portions and are the worst for you. Denny's Original Grand Slam Breakfast consists of two pancakes, two eggs, two strips of bacon, and two sausage links for $1.99. The trip to the emergency room costs extra. Also, keep in mind that while oat bran is very good for you, a ten-ounce bran muffin is merely fattening.

6. Eat "power meals" to fill you up, not out. Some foods fill you up quicker than others. Scientists have developed what they call a "satiety index" for various foods.

Oatmeal tops the index as the most filling food. Apples, oranges, and grapes are more filling than bananas. Protein-rich foods such as beef steak, fish, and beans score over eggs, cheese, and lentils. As you would expect, heavier foods leave people more satisfied than lighter foods. But researchers also found that fatty foods are less filling than those high in carbohydrates or protein. That is because fat is more calorie-dense and therefore you get a smaller quantity with your calories. The tastiest foods are the least filling. A 240-calorie serving of fish (eight ounces) will make you feel fuller than a 240-calorie serving of steak (four and a half ounces).

7. Eat a healthy breakfast. This relates to Rule 6 and taken together these two should be Rule No. 1. Fat people tend to skip breakfast. People who skip breakfast are not merely fat but also get tired and irritable by mid-morning, and almost always overeat at lunch. Most of us eat a majority of our calories in the second half of the day, just the opposite of what we should be doing. The only way to break this cycle is to restrain yourself at your evening meal so that you will be hungry in the morning. That way you can power up at breakfast. Oatmeal, one of the foods highest in soluble fiber, delivers its energy slowly into your body, so you avoid a spike and dip in your blood sugar. On the satiety index, a 240-calorie serving of oatmeal (two bowls) is four times more satiating than a much smaller 240-calorie croissant. In other words, you could cut your oatmeal serving in half (to 120 calories) and still be twice as full as you would from eating the croissant.

8. Drink a lot of water. Kidneys depend on water to filter waste products from the body. If there isn't enough water, kidneys need a reserve source, and they turn to the liver for help. The liver's primary function is to turn stored fat

into energy, and when it takes on extra work from the kidneys it can't do its fat-burning chore as well.

9. Eat like a Greek. The longevity of men and women in rural Greece goes back to their basic diets. They eat lots of whole-grain bread, at least one serving at every meal, and they make legumes and vegetables the main part of their meals rather than side dishes. They eat lots of fruit and fish. They don't drink much milk but add relatively low-fat feta cheese to salads and stews. They use olive oil as their main source of fat. And they have a little wine with their meals.

I don't mean to labor this point, but red wine keeps arteries clear by "oiling" blood platelets and increasing HDL (good cholesterol). A study at the National Institute of Health and Medical Research in Lyon, France, reports that a group of middle-aged men who drank two to four glasses a day had a 30 to 40 percent reduction in mortality compared with those who drank less wine, more wine, or no wine. Though wine is the best way I know to spark up a meal, only 16 percent of American adults drink wine more than once a week.

Remember, everything is a trade-off. This is true of dieting, of exercising, and of life itself. We trade one risk for another. Trading the calories in a few glasses of red wine for well-oiled coronary arteries seems to me to be a fair trade.

Here's another trade-off. Because I have a passion for eating and drinking well, I work out at my gym longer and harder than is necessary to maintain my weight and stay in condition. As a result, my muscles are more dense than they were six years ago, my metabolism has increased, and my body needs more fuel—more food! As I lost body fat, this process intensified: I not only lost fat, I maintained a higher ratio of muscle to fat. The more a metabolism is consistently fed, the more it lets go of its protective mechanism to hoard fat.

Paradoxically, workouts also help control appetite. From Monday through Thursday I eat mostly fruit, vegetables, pasta, bread, beans, and rice, because on weekends I like to eat steak and enchiladas and have those glasses of wine and pints of India Pale Ale that I denied myself during the week. When you are in control of your life and your attitude is right, trade-offs make perfect sense. Things have a way of balancing themselves, bad things as well as good. You will be amazed that you didn't see all this years ago.

Fourteen

Reading about the curative powers of shark cartilage, bee pollen, urine therapy, and many other quirky solutions to good health once inspired in me an uncontrollable urge to feel for my wallet and holler for a cop. I've spent nearly forty years in journalism investigating hustlers, scam artists, and charlatans, and my skepticism is sharp-edged if not chronic.

If you will indulge me for a bit, I will tell you about one of my greatest investigative triumphs. I call it "The Case of the Smoking Panties" and it illustrates my point exactly.

I happened across this case in the mid-1980s, when several Texas cities were infested with Filipino holy men who claimed that they could cure any ailment with bloodless or psychic surgery. Some of my best friends—among them Bud Shrake and Susan Walker, Jerry Jeff's wife—had ponied up hundreds of dollars in the belief these psychic surgeons could reach into their liver or heart and remove diseased tissue without leaving a trace of an entry wound. Since faith healing was a fundamentally religious concept—and since few of my friends were concerned with religion—I started asking questions.

Bud and Susan had both visited a Filipino faith healer named Angel Domingo, who had been working around Austin, Houston, San Antonio, and Lake Whitney in the spring of 1985 and was at the time doing a stint at Willie World, as we call Willie Nelson's Pedernales Country Club retreat west of Austin. Shrake had asked Angel to treat a blocked colon, and he told me that he saw a pool of coffee-colored liquid well up between the healer's fingers as Angel removed what appeared to be a piece of hog tripe from Bud's abdomen.

At a second session, Angel pulled what appeared to be a chicken bone out of Shrake's left foot, which had been aching for months. Though neither Bud nor Susan experienced much relief following their psychic surgery, both professed to believe in the concept. "I watched him work on a friend with a liver problem," Susan told me, "and saw his hand go into her liver and watched this pulsating organ going around his finger. Then I saw him take that bone out of Shrake's foot. I frigging *saw* it!"

Another friend, George Oberg, reported that Angel had fixed his neck and lower back problem. This surprised me, to say the least. George was a renowned skeptic, throughly convinced that the Apollo moon landing was a fraud filmed in a clandestine television studio, but he had no difficulty whatsoever believing that a surgeon could run his hand through a person's body and remove damaged tissue. "That seems perfectly logical," he said.

In the course of my investigation I learned that thousands of Texans regularly pay for a variety of psychic services. Austin is a mecca of psychic activity, an "energy vortex" where healers, psychics, and other denizens of the Twilight Zone come to recharge their metaphysical batteries. "Psychic" or "bloodless" surgery was only the most current example of these alternative cures. The operating room was usually in some off-the-beaten-path motel or private residence. The time and place were not advertised—advertising would be an open invitation to legal action—but were passed along by an informal network of believers.

One Sunday morning I joined the horde of true believers at WillieWorld's Condo No. 10, bringing along nothing but a bathrobe, a small reporter's notebook, and of course a completely open mind. As I entered, I could hear a voice behind a curtain singing, "How Great Thou Art!" I learned later the voice belonged to Angel.

I was greeted by a pudgy woman named Jann, founder and spiritual commander of a group called the Planetary Light Association, which acted as a booking agent for the healer. She informed me that I would need a minimum of two sessions and that a recovery time of at least two hours between treatments was essential. "You'll be receiving so much energy your body can't take it all at once," Jann explained.

I was directed to undress in the laundry room and put on the robe. Jann then had me sign a disclaimer, stating I understood that the treatment I was about to receive was religious rather than medical and that the healer—the "minister"—made no promises. There was no fee but a "love offering" of thirty dollars was requested for each session.

There were about twenty people waiting when I arrived, and more filtered in and out all morning. At least half were older women who looked as though they had read a lot of books about Edgar Cayce, but some were young, holistic New Agers with wholesome faces and startled eyes. A tall, silver-haired Hispanic wearing a VA hospital robe sat rigidly in a folding chair, his vacant eyes fixed on a fireplace as his wife and daughter comforted him. He was dying of cancer and had seen Angel more than a dozen times. A bearded, bald-headed man in a Japanese bathrobe was so weak that two women had to assist him to the sofa. He had red blotches on his thighs and I assumed he had undergone chemotherapy. Patients waiting for treatment either avoided eye contact or gave each other all-knowing smiles, as though they shared the true meaning of existence. Words like "chakra" and "karma" dropped smoothly from their lips.

Angel turned out to be a stocky little man with greasy black hair and a baggy, weathered face. He wore a flowery short-sleeved shirt with the tail out, like a Tijuana cab driver. While he worked, he sang—sometime religious numbers but more often tunes like "Spanish Eyes" or "Beer Barrel Polka." I don't know if the singing was for our benefit or his.

A woman assistant read a card that I had filled out earlier and told Angel: "This brother has some kidney damage as a result of high blood pressure. Do you want me to do a scan?" Angel said that he did, and she passed a small towel over my body. Angel held the towel to the light as though reading an X ray. "Blockage!" he declared.

As his assistant rubbed my chest and stomach with an aromatic balm, Angel directed me to face the window—"the light"—while he prayed for my recovery. I pretended to turn my head, but continued to watch as he plopped a moist piece of cotton onto my belly and began to apply pressure with his fingers. The fingers fidgeted and probed until one of them seemed to disappear into my flesh for a few seconds. Angel blocked my view so that I couldn't see any blood, even if there had been blood to see, and the next thing I saw was a small, stringy piece of gristle, which he exhibited for my brief inspection and then tossed into the trash can next to the table.

"See?" he said. "Blockage! No more bad blood."

I went back several hours later for the prescribed second treatment, paying another thirty dollars. It was no different from the first. I had seen better sleight-of-hand from grocery sackers. I didn't feel energized, I felt frustrated. I knew the operation was a fraud, but my proof was in the trash can next to the healer's table. It was clear that I had to get my hands on a piece of that gristle—"congealed energy," the Twilight Zoners call it—and have it analyzed.

Just to be certain that Angel wasn't an aberration among psychic healers, however, I flew to Mazatlán, Mexico, the following week to visit another healer who had worked Texas and was a friend of Angel's. As I expected, a number of the Zonies I'd met in Austin had also come to Mazatlán, including Jann and some of her associates from the Planetary Light Association.

While waiting see the healer, who I'll call R, I talked to a number of the Zonies, trying to understand if they really believed this or if they were part of the scam. Jann's husband, Art, an Austin chiropractor, explained that a healer's ability to penetrate a patient's skin without leaving a mark depends on "the speed of the vibration of the electrons." Oh? Tell me more.

"If you speed up the vibrations of the electrons on this tabletop," Art said, rapping his knuckles on the surface of the table at poolside, "you could stick your hand through it."

Zonies, I learned in my three days in Mazatlán, have a theory to explain every doubt. Somehow they are able to convince themselves that metaphysics is superior to literal-minded science, which they believe is a conspiracy fomented by the American Medical Association. The White Crow Theory, for example, is a handy way for the Zonies to shift the burden of proof to the nonbeliever. "If you've never seen a white crow," I was challenged, "how do you know that one does not exist?" As it turned out, Art and Jann did have a proprietary interest in these clinics. She was a professional medium or channel, in contact with a spirit named Anoah, who borrowed her voice to advise the sick and weary. Anoah, an old man with white hair and a white robe who floated through time carrying a book titled *Wisdom,* was just one of the spirits who used Jann's voice and body. Tapes of Anoah could be purchased for four dollars or they could be heard live, so to speak, during half-hour personal counseling sessions with Jann, at forty dollars a pop.

Jann was one of three psychics on R's staff in Mazatlán. All of them—in fact, every Zonie I met—had experiences with reincarnation or past-life regressions. Jann had been a Mayan priest in the Mexican seaside ruin of Tulúm. Another had been the son of an Indian chief and had witnessed her own funeral near Fredricksburg, Texas. Still another had been a young German soldier killed in the early days of World War II.

R managed to avoid me for two days, but I finally got to see him the morning before I had to fly home. He was younger and smaller than his friend Angel. Dodo, his assistant, looked like a bandy-legged, puffy-eyed Filipino bantamweight I saw fight once in San Diego. Dodo offered me a Filipino cigarette, brand-named Hope.

Except for me and a young couple from Houston, all the patients in the motel room were New Yorkers. Nick, a pious young man who walked with his hands clasped and talked almost exclusively of faith, was there to comfort his mother, Grace, who was dying of cancer. During orientation, Nick mentioned that "walking on fire" had become a popular therapy for Zonies on the East Coast and asked Dodo if he thought the practice increased faith. Dodo looked as though someone had dropped a cobra in his lap. "Walk on fire?" he said incredulously. "Me?" Nick explained that he was talking about his *own* faith, that he happened to believe that faith had no limit. Waving his hands furiously, Dodo shouted, "No, no! No walk on fire! Burn feet!"

R was quicker—and apparently smarter—than Angel had been. No love offerings here. This was a straight cash deal, eighty dollars U.S. for two sessions, no pesos, please. I asked R to remove a small knot just above my wrist; my doctor in Austin had called it a ganglion. Compared with curing cancer, removing a ganglion seemed to me to be laughably simple. I wondered if R could deal with it. The little healer rubbed oil on the knot, then shook his head. He didn't want any part of an affliction that would still be visible fifteen minutes later. Instead, he fluttered his hands in the area above my kidneys and produced a piece of gray meat. For the second time in less than a month, my high blood pressure had been cured!

Flying home that night, I kept thinking that if R had tried to pass off this act on a carnival midway in, say, Wichita Falls, he'd be leaving town on a rail, wearing tar and feathers.

By now I was more determined than ever to expose this fraud. As soon as I had landed in Austin I checked to see if Angel was still around. Fortunately, he was. I went to see a doctor friend of mine who owned Austin Pathology Associates, a laboratory that tests tissue samples for hospitals and law enforcement agencies. I told him my plan, and he gave me a bottle of formaldehyde in which to preserve my evidence.

I wasn't sure how the Zonies would react when I made my play, so when I went to see Angel the next morning I took along two big friends, Bud and Fletcher Boone.

Stretched out on the operating table, I watched Angel work. Humming a tune I did not recognize, he produced small pieces of gunk from the area of my kidneys and began to deposit them on my naked belly, not suspecting any threat. So far, so good. I waited until he had turned away, then I grabbed the tissue and leaped from the table, protecting my privacy with just a small hand towel.

Suddenly, all hell broke lose. His assistant tried to wrestle the tissue from my fist. I shoved her away. Angel was dancing about and screaming, "You'll destroy my power!"

Racing through the reception area, I observed people in fetal positions, trying to hide under pieces of furniture. "Cover yourself with the white light," someone was crying. "Surround yourself with white light before it is too late!"

Another Zonie that I had met earlier cried out a curse: "You'll regret what you did the rest of your life! It will follow you to your grave! It will haunt your karma for all of eternity!"

Fletcher had the back door open for me. Bud stepped forward to block anyone who wanted to give chase, but nobody did. I could hear Angel shouting, "Bullshit! Bullshit!" (I found out later that as soon as we'd gone, Angel complained of a sudden headache, grabbed the cash box, and caught the next bus out of town.)

I delivered a piece of tissue about the size of a pencil eraser to the laboratory and waited for the results. Several hours later I learned that the tests had proved inconclusive. The meat was connective tissue, but no one could say for sure if it was of human origin. This was the worst sort of news. I knew that I knew the truth—psychic surgery was a hoax—but I'd failed as a journalist to prove my case.

I had about given up hope when Lana Nelson called me a week later. When Angel had worked on her, removing a two-inch piece of gristle, some of the blood had stained her panties. "I still have them, if they'll help," she said sweetly. My heart sang: I had been redeemed!

That afternoon Lana's panties were on their way to the Bexar County Regional Crime Lab in San Antonio. The stain turned out to be bovine blood, diluted with water. What a surprise! Bovine blood had been my fourth guess, behind chicken, goat, and cat.

My story appeared in the December 1986 issue of *Texas Monthly*—titled "Touch Me, Feel Me, Heal Me!"—and won an award from the Texas Medical Association. It's one of my all-time favorites.

Fifteen

In the twelve years since I looked behind the curtain of psychic surgery, I've become less interested in exposing the illegitimacy of nontraditional medical claims and more interested in learning all I can about them. Maybe I'm just more forgiving, an acquired character trait common to many who have faced their own mortality. The woods are still full of charlatans and quacks, to be sure, but I understand now that perfectly legitimate therapies vary according to individual practices and cultures. As I've discovered while researching this book and seeing to my own recovery, there are many more things in heaven and earth than meet the eye.

I acknowledge, for example, that urine therapy—drinking eight ounces a day of your own urine—works perfectly well in India and would no doubt work just as well in Austin, though it would require some ingenious marketing. Nevertheless, when India's former prime minister Morarji Desai praised the benefits of urine therapy to Dan Rather on *60 Minutes* in 1978, my reaction was the same as Rather's—somebody get the net. I know now that urine is a perfectly sterile fluid that contains minerals, proteins, enzymes, hormones, antibodies, amino acids, and probably anticancer agents. Milligram per milligram, urine is said to be a better supplement to one's diet than vitamins, because the vitamins in urine have already been digested and synthesized. Having acknowledged that urine therapy is a medically reasonable alternative for millions of Indians unable to afford medical care, I'm not about to pee in a bottle and drink it, or recommend that you do so either. But I have several friends who have tried it and swear they got results.

Until 1995, terms like "beta-carotene," "phytochemicals," "free radicals," and "antioxidants" were not in my vocabulary. For that matter they weren't in the vocabularies of huge numbers of people, including, unfortunately, many in the medical profession. And yet these obscure biochemical molocules are not merely keys to good health, they are essential ingredients in our survival.

Until recently, for example, scientists didn't know about the existence of phytochemicals, biologically active compounds found in plant foods that appear to have disease-prevention and healing properties. Now mainstream publications like *Newsweek* run cover stories about phytochemicals. Four or five years ago, few physicians were concerned with free radicals and antioxidants, and most laypeople had never heard of them. Now they are becoming increasingly part of our consciousness, much the way that terms like "cholesterol" caught the public awareness in the decade just past.

"Degenerate diseases of aging such as cancer, cardiovascular disease, cataracts, and brain dysfunction are increasingly found to have an oxidative origin," reports Bruce Ames, professor of biochemistry and molecular biology and director of the National Institute of Environmental Health Studies at the University of California, Berkeley. This means that the cells throughout the body are constantly being damaged by highly reactive oxygen-rich chemicals called free radicals.

Free radicals, I know now, are rogue molecules with free or unpaired electrons, created when food is converted to energy and during other biochemical processes in the body. Everyone has them and everyone needs protection from them, especially people whose bodies are trying to fight off diseases such as cancer or atherosclerosis. Think of free radicals as electrical sparks. If you have ever felt a spark, you know that it stings and sometimes burns the spot where it lands. In the body, free radical sparks hit cells and damage or destroy them.

The cumulative damage from free radicals is implicated in many types of cancer, heart disease, and brain damage. They make us look and feel older. They cause defects in our DNA, the genetic material of the cells, and the RNA, which assembles amino acids into muscle protein chains. They attack fat cells, oxidizing fat and turning it rancid. When fat turns rancid, it sticks to the interior walls of our arteries. Our only defense against free radicals is antioxidants which catch those sparks before they hit the cells.

Antioxidants are compounds found in various vegetables and fruits. Here are the four major antioxidants, where you can find them, and how they work:

VITAMIN E (D-ALPHA-TOCOPHEROL).

The main fat-soluble antioxidant, vitamin E protects fatty acids in and around cells from free-radical (lipid peroxidation) damage. It is found in cold-processed vegetable oil, wheat germ, and whole-grain breads and cereals. Vitamin E does not work overnight, however. It takes about two years before the protection kicks in. Recommended daily dose: 400 units.

BETA-CAROTENE.

The vegetable form of vitamin A, beta-carotene protects the lipid or fatty layer of the cell, though not as well as vitamin E. Beta-carotenes are found in greatest abundance in fruits and vegetables that have a rich orange color, such as apricots, carrots, butternut squash, cantaloupe, and sweet potatoes. A study by the USDA found that people who ate two or three carrots a day with no other dietary changes lowered their cholesterol an average of eleven points. Beta-carotene is also found in a variety of deep-green vegetables such as broccoli, kale, and spinach. Recommended daily dose: 4,000–8,000 units.

VITAMIN C (ASCORBIC ACID).

The main water-soluble antioxidant, vitamin C protects muscle tissue and the brain and nervous system. It also converts depleted supplies of vitamin E back into its antioxidant form and helps stablize DNA and RNA. It is found in citrus fruits and vegetables, particularly oranges, grapefruit, tomatoes, potatoes, and broccoli. Tomatoes contain a bonus substance called lycopene, an antioxidant that "mops up" free radicals before they can attack healthy cells. Recommended daily dose: 2,000–8,000 units.

SELENIUM (I-SELENOMETHIONINE).

The chief mineral antioxidant, selenium deactivates free radicals, protects arteries by preventing platelet aggression, and forms the enzyme glutathione peroxidose, which detoxifies harmful chemicals that might otherwise lead to cancer. Selenium works best in synergy with vitamin E and so should be taken in tandem. Selenium is found in seafood, liver, whole wheat, brown rice, and asparagus. Recommended daily dose: 200–400 milligrams.

Vitamins C and E, beta-carotene, and selenium work best when they work as a team.

Science long ago recognized the value of vitamin E in preventing heart attacks. According to two Harvard scientists, Meir J. Stampfer, M.D., and Eric B. Rimm, Sc.D., "the risk [to heart patients] for not taking vitamin E was equivalent to the risk of smoking." Moreover the researchers discovered that the benefits of E far exceeded the benefits of lowering blood pressure and cholesterol levels. Imagine how many people died because of insufficient amounts of this single vitamin.

It is important to understand that vitamins can and do cause controversy among even medical experts. Generally, water-soluble vitamins can be taken with less risk because excessive amounts are eliminated in your urine. Fat-soluble vitamins, however, can accumulate in your body. Consult your doctor on the types and amounts of vitamins that are safe for you, and practice moderation in everything.

Recent research has determined, for example, that you can overdose on vitamin E supplements and cause considerable harm to your body. People who take large amounts of vitamin E *supplements* may actually be depleting their bodies of another form of the vitamin that performs unique and vital chemical tasks. Supplements of vitamin E contain a form of the vitamin known as alpha-tocopherol. Ordinarily, about 80 percent of vitamin E in the human body is made up of alpha-tocopherol and about 20 percent is made up of another form of the vitamin, gamma-tocopherol, which is not contained in supplements. The differences are highly significant. Gamma-tocopherol removes from the body toxic chemicals that cause cancer and heart disease that aren't affected by the other form of vitamin E or other antioxidants. Large doses of alpha-tocopherol cause the concentration of gamma-tocopherol to drop by as much as twenty times. Though scientists disagree on the amount of vitamin E supplements a person should take, 400 units seems about right for me.

Some antioxidants have the ability to facilitate the production of cellular energy. Heart patients in particular need to be aware of these antioxidants. In every cell in your body there are small subcomponents called mitochondria, miniature energy stations that fuel life. Ninety-five percent of the total energy in your body comes from your mitochondria. In her book *Stop Aging Now*, Jean Carper says that the relentless damage from free radicals over the years to heart mitochondria can lead to an enlarged heart, diastolic dysfunction (when blood flows back into the ventricle), and congestive heart failure. There may be a window of time between ages fifty and eighty, however, in which antioxidants can reverse the dysfunction and save the mitochondria.

There are a number of natural antioxidants that we're just becoming aware of—partly because the federal government and the traditional medical and pharmaceutical communities haven't seen fit to inform us—which may prove as important as the big four mentioned above. Science is only now discovering that each of these antioxidants is important in its own way and that a wide variety of antioxidants is a better tonic than merely the big four. One of most effective (and lately recognized) is melatonin, a powerful and popular antioxidant used by older people to help them sleep.

One of the ways melatonin promotes sleep is by lowering the body temperature in the early-morning hours when we enter into the deep hibernationlike sleep that revitalizes and rejuvenates us. Phyllis and I have been taking nightly doses of three milligrams of melatonin since 1995, with very good results, and have recommended it to all of our aging friends. New studies reveal that melatonin can also protect brain cells against free radical assault and age-related degenerative changes, and is in addition a powerful cancer-fighter.

Brain cells have an extraordinarily high need for energy, and the by-product of energy conversion is free radicals. Since it has a high fat content, the brain is especially vulnerable to lipid peroxidation. Melatonin is one of the few antioxidants that can penetrate the "blood-brain barrier" that shields the delicate structures within the cells of our brains.

Though melatonin's effectiveness as an adjuvant cancer therapy has been documented by several hundred research papers, it has only recently been touted to the public as a cancer-fighter. Melatonin boosts the components of the immune system that attack cancer cells and also inhibits cancer-cell proliferation while promoting cancer-cell differentiation into normal cells.

Preventive medicine is not a new concept—Benjamin Franklin preached it more than two hundred years ago—but until the 1990s it was not widely accepted by either politicians or medical professionals. One study I read reported that less than half the primary care physicians in America bothered to recommend vitamin and mineral supplements to their patients. A lot of doctors may not have realized vitamins and minerals were important: these were not sexy subjects in med school. My own doctor, Thomas Blevins, is a strong advocate of vitamin therapy and tells me that many of his colleagues are beginning to get the message, but too many doctors still regard alternative therapies as quackery.

The dramatic changes in our broad system of medical care are partly due to the public's disenchantment with modern, high-tech medicine, but more than that to increasing awareness that such things as diet and nutrition are directly related to the chronic diseases of aging—and to the process of aging itself. A landmark study by Harvard Medical School in 1993 showed that one in three Americans used nontraditional treatments and that $14 billion a year was spent on them. Americans are voting for better health care with their pocketbooks, and the market is getting the message. Look at the number of best-selling books targeted to health and fitness. Newsstands display a dizzying procession of magazines like *Self*, *Prevention*, *Health*, and *Fitness and Shape*, all dedicated to improving and prolonging life. This trend is equally evident in the proliferation of health food stores and organizations like Life Extension Foundation, all competing for attention in the marketplace.

Even traditional neighborhood pharmacies are stocking up on supplements like ginkgo biloba and coenzyme Q10, both of which have been popular for years in Europe and Asia. CoQ10 is one of the more remarkable supplements I've read about: it induces regressions of breast cancer, protects the heart from cell energy depletion, and provides varied health and longevity benefits. Since it is a natural substance that cannot be patented, American pharmaceutical companies didn't consider CoQ10 economically viable until it became a billion-dollar export for the Japanese.

Drugs once prescribed only by doctors are being promoted in television commercials as though they were toothpaste or deodorant. At last count there were more than a thousand homeopathic medicines sold over the counter, and a staggering variety of vitamins, minerals, herbal remedies, fat burners, allergy preventers, and sexual stimulators.

Chains of potency clinics are sprouting up around the country, many of them funded by groups of urologists and their investment bankers. Pharmaceutical companies are racing to promote drugs that claim to restore youth, improve memory, or enhance sexual desire. Mainstream physicians, clinics, and medical research organizations are experimenting with heretofore radical treatments. Harvard Medical School has endowed a Mind/Body Medical Institute chair. Relaxation techniques and biofeedback are routinely taught to medical students all over the country.

So, too, is spirituality. There is now considerable scientific investigation into the power of prayer and faith healing. Some highly respected scientists are staking their careers on the idea that prayer works better than many traditional therapies. Larry Dorsey, M.D., has written several best-selling books about the capacity of prayer to heal, even over long distances and even when the recipients didn't know they were being prayed for.

A cardiologist at the University of California School of Medicine in San Francisco tested the impact of distant prayer much as he would a new medication, recording its effects on 393 heart patients, half prayed for and half not. Those who were not prayed for required five times the antibiotics and experienced more than twice the number of congestive heart failures and four times the number of cardiopulmonary arrests as the patients who were served by prayer. Some scientists are beginning to suspect that we are actually engineered for religious faith.

Praying and meditation both affect so-called stress hormones, leading to lower blood pressure and more relaxed heart rate and directly impacting the body's immunological defenses against diseases. In the June 24, 1996, issue of *Time*, Claudia Wells writes: "Many researchers believe . . . neuronal and hormonal pathways are the basis for the renowned and powerful 'placebo effect.' Decades of research show that if a patient truly believes a therapy is useful—even if it is a sugar pill or snake oil—that belief has the power to heal."

HMOs are beginning to understand that people who favor holistic cures tend to be healthier than people who do not, and are therefore more attractive patients. Most HMOs offer chiropractic coverage, and many are adding acupuncturists, massage therapists, and even practitioners called naturopathists who emphasize the body's ability to heal itself. Naturopathists use vitamins, nutritional supplements, herbal remedies, relaxation therapies, and yoga to improve circulation and boost the immune system. Some also employ homeopathy, touch therapy, music therapy, and biofeedback. Biofeedback, a method of learning to regulate consciously normally unconscious bodily functions, is popular with several of my friends who a decade earlier would have laughed at such notions.

Even the government is starting to catch on. In 1992, Congress created the Office of Alternative Medicine, largely because Senator Tom Harkin of Iowa believed that bee pollen cured his hayfever. To date, Congress has shown little willingness to fund OAM; it gets $7.3 million yearly, compared to the $12 billion appropriated to the National Institute of Health. In 1994, because of pressure from citizens' groups like the Life Extension Foundation, Congress deregulated products sold as dietary supplements, meaning that the FDA could no longer arbitrarily ban the sale of popular and harmless supplements like melatonin and CoQ10.

The most exciting area in medicine as far as I'm concerned is the research being done on hormone replacement therapy as a method to slow or reverse the aging process. As we age, our bodies not only lose muscle mass and bone density, they produce hormones at a lower level. This is nature's way of saying "you're not needed anymore." Until recently, the medical profession tended to agree with nature. The rapid decline of hormones was considered a natural process, best left unchecked. Old people generated less of the natural hormone melatonin, for example, because they didn't need as much sleep as kids did. After menopause, women had no use for the female hormone estrogen. Men over the age of fifty didn't need the male sex hormone testosterone or its parent hormone, DHEA. Fortunately, medical science is taking another look at the situation.

"We know now that when women reach menopause and the production of the estrogen rapidly declines, women experience escalating amounts of heart disease, memory disorder, osteoporosis, and negative changes in cholesterol levels," Dr. Tom Blevins told me. Estrogen replacement therapy, however, has been a high-stakes trade-off. While postmenopausal women who took estrogen protected their heart, bones, and brains from the ravages of age—and reclaimed their sexual appetite—they were also at increased risk of breast and uterus cancer. In the spring of 1997, however, scientists announced that they were not on the trail of wonder drugs that offered the benefits of natural estrogen without the serious risks that dissuaded many women from taking replacement hormones after menopause.

Men, of course, do not experience menopause, but they do experience a gradual decline of strength, sexuality, and general sense of contentment as they age. Viropause, some call it. Between the ages of forty and seventy, a man loses twelve to twenty pounds of muscle and 15 percent of his bone mass. At viropause men begin losing testosterone, though the decline is far more subtle than in menopause, when a woman's ovaries shut down entirely and estrogen levels crash. Men's levels of testosterone drop about 1 percent a year after forty. By age seventy, a man's testosterone level has dropped about 30 percent. Testosterone replacement therapy, in the form of injections or patches applied to the skin, helps men maintain muscle and increase energy and libido. There is a small risk that the therapy can trigger prostate tumors.

Testosterone, incidentally, kindles sexual desire in both men and women. Although estrogen is the primary hormone for women, a small amount of testosterone is essential for them as well. It stimulates sexual desire, energy, assertiveness, elevated mood, and a sense of well-being. While the decline of testosterone in men is gradual, women's testosterone levels drop rapidly after menopause. The loss is not as urgent as the loss of estrogen, but it does matter. Some doctors treat postmenopausal women with small amounts of testosterone and report renewed sexuality, sensuality, and vitality. Other doctors believe that such side effects as the growth of unwanted facial or body hair make testosterone replacements for women unwise.

The hottest hormonal replacement on today's market is DHEA, the so-called fountain-of-youth hormone and the "mother hormone" of both testosterone and estrogen. Like other hormone levels, DHEA levels decline with age, starting at about thirty. Scientists have known about DHEA since the 1930s and have done thousands of studies using lab animals, demonstrating that the hormone can help prevent heart disease, cancer, diabetes, weight loss, lupus, and a variety of conditions—and can restore youthful vigor and vitality. But until recently the public knew nothing of this remarkable hormone.

Since 1994, however, we have been deluged by reports on DHEA in newspapers and magazines and on television. That's when the results of an experiment on human volunteers at the University of California at San Diego were published. An endocrinologist, Samuel S.C. Yen, M.D., gave fifty milligrams of DHEA to thirty men and women, ages forty to seventy, nightly for three months. The subjects experienced an increase in physical and psychological well-being, enhanced energy, deeper sleep, and an improved ability to deal with stressful situations. The publication of Yen's study coincided with federal deregulations of products sold as dietary supplements. Within a year most vitamin manufacturers started marketing DHEA. Since there have been no long-term studies, most doctors are hesitant to prescribe DHEA. Men with prostate cancer should definitely avoid this hormone.

The shelves of health food stores are full of extracts and supplements that elevate levels of glutathione, a compound composed of three amino acids that is present in every cell of our bodies and is essential for life. Many antioxidants work by increasing the production of glutathione enzymes. For example, the effectiveness of melatonin is increased because it stimulates the production of glutathione peroxidase, one of the principal enzymes for controlling free radical damage to our brains. Though it's easier to take it in supplement form, gluthathione can be acquired by eating foods such as broccoli (particularly the flower), brussels sprouts, cauliflower, cabbage, kale, bok choy, cress, mustard, horseradish, turnips, and rutabagas. Some of the best-known supplements for elevating levels of glutathione are green tea extract and grapeseed extract, both powerful antioxidants and scavengers of free radicals; and l-arginine, an amino acid that appears to reverse the aging effect that causes blood vessels to narrow and lose their ability to relax, and that also may improve memory by increasing the blood flow to the brain.

A herbal supplement that appears to work even better than l-arginine in improving the circulation of blood in the smaller capillaries is ginkgo biloba. Taken from the bark of the ginkgo tree, this potent antioxidant may be an effective treatment for several conditions associated with aging, including impotence. It has been found to inhibit the abnormal stickiness of blood platelets, increase blood flow to the brain, and shield the nervous system from damage. Gingko biloba extract (GBE) may also be a powerful tool in treating Alzheimer's disease, as well as sleeping problems.

What caught my attention was an experiment in Germany in which patients suffering from arterial erectile impotence were treated with large doses of GBE. The results were startling. The test subjects fell into two groups, those who had been able to achieve erections when given penile injections and those who hadn't responded to injections. Both groups were given 240 milligrams of GBE daily for a period of nine months. In the first group every patient regained spontaneous and sufficient erections after six months. In the second group, improved penile blood flow and rigidity were noted at six and nine months. After these improvements nearly two-thirds of the patients could get an erection when given penile injections. The final one-third of the second group remained impotent.

Although GBE therapy may not be effective for every case of circulation-related impotence, it is a safe, easy treatment for many.

It's not cheap—a month's supply of extract costs twenty-five to forty dollars. Be warned that you may not notice results for three to six (or even nine) months. Those arteries didn't get clogged overnight, and neither will they get unclogged quickly.

I started using 240 milligrams of GBE on September 1, 1996. By the end of October, there was a noticable improvement, and by the end March 1997, the improvement was, shall we say, large. On a scale of one to ten my sex life has improved by about eight. In general I feel much better than I've felt in a long time. My energy level is higher than it has been in years, and I seem to be thinking more clearly. I should mention that I also started using the so-called youth hormone DHEA a month after I began GBE, so I'm not sure how much to attribute to the extract, but I'm feeling too good now to worry about it.

Some doctors prescribe the herbal extract yohimbine to improve sexual function, and several friends swear that it works like magic. The downside of yohimbine is that it can trigger serious side effects like erratic heart rate and elevated blood pressure. People who suffer from hypertension should definitely avoid yohimbine.

Not all the supplements on the druggist's shelf are safe, and some are downright dangerous—mahuang, for example. Mahuang, an ancient Chinese herb that boosts energy and brings on euphoric effects similar to those of amphetamines, is largely unregulated, even though it contains a regulated drug called ephedrine. An active ingredient used in hay fever and asthma drugs, ephedrine is a botanical amphetamine that suppresses appetite, stimulates the central nervous system, and promotes wakefulness. It can also raise blood pressure and cause palpitations, nerve damage, muscle injury, or stroke if used in excess. Legal stimulants like Herbal Ecstasy, Diet Pep, and Formula One also contain ephedrine. Some of them also contain kola nut, a source of caffeine, which speeds up the heart and is doubly dangerous when combined with ephedrine.

Again, always keep in mind that there are theoretical risks to taking vitamins, supplements, and especially hormones without consulting your physician. Even small amounts of hormones can have profound effects on the body, an extremely complex mechanism in which thousands of chemical interactions take place constantly to keep the systems in harmony. No one understands all of them. I'm pretty sure it was Aristotle who said, "Moderation in everything." If he didn't, he should have.

Both the mainstream and alternative medical communities recommend that whenever possible you get nutritional components from whole foods rather than supplements, but there are some caveats to this good advice. Supplements are easier to take than natural food and, generally speaking, more powerful in terms of nutrition. Also, only about 9 percent of the people in this country eat the kind of diet necessary to get the full spectrum of nutrition. On a practical level, it's difficult to eat enough of the right things to reach therapeutic levels—and even if you did, the fats and calories would more than offset the nutritional benefits.

Eating sixteen pounds of blueberries, for example, would give you just 100 milligrams of vitamin C. A high-dose vitamin C capsule has ten times that. You would need to eat two hundred avocados or five pounds of nuts to get four hundred milligrams of vitamin E, nature's best defense against a heart attack. Research by Harvard scientists shows that you can't get enough E from food to suppress a heart attack.

Potatoes are the main source of vitamin A in America. Without french fries, we'd have an epidemic of scurvy. Our main source of the powerful antioxidant lycopene is the tomato sauce on pizza. Some compounds appear to be more bioavailable in supplement form than in food. For example, beta-carotene levels in people who take supplements have been found to be six or seven times higher than in people who consume an equivalent amount of beta-carotene in carrots.

On the other hand, we can't live by supplements alone, nor do we want to. Food is one of the supreme pleasures of life. Long before we realized that food is an irreplacement source of fiber and phytochemicals, dining was part of the institution of family and of gracious living. Meals were designated gatherings, the anchor that kept us from being swept away, a statement of purpose and a declaration of being. Somehow, in modern times, we've gotten away from the gentility of dining and moved in the direction of science fiction where a proper dinner is four brightly colored pills on a platter. We've become so neurotic about weight that eating has become either a fast or a binge. We're approaching the unthinkable: making ourselves feel guilty about enjoying food.

Sixteen

*N*utrition isn't rocket science, it's common sense. Food should serve three purposes: to satisfy hunger, enrich life, and improve health. Remember, there is no such thing as good food and bad food, but there are some rules you need to learn in selecting and preparing what you eat.

Removing the skin from chicken doesn't hurt the flavor and it eliminates a huge part of the fat. Skinless chicken smoked over charcoal is infinitely better in every way than those greasy buckets you used to buy at KFC. On the other hand, keeping the skin on a sweet potato makes it tastier and healthier, and gives you more fiber. Some vegetables are better for you than others. In particular you need to make an effort to eat the four Power Vegetables—spinach, carrots, sweet potatoes, and broccoli.

Six years ago when I got serious about health, fitness, and weight loss, I either hated most vegetables or was monumentally indifferent to them. The only exceptions were tomatos, onions, and dried beans—and I know now that beans are not vegetables (nutritionally speaking) but grains. Nevertheless, I forced myself to eat a variety of vegetables, and in the course of my heroic suffering discovered that vegetables actually taste good. Not good like steak, understand, but good nevertheless. By forcing myself to eat a daily quota of fruits and vegetables, I could, from time to time, enjoy a giant slab of red meat. The more fruits and vegetables I ate, the better I felt and functioned, and the easier it got to make myself believe I actually *liked* broccoli. After a time this new way of eating stopped being a sacrifice and became my diet of choice.

My original solution to the vegetable problem was to sprinkle large amounts of Louisiana Cajun red sauce on broccoli, carrots, spinach, and sweet potatoes, and sometimes on other vegetables. Later I experimented with other vinegar-based pepper sauces. My current favorite is Tabasco green sauce, made from jalapeños and milder than the fiery red Tabasco. Phyllis and I buy it by the case.

More recently I discovered that roasted vegetables sprinkled with olive oil and sea salt are delicious, so good in fact that I wouldn't dream of tarnishing them with pepper sauce. Vegetables are also great when stir-fried with a small amount of oil, with garlic, ginger, peppers, soy sauce, and pineapple juice. Vegetables mixed with various salad dressings can be eaten raw; marinated vegetables, served with pasta, French bread, and a piece of fruit, make a great and very healthy lunch.

Optimal nutrition should include supplements, a variety of the five food groups, and the healing compounds in "functional foods," to use a term currently in vogue. Garlic is a good example of a functional food. Eating garlic or taking garlic pills has been found to reduce cholesterol levels 10 percent and raise good cholesterol (HDL) by 23 percent.

Beans are another functional food, I'm happy to report. They are rich in cholesterol-fighting fiber and heart-healthy folic acid—which has been proved to lower levels of homocysteine, a blood factor linked with artery disease. Pinto and kidney beans beat out vitamin C at preventing fat in the blood from becoming oxidized. People in Mexico have less heart disease than people in this country, even though their diets are much higher in fat than ours. The reason is beans and peppers.

I cook two or three pounds of dried beans at a time and keep them in quart-size containers in the freezer. To prepare world-class chili beans, place two pounds of dried pintos in a large pot or pressure cooker and wash them thoroughly, at least four or five times. Refill the pot almost to the rim with water—you need a lot of moisture to cook and keep dried beans. Add one coarsely chopped onion, five or six coarsely chopped cloves of garlic, three or four dried chili peppers, and a small (no more than three ounces) piece of lean ham or Cajun tasso with the fat removed. Season to taste with chili powder, cumin, onion, and garlic powder. (I use at least a heaping tablespoon of each.) Don't salt the beans until they are cooked. If you use a pressure cooker, cook at maximum pressure for about ninety minutes. Or bring a covered pot to a boil and simmer for at least four hours, or until the beans are tender. Make certain that there is always plenty of water covering the beans.

As long as they have plenty of moisture, chili beans can be re-fried, Mexican-style, in a Teflon-coated or well-seasoned skillet, using no oil. Simply simmer and mash with a fork or spoon, then allow the refries to cool and thicken. Crumble a little goat cheese on the top and serve with baked (low-fat) yellow corn tortilla chips or tortillas.

Chili peppers appear to have even greater magical qualities than beans. Researchers are learning that chilies can heal you, make you euphoric, even help you lose weight. Capsaicin, the odor-less and tasteless compound that controls the heat level of chilies, causes the brain to release painkilling endorphins. This produces a natural high and may explain why some of us believe that we are addicted to spicy food. The ability of capsaicin to neutralize pain in the body's mucous membranes has made it a treatment for mucosi-tis, a side effect of chemotherapy. The extract from hot peppers is effective against diabetic neuropathy, a burning pain in the ex-tremities that afflicts long-term diabetics. It can actually help sur-gical wounds heal faster than they would heal with antibiotic ointments.

Peppers aid digestion by sending signals to the brain to pro-duce salivation and the secretion of gastric juices. Chilies may help control cholesterol levels by causing cholesterol to bind more easily to bile acids which carry it out of the body. Hot spices accelerate by 25 percent the temporary increase in the body's metabolic rate. In theory, you could lose a pound a month merely by eating a diet of spicy food.

Contrary to popular belief, the fiery taste of peppers does not erase other flavors and may even enhance them. Peppers are a form of sensory excitement apart from taste and smell. The hotness of chilies is measured in Scoville units, named for the pharmacologist who invented the system. A bell pepper has zero units, a jalapeño 5,000, and a habanero 300,000. My favorites are the jalapeño, which snaps the front of the mouth to attention and stings the lips and tongue, and the New Mexico green chili, which has a midpalate burn and ranks closer to the bell pepper than the jalapeño on the Scoville scale.

Many of my favorite recipes use a green sauce I discovered years ago in Taos, made from New Mexico green chilies. Heat a tablespoon of olive oil in a medium-size kettle or skillet and sauté one finely chopped onion, two finely chopped cloves of garlic, two finely chopped shallots, and one pound of fresh roasted New Mexico green chilies or four four-ounce cans of Old El Paso peeled green chilies. Add three cups of chicken stock and one tablespoon of chopped fresh oregano. Bring mixture to a boil, reduce the heat, and allow the chili sauce to simmer twenty-five or thirty minutes. Thicken with one to two tablespoons of cornstarch, dissolved in water. Add salt and pepper to taste. This sauce is great on omelets, enchiladas, or refries.

Fish is an almost perfect functional food, low in fat and calories and great for your heart. Since I have never been especially fond of fish, I had to work on this one. I solved the problem with another Mexican standby—seviche. Seviche is fish "cooked" in lime or lemon juice rather than with heat, and mixed with onions and chilies. Cut one pound of sea bass, snapper, or rock cod (or any type of white, firm-fleshed fish) into bite-size pieces and cover with half lemon and half lime juice. Marinate at room temperature for about three hours. Drain off all the juice. In a large bowl, stir the fish with one large chopped onion, one chopped tomato, five chopped cloves of garlic, two or more chopped jalapeños, one chopped red bell pepper, one chopped Anaheim pepper, one bunch of chopped cilantro (note: the cilantro will cut the fiery taste of the jalapeños), and twenty pitted, chopped kalamata olives. Mix the fish and vegetables well. Season with three tablespoons of olive oil, two small (five-and-a-half-ounce) cans of V-8 juice, one tablespoon of chili powder, one tablespoon of cumin, two ounces of fresh lemon juice, two ounces of fresh lime juice, and salt and pepper to taste. Serve with slices of avocado, wedges of fresh lime, baked tortilla chips, and refried beans.

Of all the vegetables, the carrot has the most amazing medicinal qualities. Early Greek writings around 200 A.D. mention methods used to prepare carrots for culinary and medicinal use. Because it has many of the same protective and therapeutic benefits as ginseng—and because it costs a fraction of what ginseng costs—

the carrot has been called the "ginseng of the masses." Carrots contain not only beta-carotene but alpha-carotene, epsilon-carotene, gamma-carotene, lycopene, and many more compounds that have yet to be identified. Grated carrots work nicely in salads and soups.

As a rule, raw vegetables contain more powerful doses of antioxidants than cooked vegetables, but there are a couple of exceptions. Cooked carrots are better than raw ones because cooking releases more of the carotenes. Tomatoes are also more nutritious when cooked. Cooking appears to release lycopene from the cell walls of the tomato and increases the yield.

So what vitamins, minerals, and antioxidants should you be taking? The important thing is to make certain that you eat a balanced diet and, *in addition to your diet,* take a supplement that by itself assures that you get your recommended daily allowance (RDA) of all vitamins and minerals. This usually requires more than a single multivitamin tablet. I would suggest also that you take extra amounts of all four major antioxidants, plus any other supplement your doctor might suggest for your particular condition.

Garlic is one of several supplements I take on the advice of Dr. Blevins. Phyllis takes at least a gram of calcium in tablet form; it would be difficult for her to get enough calcium in her daily diet. We both take a once-a-day packet of vitamins and minerals purchased from the Whole Foods chain, which has its headquarters in Austin but owns more than a hundred stores nationwide. The packet costs about a dollar. Similar packages of across-the-board supplements can be found at almost any health food store.

Whole Foods calls this particular packet a Stress Pak. Stress depletes the body of the all-important B and C vitamins as well as several key minerals. The formula provides a full day's supply of necessary vitamins and minerals, but is especially potent in the key nutrients required during periods of stress: pantothenic acid, vitamin C, calcium, and magnesium. It also includes beta-carotene, selenium, and the recommended 400 international units of vitamin E, along with valerian, skullcap, and passiflora for herbal support.

In addition to the Stress Pak, I also take three caps of saw palmetto for my enlarged prostate and 240 milligrams of ginkgo biloba. Phyllis and I both take twenty-five milligrams of DHEA two times a day, coenzyme Q10, and melatonin at night. That's a lot of pills, but we always prefer to err on the side of excess. And neither of us has ever felt better.

Seventeen

Given that aging is far better than the alternative, there has never been a better time to grow old than this final decade of the twentieth century. In 1900, life expectancy in the United States was forty-seven. Today it's seventy-five plus. By the middle of the next century, 20 percent of the population will be sixty-five or older. Nearly four million seniors—the "old old"—have already celebrated their eighty-fifth birthday; they're the fastest-growing segment of the population. By 2030, some demographers predict, the old old will number 48 million. What we're witnessing isn't a revolution but a form of evolution, a transformation in which life expectancy is more than just a number.

Old age doesn't look or act like it used to. Through the wonders of science and the gravity of our media-addled times, we are becoming experts at making old age an interesting time of life—maybe even the *most* interesting time. Retired people don't spend their last days sitting on the front porch anymore, they take up golf or skydiving or archaeology.

On trips to Europe in the 1990s, Phyllis and I noted that most of our fellow tourists weren't college kids as one might have expected but seniors like ourselves. Our old pal June Jenkins and my agent, Esther Newberg, both of whom are—how to say this?—*mature* women, spent their 1996 vacation walking across Tuscany.

Another friend, Warren Burnett, one of the best attorneys in Texas until he retired a few years ago, observed his seventieth birthday in the spring of 1997 by forgoing his usual visit to St. Petersburg, Florida, for baseball spring training and traveled instead with his wife, Kay, to London to fullfill a cherished dream: to sit in the House of Commons and listen to members of the Labour Party berate the Conservatives in the days just prior to England's national election. On the trip he managed to meet with Tony Blair, the new prime minister, at which meeting I'm sure Warren reminded the new head of Labour of the pitfalls encountered by our own Industrial Workers of the World (the Wobblies) shortly before World War I. For many years, Warren has been a card-carrying member of this archaic turn-of-

the-century labor movement, dedicated to the overthrow of capital-
ism. Is ours a great age or what? At what other time in history could
a wealthy lawyer sacrifice spring training in the vain hope that Lenin
might reappear at No. 10 Downing Street?

The social constraints and age-based limitations that hobbled
our parents and grandparents look as quaint today as the horse and
buggy. Our generation, for example, doesn't feel compelled to dress
old as did previous generations. My dad wore a suit and tie nearly
every day of his life. I never saw him in a pair of jeans. He wore only
black wing-tipped shoes of a particular brand, never loafers, much
less sneakers. Phyllis noted a similar fashion manifesto while visiting her widowed mother, Lucy Mae McCallie, in Wetumka, Oklahoma, last year. Phyllis tried to buy Lucy Mae a comfortable, stylish
Empire-waisted dress like the one Phyllis was wearing, but her
mother refused, protesting, "Nobody dresses like that around here."

Our society is far less hierarchical than it was even thirty years
ago. As recently as the 1960s, after a woman's children left home,
she was expected to spend her twilight years playing bridge, baking
cakes for charity events, and caring for the sick and needy. Not anymore. Today, many of my oldest and best women friends have celebrated their maturity by taking on new and demanding careers,
frequently becoming more successful than their husbands and male
friends who started years earlier.

After her children were grown, Ann Richards divorced her husband, David, and became Travis County commissioner, then trea-
surer of the state of Texas, and finally the first female governor of
Texas since the 1930s, when Ma Ferguson was a surrogate for her im-
peached husband, former governor Pa Ferguson. When she was in
the Governor's Mansion, Ann promised herself that when she turned
sixty she would learn to ride a Harley-Davidson motorcycle. And so
she did. Readers of *Texas Monthly* will recall the classic July 1992
cover, with the governor in a sequined white outfit, astride a hog
powerful enough to suck the doors off a Buick.

Sue Sharlot, wife of University of Texas law school dean Mike
Sharlot, got her own law degree after her kids left home, graduating
with honors and jumping instantly to a job with a major law firm
only too happy to pay her six figures. Sally Wittliff, whose husband,

Bill, is a successful screenwriter and producer (he wrote and produced the great television miniseries *Lonesome Dove,* among many other accomplishments), graduated from the UT law school in June 1997, also with honors.

The old truth that we're only as old as we feel has never been so acutely apparent, at least to me. Most of my friends who don't feel bad feel great—and those who feel great also feel young. When I run into a group of people I went to high school with, I can't help thinking, Who are all those old farts? Historically, age has always been associated with dysfunction: the interplay of physical health and chronological age is powerful. If you aren't in good health, it's hard to think young even if you are. And if you are in good health, it's hard to think old even though you might be eligible for Medicare.

Youth is wasted on the young, as Oscar Wilde famously reminded us. Who among us has not daydreamed of having the vigor and vitality that we had when we were twenty, combined with the wisdom and experience that we've accumulated along the way? We could have made out like bandits, eh? Our dreams may yet come true. Medical science is on the brink of discovering what makes us age—why and how the aging process triggers diseases like strokes, heart attacks, and Alzheimer's.

Aging seems to take place at the cellular level. If cells didn't grow old, scientists hypothesize, biological aging might be slowed or even prevented. Until 1990, scientists believed that given proper care, individual cells could live forever, at least in the laboratory. Today we understand that all human cells age and die—and, more important, we now know that *they don't have to.*

An article on aging in *Time* in the fall of 1996 reports that gerontologists are pursuing two different strategies to retard the aging process. The more conservative of the approaches accepts biological aging as nature's way but holds that the diseases and disabilities that signal our decline can be delayed through exercise, diet, and medical breakthroughs. A more radical strategy challenges nature by attempting to halt and even reverse degeneration of the body's cells.

The most exciting trends in the anti-aging process in recent years are the increased use of anti-aging medicines to replace the natural energy-producing hormones and enzymes that are lost in the cellular energy factories of our brains, heart, and muscles with advancing age, and the perfection of surgical techniques to replaced injured or worn-out joints. Warren Burnett has had both hips replaced. Science is also on verge of being able to use small pieces of tissue to duplicate the organs of our bodies. Imagine shelves of human replacement parts!

For some time now, gerontologists and gene theorists have speculated that aging is a process of the genetic programming of cell division. If they are right, we can increase life spans by altering genetics. Over the course of a lifetime, healthy cells complete a specific number of divisions before aging and dying. When this natural process is disrupted (as happens often in older cells), problems like immunological failure set in. Conversely, so-called immortal cells that continue to divide past their allotted time turn cancerous and can proliferate indefinitely. Before scientists can prevent or slow this dysfunction, however, they have to locate the proper genes.

What causes us to age is a genetic clock, or more precisely a series of clocks that tell time in every cell in our bodies. If we can manipulate these clocks—and science is sure that we can—we will not only stop the aging process, we will reverse it. We would live for several centuries, with the bodies of twenty-year-olds and the wisdom of the ages.

In his book *Reversing Human Aging*, Michael Fossel, Ph.D., M.D., explains that what determines the life span of a cell is its chromosomal clock. When the clock runs down, the cell dies. Cancer cells, however, have the ability to reset their clocks and so keep on dividing forever.

"If we reset the clock of a normal cell, it lives anew," Fossel writes. "If we stop the clock of a cancer cell, it dies. When we reset the clocks, our cells need not age and cancer can be cured. In other words, life as we know it will change beyond recognition."

These clocks, Fossel tells us, are the telomeres, which are the ends of a chromosome's arms. As cells divide, telomeres shorten and the production of proteins in the genes changes. Eventually cell function begins to break down and deteriorate. The telomere is the only place in the body where all the mechanisms of aging come together. Although it would be impossible to prevent the thousands of biochemical breakdowns that occur within and between cells, it is possible to reset the telomeric clock or stop it.

In laboary experiments, researchers at the University of Texas Southwest Medical Center in Dallas have reset the telomeric clocks by lengthening the telomeres, which allows the cells to continue to grow indefinitely. In theory, resetting the clocks will prevent age-related diseases such as strokes, heart disease, and Alzheimer's. Diseases such as cancer, on the other hand, can be prevented by shortening the telomeres and stopping the cell clocks.

"Cancer cells are biologically immortal," Fossel says. "They never age, because they continually reset their telomeric clocks. They do so by producing telomerase, the enzyme that relengthens the telomere and allows these cells to divide endlessly."

By blocking the enzyme telomerase, scientists can cause cancer cells to age and die. Researchers have already insolated inhibitors that do the job. Unfortunately lengthening the telomere is more difficult than shortening it. To date, the only experiments in which the telomeres were extended have been in the lab. Fossel estimates that it may be two decades before the procedure of resetting clocks is ready for clinical use. "But the clinical benefits are staggering," he tells us. "The final result may be a treatment to be administered intravenously once a decade or so."

An equally vexing problem is finding a way to prevent the progressive slowdown of the brain. Brain aging is the number one cause of disease, disability, and death in the elderly. Literally the seat of the self, the brain has been described as a three-pound universe. It is wired with billions and billions of neurons, as many neurons as the universe has galaxies and the galaxies have stars. When the metabolism of neuronal cells drops below a level necessary to support such cellular functions as the intake of glucose for energy production and the excretion of cellular debris, the neuron cells of the brain die or lose their connections with one another.

The dying off of these cells has been likened to leaves falling from trees until the entire forest is naked. These falling leaves lead to loss of memory and other cognitive functions—and to a sharp decline in the regulation of essential life systems. At least one-fourth of people over eighty-five suffer from dementia, which includes not only memory loss but the inability to understand words, carry out motor activities, and recognize or identify objects.

Until the 1960s we thought Alzheimer's disease was a radical version of the normal process of aging. Today we recognize it as a disease with a distinct pathology. In other words, the degeneration of the brain is not inevitable or even normal.

Neuroscientists are heralding a new generation of designer drugs, psychiatric medications, nutrients, hormone replacements, and "smart" drugs that are more powerful and quicker-acting (and have fewer side effects) than current anti-depressant and anti-anxiety drugs. Many of them help the brain maintain a healthy metabolic rate. A few are already on the market.

Another new drug, one of a class of chemicals known as ampakines, can improve memory in healthy older people by clearing a path for neurotransmitters in the brain. It may even be able to reverse the devastating effects of Alzheimer's, Parkinson's, and schizophrenia. Neurons signal each other by sending tiny electric currents down long, wirelike extensions called axons. When the current reaches the tip of an axon, it sends a chemical messenger—a neurotransmitter—across the narrow gap to the neighboring neuron. The message docks on the receiving neuron in a niche known as a receptor, which opens a passageway for the signal and then closes it until another message comes along. Ampakines hold the receptor open longer than usual so the signal has time to get through.

Scientists at the University of California at Irvine found that ampakines improved the memories of younger people by 20-25 percent, and that people over sixty-five were able to double their test scores after taking an ampakine drug. The improvements were in "parking-lot memories"—the ability to recall recent events. Nobody knows yet if ampakine drugs can strengthen long-term memory. At any rate, they won't be available to the public for another three to five years.

Researchers are discovering new anti-aging techniques every day. The degree to which we seek out mental and physical challenges and even the way we prepare our food can affect the aging process. Students and others who work with their brains stimulate neurons through the process of problem-solving, thereby making their brains more fit and agile and better able to solve more problems. Along similar lines, those who exercise on a regular basis stimulate blood flow to the brain and nerve growth, both of which create stronger, more densely branched neurons, which are better able to resist disease. Neither of these revelations comes as a jarring surprise. But did you realize that you can accelerate aging merely by eating well-done roast beef?

The "caramelization effect" of cooking foods at high temperatures for long periods of time can make you older sooner, scientists now tell us. This form of cooking bonds protein and sugar together into a sticky substances that gum up the inner workings of our bodies. Soon we may have drugs available to control the carmelization effect, but in the meantime you're better off grilling or broiling your meat.

Finally, science is learning that people who are happily married and believers in God live longer, happier, and better lives than those who don't. Love isn't a cure-all, but it comes close, and it makes the other aspects of aging far more pleasant.

Part Five:

Move It or Lose It

Eighteen

A motivation survey by *Self* in January 1997 throws a revealing light on why some people exercise and others don't. Though the survey was directed specifically at women, I'm certain the results would be much the same for men. People who responded to the magazine's survey said that the three main reasons they didn't work out were that they were too tired, that their work took up too much of their time, and that they lacked discipline.

All of these reasons would have been at the top of my list, too, six years ago. Today I see clearly that two of the three are the products of convenient misconception and the third is an obstacle that can be overcome with some small adjustments.

The reason people feel too tired to exercise is that they *don't* exercise. The truth of this statement becomes evident as soon as you start working out. Almost all those who begin a regular exercise program after a long spell of inactivity are amazed by their new surge of energy and bolstered by an unexpected bolt of self-confidence. What startles them is not necessarily how much better they look—that takes time—but how much better they *feel*. Exercise is one of the two great stimulants for increasing energy and elevating a sense of well-being, right up there with sex—which if done right can be another form of exercise.

As for lack of discipline, the simple act of doing any kind of regular exercise is the beginning of discipline. Complaining that you lack discipline is a cop-out—discipline is not something you're born with, like blue eyes and dimples. You build it a day at a time, until it becomes second nature. At that point it doesn't seem like discipline anymore, not in the old begrudging way you interpreted that word. Discipline is merely another interesting thing you do. People who exercise soon realize that the reason they keep working out is that they enjoy the sensation of being in touch with their bodies and the dramatic release of tension and the accompanying feeling of well-being that follows a workout.

During high-intensity workouts, you will also feel the rush of the

brain chemical beta-endorphin, a natural painkiller similar to morphine that the brain releases in response to the pain of resistance
training. Endorphins explain the "high" that many people experience during a rigorous workout. This is the same endorphin surge
you feel after an orgasm, a different sort of pain masked by pleasure.
The release of beta-endorphins is the body's way of rewarding itself
for good work.

Accommodating your job or professional schedule to regular exercise is more difficult than overcoming the first two excuses for not
exercising—but not much. It depends, of course, on what kind of
work you do and on whether you set your own hours or follow the demands of a boss. Most people over the age of fifty, however, are in a
position to adjust when and how they practice their profession. In the
beginning, I believed that I didn't have time to go to the gym three
days a week. Now I realize that I don't have time not to.

What I did was rearrange priorities. Before joining Big Steve's,
I wrote in the afternoon, because that was the time writing seemed
most natural. Two or three days a week, after work, I walked my dogs
on the hike-and-bike trail. Now I write in the mornings and go to the
gym in the afternoons. I walk my dogs on the afternoons that I don't
work out. I have so much extra energy now that I walk them weekends, too, and in warm weather, I also give them a bath. Except for
the bath part, Mitzi and Nicky love my new routine.

After a few months, this schedule felt natural. After a few more
months, the workouts became an indispensable part of my life, an addiction. I discovered that if I went to the gym regularly my work took
care of itself. In fact, for the first time in my life, I began to look forward to work, to find the actual process of writing (as opposed to what
happens once the writing is published) pleasurable and rewarding.

What divides those who are motivated from those who are not,
the article in *Self* reveals, is a passion for "instant gratification."
Some of us are particularly partial to instant gratification and understand well its rewards and potential, which is the opposite of pro-
crastination.

The magazine reports: "Our survey reveals that the single greatest motivating factor for active women is 'enhanced psychological

well-being.' Exercise makes them feel good. By contrast, the single great stimulus for the inactive is 'weight loss.' Exercise, for them, is something to be endured on the way to a long-term goal. So while the actives are compelled by the here and now [i.e., instant gratification], the inactive women are driven by hopes and dreams."

The magazine goes on to note that the extra weight that inactive people have accumulated won't melt away in a week or two. Those who start an exercise program motivated only by weight loss are always disappointed and usually drop out after a few workouts.

What I found most amazing about the magazine article was the revelation that the barriers to exercise between the active and the inactive are pretty much the same. The difference is how the two *perceive* the barriers. One views them as merely another wall to be scaled on the path to success, while the other sees them as insurmountable.

Let me stress that any kind of regular exercise will make you feel better and help you live longer. Simple acts such as taking the stairs instead of the elevator, parking as far as you can from the entrance to a shopping mall, or walking for ten minutes after lunch can lower health risks. Thirty minutes of any physical activity can make a big difference in your overall well-being. People who exercise are about half as likely to die prematurely as layabouts, *regardless* of other risks. By the same measure, otherwise healthy people who do little exercise are as likely to die as smokers and more likely to die than people who have high cholesterol or high blood pressure.

Of all the aerobic exercises, the safest, the easiest, and the least likely to cause burnout is the simple act of walking. Regular walks help lift depression, lessen tension and confusion, and increase optimism, hope, self-esteem, and energy. Like all moderate exercise, walking produces a holistic pattern of change, a general body arousal. Metabolism increases, and so does heart rate and breathing. Muscle tension drops. There are even changes in hormones and in brain neurotransmitters, which greatly influence thinking and mood. "If you're not exercising at all and you develop a habit of walking about thirty minutes a day most days of the week," says Steve Blair of the world-famous Cooper Institute for Aerobics Research in

Dallas, "you'll cut your risk of heart attack by about fifty-five percent. That's an *enormous* reduction." The Cooper Institute has discovered that walking is almost as good as running. Blair explains: "If you get into really vigorous exercise like running instead of walking you will on average cut your risk only another five to ten percent."

Long before I joined the gym, I walked regularly, which probably accounts for the fact that my heart attack in 1988 wasn't fatal. There was a time when I enjoyed walking almost to the exclusion of everything else. When I was living alone in a cabin at the edge of the Gila Wilderness in Arizona in 1971, working on my second novel, *Thin Ice,* I walked up to ten miles a day, partly as an excuse not to write. (This is a type of obsessive-compulsive behavior that I have to watch out for and modify from time to time.) Later, when Phyllis and I lived in Taos, we took our dogs to Kit Carson National Forest and hiked the logging roads to the top of mountains, walking five or six miles at a stretch. That was too much. We felt so good that we usually followed the walks with long naps. What finally got me to the gym was the realization that walking wasn't enough, that I needed some kind of resistance training to transform fat to muscle and to improve upper-body strength.

Which type of exercise is best, aerobic or weight training? The question is hotly debated but is beside the point, particularly for men and women past the age of forty. People who are beginning to feel their age need to do both. Aerobics exercises, which include running, walking, swimming, skiing, and any other activity that requires moving your arms and legs, are essential for a healthy heart and for weight loss or maintenance. Weight or resistance training builds muscle mass and boosts your metabolic rate. As I explained earlier, the only way to lose weight and keep it off is to build muscle mass.

I saw a bumper sticker the other day that said it all: "Old Age Is a Bitch!" Think about this: As you age, you began to literally *shrink.* True! The reason old people look shriveled-up is that they are. After age forty our bones thin, our vertebrae weaken, and our spinal columns start to curve. We actually lose height and become physically smaller. According to a report from the Pennsylvania State

University's School of Sports Medicine, men and women who are inactive also begin to lose muscle by age forty. By age sixty the loss is
significant, and by age seventy it is pronounced, particularly in the
large muscles used for strength and power. For example, the report
says that the quadriceps (thigh) muscles of women in their seventies
are 77 percent smaller than those of women in their twenties. As
muscle fibers decline in number and size—a condition known as atrophy—we lose the capacity to perform many of the tasks that made
life pleasurable. Climbing a flight of stairs or lifting a grandchild becomes burdensome and finally unthinkable. After a while, it's a chore
just getting out of bed. One senses that soon the entire body will atrophy, and it will unless we get moving. "Move it or lose it" is a
motto you should copy and pin to your bedroom wall.

Weight training is the best (and just about the only) method for
maintaining or increasing the size and strength of all our muscles.
Pumping iron increases muscle strength, muscle size, bone density,
and metabolism. It works for women as well as men, and it works for
all ages: nobody is too old to begin pumping iron. "Muscle mass and
body fat are really dictated by how active you are, not what your age
is," says Dr. William Evans, director of the Noll Physiological Research Center at Penn State. A fair number of the members at Big
Steve's Gym are in the sixty-to-eighty age range, and some of them
didn't start pumping iron until they were already in their fifties. Lynn
Helton, Big Steve's charming, live-wire wife, told me about a woman
who had never worked out in her life but at age seventy-three began
power-lifting. By seventy-five she was the power-lifting champion of
her age group and body weight. Studies consistently show that even
people over age ninety can make strength gains in about two months.

In her book *Alternative Medicine: What Works,* Dr. Adriane Fugh-
Berman reports the spectacular gains made by a group of senior citizens at a nursing home who were put on a high-intensity
weight-lifting program for eight weeks. These old-timers, in the
eighty-to-ninety-six age group, increased their strength 174 percent,
sped up their gait 48 percent, and increased their lower-extremity
strength up to 374 percent.

Everyone's metabolism slows down with age, which is the reason most people gain a pound or two each year. The slowdown in metabolism is probably a function of evolution, a built-in safeguard that allows older, more vulnerable people to store fat during times of famine. When men in their twenties overeat, their bodies automatically speed up metabolism to burn off extra calories. Men in their fifties and sixties, on the other hand, must consume fewer calories each year merely to maintain the same weight. Why? Nobody is really sure. Something in our sympathetic nervous system changes with age, something that short-circuits the signal for our caloric furnaces to stoke up.

The differences in muscle mass between older and younger guys is largely responsible for older guys' getting fat. As total muscle mass reduces with age, so does the body's ability to burn fat. Our bodies have a dramatic need for calorie energy—approximately one-third of our energy expediture is due to muscular activity—so it becomes apparent that muscle plays a major role in metabolism.

Similar fat buildups have been observed in women. Over the age of forty, women usually lose about a half pound of muscle mass a year, while gaining about one and a half pounds of body fat. With each passing year, women find it more difficult to lose weight merely by eating fewer calories. Between ages forty and fifty, a woman would have to cut her weekly calorie intake by more than a thousand calories—or increase her weekly walks an extra ten miles—*just to maintain* her target weight.

The best option for both sexes is to add sixty minutes a week to weight or resistance training. It's the only way to prevent muscle loss and maintain metabolic rate. I think sixty minutes a week is not enough, but the experts claim two half-hour workouts can cover the essential muscle groups. People who exercise twice a week—doing twenty-five minutes of aerobic activity on a treadmill or stationary bike and twenty-five minutes of strength training using a Nautilus machine—get nearly 90 percent as much benefit as those who follow that same exercise program three times a week. In other words, two hours of exercise a week is nearly as beneficial as three. In one study, those who worked out on Tuesday and Thursday averaged a loss of 4 pounds of fat, compared with the 4.6 pounds of fat lost by the Monday-Wednesday-Friday exercisers.

I work out on Monday-Wednesday-Friday because that's how I learned, but two workouts a week make sense for beginners. At most gyms and health clubs, Tuesdays and Thursdays are the least crowded days of the week. Anyone working out for the first time is likely to be self-conscious about his or her appearance and feel intimidated sharing equipment with veteran exercisers. When beginners see the gains they can make in just two days a week, however, it is likely to pump up their confidence and inspire them to add an extra day to their routines.

There is at least one additional benefit to weight lifting, especially for those who need to lose weight. Resistance training, it has been demonstrated, is the most painless way to curb your cravings for fat. Researchers at Brigham Young University, testing two groups of women to determine if strength training affected eating habits, discovered that the group that lifted weights cut back their fat intake to 30 percent of total calories—*without being told to cut back!* By the end of the twelve-week study, this group's daily consumption of fat actually fell below 30 percent. Women who lifted weights changed the composition of their diets without actually "dieting" in the traditional sense. By contrast, the second group, which did only stretching exercises, showed no change in diet.

What is there about weight resistance exercise that lessens cravings for fat? Again, nobody is really sure. Some have speculated that it has to do with the noticeable and measureable results of the weight training. Though beginners don't detect the slow buildup of muscle mass, they do notice that in a few weeks they are lifting much heavier weights than they did at the start. Such obvious gains in fitness apparently spark other aspects of life, like diet. The compulsion to eat fatty foods doesn't disappear completely when you began to work out, but it becomes much easier to manage.

A few words of caution before you begin your exercise program. Forget those spot-reducing gadgets you see advertised—waist trimmers, fat melters, thigh melters, butt busters. Melting off fat in one particular spot is impossible. You need a complete and well-balanced body workout, which is the reason I think it's important to join a gym, health club, or YMCA. Call the Y or your local fitness center for a schedule of beginning exercise classes and find out what times the club is less crowded. Consult with your physician before beginning any exercise program. And use common sense.

"My advice to anyone over the age of fifty," Big Steve told me, "is find someone knowledgeable [i.e., someone like himself] to start you on a light weight-training program, three times a week, thirty to forty-five minutes each workout. Once they start feeling their strength and get their confidence built up, they can increase the time and amount of weight. But they need to start light and with the right form." Steve recalled a man that he met in Beaumont some years back, a fifty-year-old bookkeeper who had never lifted weights. On Steve's instruction, this man began by bench-pressing a hundred pounds. After one year he could lift three hundred pounds. That's pretty extreme, but it illustrates what people can do with some determination.

There is something about a gym that is conducive to exercising, an atmosphere of dedication that you can't find at home. Even if you can afford to buy all the machines, weights, and aerobic devices that gyms provide, the environment of being around other people interested in body-building and good health is highly energizing. It's also instructional. Everyone is there for the same reason, to better himself or herself. The mental as well as the physical is part of everyone's program. The conversation is usually about things you never knew you needed to know. I learned a lot of new exercise techniques at the gym and why supplements like coenzyme Q10 and ginkgo biloba were important for me. I learned, too, that the problems that sometimes got me down weren't much different from the problems experienced by everyone else. After a while, spending three hours at the gym became a sort of spiritual experience.

Do not be intimidated just because you're the new member. Everyone was new once. Remember, the only person you are competing with is yourself. People who work out regularly are almost always sympathetic to newcomers and willing to help them. Just being around people in good shape made me want to improve. Don't worry about becoming muscle-bound. No matter how hard you train you're in no danger of looking like Arnold Schwarzenegger. The muscle mass that you accumulate will barely show. But you will know it's there, I promise.

A final warning: Don't start with a lifetime or even a multiyear membership. It zaps motivation. It's too easy to tell yourself you'll get serious about exercising tomorrow. The best way to live to see tomorrow is to forget about it. Just have fun. Take care of the minutes and the days will take care of themselves.

Nineteen

I can admit now that when I climbed the stairs for the first time in the winter of 1992 and prepared to enter Big Steve's Gym, my knees were knocking and my palms were greasy with sweat. My anxiety level soared like a hot-air balloon. What was I about to do?

The first thing that caught my eye as I opened the door was this beefy man with graying hair, glasses, and an expression that said what he really enjoyed most in life was being pissed off. If I'd had to take one guess, my guess would have been that he'd spent most of his life traveling with the carnival. The muscles in his arms and chest were the size of cantaloupes. His black T-shirt appeared to be spray-painted across the contours of his upper body, and the veins of his neck throbbed. I heard him barking insults to a scrawny young man who appeared to be new to the program:

"You chicken-breasted, bird-legged little shit, shut up and work!" the instructor yelled. "You pitiful dumb-ass! My big toe could lift more than your whole body, you puny toad! One more set or get the hell out of my gym."

The instructor, I learned presently, was Big Steve Helton—the man into whose hands I was about to deliver myself.

First appearances, as is often the case, were deceiving. The tongue-lashing was part of a running joke between Big Steve and one of his members. Insults, barbs, and caustic comments pass as humor at this gym, and the young man who I had thought was being harshly abused could dish it out as well as he could take it. The bickering is a little unsettling at first, but after a while it becomes part of the fabric. Good humor is the essence of the insults and barbs, you come to realize, an acknowledgment that since everyone here deserves respect, the only self-respecting way to give it is with a sugaring of derision.

Once my eyes became accustomed to the dank light that first afternoon—once I had surveyed the premises from end to end, upstairs and down—my next reaction was to wonder why all these people weren't in prison. There was an abundance of bad haircuts, long, short, and indifferent, and an inordinate number of tattoos on a wide assortment of body parts. These people looked as though they'd just eaten a lunch of ground glass. Today, I understand how my first reaction could have been so far off target. I was looking at the gym through the warped lenses of one who had been too long on the outside, in the world of soft flesh and weak wills.

Serious bodybuilders, I know now, develop hard appearances, a mental as well as a physical toughness. What initially appears as cockiness or arrogance is gradually transformed in the eyes of the beholder into a disarming nonchalance, a disdain for the rigors of convention inspired by mounting self-confidence. Builders shrug their shoulders at adversity. Nothing seems to perturb them. They exude cool, dressing down, not up, and studiously avoiding the slightest appearance of the uniform or orthodox. Outside the gym, they look the same as anyone else, but in the holy sanctuary they become as single-minded as monks. I heard about a gym in El Paso that was suddenly left leaderless when the cops hauled away the owner. For the nine weeks that he was in jail, the place remained exactly the way he'd left it. The door was never locked, the lights never turned off—at least until the electric company extinguished them because no one had paid the bill. All that time, the members continued to work out, the same as before. When a piece of equipment broke down, they moved to the next one. When the lights were turned off, they brought kerosene lanterns. Dust accumulated in thick layers, but still they came, doing their daily routines and recording progress. In all that time, nothing was ever stolen or vandalized.

At Big Steve's Gym, Steve sets the tone. He's an American original, a throwback to a frontier where folks either learned from the school of hard knocks or didn't learn at all. He grew up in Washington State, a sickly, skinny runt with bad tonsils. Neighborhood bullies regularly beat the stuffing out of him. At the age of sixteen, his tonsils having been removed, Steve and a friend studied some muscle-man magazines and began to work out with homemade weights in the friend's garage. In one year Steve went from 137 pounds to 197 and joined a real gym in Tacoma.

In the thirty-something years that followed, he became a double handful—a drunk, a pillhead, and a barroom rowdy known from Seattle to Muscle Beach to Beaumont. He wrecked more bars than this book has pages to record, sometimes after playing his guitar and singing country-and-western songs to a captive audience in his unforgettable off-key baritone. He was a man of constant appetites, drinking and carousing all night, and working all day on loading docks in Beaumont and Houston. In his spare time he became a serious power-lifter. At one time or another he held fifteen Texas state records in the bench press and six national records. In 1979, with the help of a twelve-step program, he stopped drinking and popping pills. By 1997 he had been sober for eighteen years.

The same year that he sobered up, Steve met a comely bank clerk named Lynn, and after serenading her with a version of Lefty Frizell's "I Love You," persuaded her to marry him. In 1982 they moved to Austin and opened Big Steve's Gym in a two-story building in a shopping center at the top of a steep hill across the Colorado River from downtown Austin. The gym is a sort of blue-collar country club. Nothing fancy about this joint. No swimming pool, no sauna, no steam room or whirlpool, just the ignorant tools of iron necessary for a solid workout: Nautilus and other machines, various barbells and dumbbells, aerobics machines, plenty of mirrors in which to admire oneself, and the required number of *No Pain, No Gain* signs for attitude adjustment.

Steve is self-made to a fault, blunt, impatient, and impulsive, a man whose attitude is constantly in need of adjusting but whose bark is several degrees of magnitude worse than his bite. If Charles Dickens had lived in the Big Thicket of south Texas instead of London, you'd have to say that Steve is a character of Dickensian proportion. Most people in South Austin have known Steve for years, and he's been a favorite of the media since Governor Ann Richards, a member of the gym, appointed him to her Physical Fitness Council in 1992.

Until Big Steve was seated, the governor's Physical Fitness Council consisted mainly of political favorites with college degrees but little knowledge of what it took to get in shape or stay that way. A grade-school dropout, Steve was at first afraid to open his mouth in such august company. Then somebody said something about being "too old" to worry about physical fitness, at which point Steve erupted.

"I've worked out every day for the last forty-five years," he roared, his face turning red and his voice cracking. "And I'm here to by God tell you that a body don't get too old to exercise!" He looked around the room, a little stunned at his own temerity. But the wide eyes and slack jaws around the council table emboldened him to continue. "I'll tell you people something else. On December 20th of this year I'll be sixty years old, and on that day I'm by God gonna do something no man my age's ever done before! I'm gonna bench-press four hundred pounds!"

The words just kind of slipped out. Later, in the cold light of reason, he thought to himself: I said *what?* Steve hadn't lifted competitively for more than a decade. But it was too late for apologies or second thoughts.

On December 20, all the TV stations in Austin showed up at Big Steve's Gym, as did Ann Richards, members of her Physical Fitness Council, and a collection of other luminaries. Nothing gets Steve pumping like a crowd. At the appointed time, he took a big slug of Turbo Tea, positioned himself under the weights, and did exactly what he had promised. Later, he treated the crowd to several country-and-western songs and pledged that on his sixty-first birthday he would break his own record by lifting 410 pounds. Which, of course, he did. The date of December 20 has become, at least in South Austin, a testament for aging. Each year Big Steve promises to lift ten pounds more on his birthday than he did the previous year, and for four years running he has been as good as his promise.

The five hundred members of Big Steve's Gym and Aerobics Center (membership fee $300 a year) are a mixed bag, more or less typical of what locals like to call "Old Austin"—meaning to the current generation the slacker attitude that was popular in the seventies and to my generation the laid-back, drugged-out Austin of the late fifties. Not surprisingly, a number of members are recovering alcoholics or drug addicts. Tough programs such as weight resistance training are excellent substitutes for people who have any kind of addiction. Drugs, alcohol, and other abused substances cause the brain to create endorphins, the brain's natural upper. So does lifting weights and other rigorous exercise. Most have faced serious illness at one time or another, and many have lost someone they loved to premature and sometimes violent death. Hard training has kept their bodies comparatively young, but you can read the aging in their eyes, the bitter chapters of a life rescued at the brink and the deep hurt of losses that can never been replaced or recovered.

A few of them have lifted competitively, but the vast majority joined because they wanted to feel or look better. Some joined because they were afraid of the world. Roughly 40 percent are women, and some of them have been victims of abusive husbands or rape. In age the members range from a group of sixteen-year-olds who are enrolled in Steve's "Teens in Trouble" summer program to a seventy-nine-year-old couple who retired a few years ago from the grocery business. They come from all walks of life and all professions—musicians, writers, artists, lawyers, doctors, nurses, politicians, businesspeople, policemen and firemen, a number of retired people. Phyllis and I joined because two of our oldest friends, Bud Shrake and Jodi Gent, were members. I was fifty-seven and Phyllis was fifty-one when we joined, and neither of us had worked out in twenty years. Joining was a landmark occasion in both our lives: we date our current overflow of happiness by it.

People are drawn to the gym for some of the same reasons they are drawn to church, because they feel a need for something beyond their present life, something redeeming and uplifting. The magic of a gym isn't so much that it permits self-improvement but that it enables people to find themselves within themselves. Self-discovery is a type of salvation, a reward larger than the sum of its parts. Whatever they came looking for—weight loss, strength, inner peace, confidence, relaxation, big biceps, a hard belly—they found something more than they imagined in their weekly routine of sweat and work.

The hardest part is making the commitment.

Betty Maxwell was seventy and had never worked out with weights before. She visited six other gyms before deciding that Big Steve's was her place. What caught Betty's eye when she first walked through the door was the ambience—or rather the lack of it: "I didn't see any glamour girls sitting around polishing their nails." Tiny as a splinter—about four feet eleven, a hundred pounds—Betty grew up working on a ranch and for years had trained equestrian horses and taught riding. Her husband, Jack Maxwell, was a retired naval pilot but not a horseman. When congestive heart failure forced his retirement, Betty had to do the work of two.

"I knew I had to muscle up," she tells me. "I couldn't risk breaking down and spending the rest of my life in a nursing home. The other gyms wouldn't take me seriously. They'd pat me on the head and tell me to try aerobics or swimming. I didn't want to do aerobics. I wanted to lift weights. Big Steve was the first one who looked me straight in the eye and put me to work." In six months Betty more than doubled her strength and endurance level.

Nancy Davis tells me a similar story. "Walking up those steps into this place was the most serious thing I'd ever done. My heart was thumping like crazy," Nancy says. She was forty-eight when she joined four years ago, an exceptionally attractive woman married to a highly successful but somewhat domineering car dealer. She had been exercising at home, using Jane Fonda tapes, but wanted to work with weights even though her husband had told her that weights were "a man's thing." Without telling him, she took out a three-month membership, sure that she wouldn't stick it out. After three months she still hadn't told her husband where she was sneaking off to every afternoon.

"The hardest part of the whole experience was telling him," she admits. "He didn't like it *one bit,* and he told me so. It must have been one of my PMS days or something, because to my surprise I stood up to him. I said, 'Larry, I'm sorry you feel that way. But I enjoy what I'm doing, I'm not hurting anyone, and I'm not going to *stop!*'"

Watching Nancy Davis's self-awareness blossom along with her physical fitness was one of joys of belonging to this gym. I do not make friends easily, but it was surprising how quickly I got attached to Nancy, Betty, Jim Peters, Bob Guest, Peggy Box, Jean Mitchell, Darlene Utos, and a number of other regulars at Big Steve's. We don't see each other socially, but for six or eight hours each week we share an *esprit de corps,* comforting and consoling each other and watching each other's backs through the unique pleasure/punishment of our workouts. We share one another's triumphs—and sometimes defeats—as we gain, grow, improve, fall back, struggle, and constantly acquire a new sense of who we are and what we can be.

The dynamics of this blue-collar country club are such that it *sustains,* day after day, month after month, a continuum unlike any that I can remember. The one constant in my life, aside from my love for Phyllis and family, is that three days each week, for as long as I'm able, I'll be at Big Steve's Gym. As Bob Guest put it, "My goal is to be on my feet till the day I die."

Twenty

Once you decide to muscle up, the next thing you need is a good trainer to design your program. No single program works for everyone, nor is there just one right way to exercise with weights—though there are a number of *wrong* ways. With time, you'll learn what routine works best for you. But first you need professional help.

Like all good professionals, Big Steve and his staff start newcomers on about twelve basic exercises, using both machines and free weights. The first day, after a ten-minute warm-up, you'll be asked to do ten or twelve repetitions of each exercise, using weights that are lighter than you were prepared to handle. The first workout is a breeze and lasts about a half hour. After a week or so, you may be asked to do more than one set of each exercise, and the workout time will get correspondingly longer. For the first six to eight weeks, you'll probably follow this routine three days a week, with a day's rest between sessions.

Once you learn the routine, the instructor will no longer follow you around but will keep an eye on you and correct your form when necessary or suggest new methods and techniques. As I mentioned, some researchers believe that exercising just two days a week can achieve nearly the same results as exercising three days a week. Use your own judgment.

The emphasis for beginners is to take it slow and easy. It's important to learn technique first, to find your groove and get the feel of weight lifting. Each lift should be a slow, even motion, with full attention directed to your "target" muscle or muscle group. Don't try to heave or jerk the weight or use body English. This can damage muscle and tissue, and it doesn't do much good as far as building muscle. The object is to isolate and work the target muscle, not see how much weight you can lift. The game is bodybuilding, not weight lifting.

From your first day at the gym, concentrate on controlling your motion through all phases of the lift. Maintaining control is extremely important. Focus on the muscle you are exercising. In your mind, picture it getting bigger and flooding with the anabolic hormones that make muscles grow. A huge part of pumping iron is mental.

You will learn terms like "sets" and "repetitions." Normally, twelve repetitions of the same exercise is one set. You'll do two or three sets before moving on to the next exercise. Your proper weight in a given exercise is one that tires the target muscle in eight to twelve repetitions. The object is to tire the muscle, or as body-builders say, "achieve muscular failure." The eight-to-twelve-repetition pattern isn't arbitrary but has been time-tested and is based on science. Researchers have found that most of us can handle about 70 percent of our one-repetition maximum from eight to twelve times before exhausting the muscle. When you can do twelve reps easily, it's time to increase your weight load about 10 percent.

Bodybuilding operates on the principle of "overload." When you demand that a muscle do more than it's accustomed to doing—i.e., 70 percent of maximum strength—the muscle compensates by adding protein to its cellular structure. The additional protein causes the muscle to thicken and get stronger. By progressively making more demands on the muscles during your training routine, you force them to continue developing.

Rest between sets for as long as it takes you to feel recovered, usually forty-five to ninety seconds. It will take longer when you're exercising large muscle groups such as legs, back, and chest, which require more energy and intensity. Smaller muscles like triceps ideally should come late in your routine, when you're beginning to run out of gas. Some days you'll be able to lift more weight than other days. Some days the workout will actually energize you—you'll feel stronger at the end than at the beginning—and other days you'll strain to get all the way through your routine. Listen to your body. Push it but don't punish it.

Remember, too, to eat right and take vitamins and minerals. Bodybuilders on really intense programs don't eat within two hours of a workout, but personally I like to eat a light lunch—pasta and fruit, for example—about an hour before going to the gym. It keeps me energized. Most gyms sell high-energy drinks such as Turbo Tea (I prefer the sugar-free, calorie-free kind), many of them spiked with caffeine. Recent research has shown that caffeine increases work capacity, both by altering your perception of your degree of effort and by actually increasing your strength during workout. In other words, a jolt of caffeine allows you to train harder and hence achieve bigger gains. A dose of eight milligrams of caffeine per kilo (2.2 pounds) of body weight is considered safe and effective.

And always remember this: *Exercise should be fun.* If it's not, you're not doing it right.

THE WARM-UP.

For the first ten to fifteen minutes you need to warm up on a stationary bike or with some type of light aerobic exercise. This gradually increases your heart rate, blood flow, and body temperature and improves the oxygen exchange in the muscles. Next do some bending and stretching exercises to limber up muscles and connective tissues and make joints more pliable and less prone to injury. Think of the warm-up as part of your routine, a time to ease mentally into your weight resistance training.

SPARING THE BACK.

Almost everyone who works out experiences back problems. Ask your instructor for warm-up exercises to strengthen your lower back. Many people also experience pain in the sciatic nerve, which runs from the hip through the muscles of the thigh. To stretch the sciatic nerve lie on your back, lock your hands around your knees, and pull them up toward your chest, feeling the pull in your thighs, buttocks, and lower back. Hold for a fifteen-to-twenty count. Or you can stretch one leg at a time.

THE ABDOMINAL CRUNCH.

I do stomach crunches as part of my warm-ups, but you can do them during any part of your routine. Crunches are far superior to old-fashioned sit-ups, not only to harden the abdominal muscles but to prevent back injury. Most people learn to do abdominal exercises the wrong way. Like sit-ups, sloppily exercised abdominal crunches are mostly wasted motion, because they exercise two muscle groups that you're not interested in at the moment—the hip flexors and part of the quadriceps (thighs). Instead, you need to concentrate on just one target group, the abdominal muscles. Try to picture them in your mind.

Here's an exercise that will let you focus on your abs:

Stand in place with the thumb of your left hand on your rib cage. With your fingers wide, place the middle finger of the same hand on the front of your hipbone. Slowly kick your left foot forward so that it's eight or ten inches off the floor. You've just executed a *hip flex*. The distance between your thumb and middle finger—which is to say between the ribs and the pelvis—shouldn't change.

Now do a true *abdominal flex* by shifting the weight to your right foot until the left foot is lightly touching the floor. Keeping your left leg loose, contract your abdominal muscles by pulling the rib cage and pelvis toward each other. Your leg may move a little. You've just done a mini-crunch from a standing position, with nothing above your chest moving. If you did it right, the distance between the thumb and the middle finger should decrease about a half inch. This exercise teaches you what a real abdominal contraction feels like. If electrodes were attached to your stomach, you'd see bursts of activity in your abdominal muscles.

There are several variations on the abdominal crunch, all of them effective once you've isolated your abs. Many gyms have abdominal brackets that help beginners get the full motion of the exercise. If your gym doesn't have an ab bracket, you can buy one at any sporting goods store for about sixty dollars.

OTHER BELLY TIGHTENERS.

Most gyms have leg-lift devices to supplement the crunches or exercise other areas of the abdominal muscles that the crunches miss. One standard Nautilus model is a chair with a bar to lock your feet, a hand grip behind your head, and weights that can be adjusted. The object is to bend forward, holding on to the hand grip, while using your abdominal muscles to pull the weights behind your neck, and touch your elbows to your knees. If you can't stretch that far, don't worry. It gets easier with time. One warning: if you have any kind of back injury, avoid this one.

Another model is a metal frame with pads about waist high on which you plant your lower arms and elbows, and a platform to support your feet. It also has a back support, so you have something to push against. Supporting the weight of your body with your arms and elbows, step off the platform and at the same time bring your knees up to your chest slowly. Then slowly lower your legs, allowing them to dangle beneath you. Repeat five to ten times. This is a safer one for people with back problems.

The variation that I prefer, which also spares the back, is an overhead bar with two leather arm straps to support your body weight and a platform to stand on which you adjust the straps. Standing on the platform, secure your upper arms through the straps and hold on with your hands. Step from the platform and allow your legs to dangle beneath you. Slowly bring your knees to your chest, hold them there for a beat, then slowly lower your legs to the starting position. Going slow helps you maintain control so that your legs do not swing. Think of the raising and lowering of your legs as a series of small movements.

In all of these variations you will feel the burn in the front wall of your stomach. They don't work the sides of your abs, however. To work the sides—or love handles—do side bends with a light weight. Stretch only as far as is comfortable.

You'll never again have the hard belly of a twenty-year-old, but you can get damn close if you do crunches and side bends three times a week.

THE ROUTINE.

In the beginning you should do about a dozen exercises, which is enough to cover your entire muscular structure. The leg press and leg extension work the quadriceps (thighs) and gluteus (buttocks). The leg curl works the hamstrings, and the standing calf raise exercises the calves. The bench press and pec deck work the chest. The overhead press and upright row exercise the shoulders. A back extension stretches your lower back, and front pull-downs exercise the deltoid muscle below your shoulder joint. Biceps are worked with either a standing or sitting curl, and triceps with a standing press-down.

The bench press, overhead press, and barbell curl can all be done with either free weights or machine. A variation of the triceps press-down is an exercise in which you hoist a dumbbell over and behind your head and neck. Slowly raise, lower, and raise it. Most people prefer to do this exercise seated, with a chair back for support. Consult with your trainer on the proper technique for all these exercises.

Lifting weights can do serious damage to your body, and everyone who works with weights needs to use caution and common sense. People with lower back problems, for example, should avoid any bent-over movement without some type of support for the upper body. If you have a history of shoulder problems, don't try any behind-the-neck barbell presses or any of the machines that require you to reach back behind your neck and shoulders. Over the last six years I've seen dozens of people who have been injured doing the bench press.

Injuries to the rotator cuff—the muscles, tendons, and ligaments that operate your shoulder joints—are common for people who do over-the-head exercises, particularly for people over fifty. "Your muscles might develop to support all that weight, but your tendons can't keep pace," an orthopedic surgeon told me. "The older you get, the more susceptible you are to injuries to the rotator cuff." I tore a rotator cuff tendon in my right shoulder in the spring of 1997 on the inclined bench press, using a pair of thirty-five-pound dumbbells. I had been aware for some time that my right arm was weaker than my left arm, and when I tried to do an extra repetition with weights that were heavier than the dumbbells I was accustomed to using, I felt a slash of pain in my right shoulder at the top of the movement. I assumed at the time that the pain would go away in a few days, but it just got worse. Eventually I had to have surgery to repair it. In the meantime, my right arm was almost useless and the pain was always present.

The first sign of a rotator cuff injury is usually tendinitis—inflammation of a tendon. I'd felt the tendinitis in my right elbow but had dismissed it as nothing of consequence. That was a bad mistake. Do not attempt to ignore or "work through" any kind of persistent pain. At the first sign of shoulder pain, rest. If it persists, seek medical advice.

Once you have mastered the dozen basic exercises and managed to do three sets of each, you may want to find variations or go to more complex types of training. Exercises with compound movements work two or more joints and a number of assisting muscle groups at the same time. The squat, for example, works hips, legs, knees, and ankles. Some trainers advise elevating the heel on a one-inch board for maximum leverage, but Peggy Box, a world-class lifter who works out at Big Steve's, tells her students to squat flat-footed. The squat is especially good for women with too much flesh on the butt, legs, and hips. A machine version of the squat called a Butt Buster is available at some gyms.

Some bodybuilders do what they call "circuit training," moving quickly from station to station with little rest in between. While this is good for overall health, it doesn't maximize muscle growth. Veteran lifters train one muscle at a time, usually with two or sometimes three exercises that target the muscle from different angles. For example, a bench press from a flat bench or a Nautilus machine builds chest muscles, but a bench press from an inclined bench is better for the upper pectorals.

The language of body parts—quads, lats, traps, delts, abs—is a shorthand that you hear constantly at the gym. It will seem normal before long. You'll hear one builder explain to another, "I'm pyramiding my quads and lats today." Pyramiding is a technique whereby weight is added on successive sets. It's an effective way to gain muscle mass.

Once they have established their weight base, some bodybuilders will "cycle," alternating large numbers of repetitions to build muscle endurance, medium numbers of reps to build muscle mass, and low numbers of reps to improve strength and power.

In the beginning, anyway, do not worry about any complicated techniques. Your aim right now is a well-balanced program in which all muscle groups get equal attention. Some exercises will be easier for you than others, so be careful that you don't overemphasize the easy ones. This is a natural response. Researchers know that muscles get "lazy." Without your realizing that it's happening, muscles can precondition themselves to certain amounts of stress. (Veteran lifters change their routine from time to time to "confuse" their muscles and keep them alert.) In the beginning, Phyllis devoted an inordinate amount of her time and energy to the leg press—she's "very strong in the legs," remember?—instead of exercising her upper body muscles, which needed the most work.

Commit yourself to at least three months of weight resistance training before you make a judgment on whether it's working or not. Even three months isn't enough to notice significant changes in strength and size. This program is designed for the long haul—just like your body.

You'll discover your own pace, finding bonuses and the flaws in day-to-day practices. Nothing should be set in stone. Everything should be questioned and nothing ignored. One warning—beware of burnout. You can get too much of a good thing. After a couple of years at Big Steve's I noticed that my workouts had gradually increased in duration, from an hour to ninety minutes to two hours and finally to more than three hours! As a previous victim of obsessive-compulsive behavior, I should have seen it coming. What had started out as a way to improve my quality of life had become life's very focus. I had it backward. Once I'd come to grips with that, I cut back to about two and a half hours, which may still be too much.

The secret of success is finding a level of exertion that makes you feel good, both during and after your workout. How hard is hard enough? On the wall behind the treadmills and exercise bikes at Big Steve's Gym is a copy of the Borg Scale for Rating of Perceived Exertion. Curiously, measuring "perceived exertion" works the same for people of all ages and all physical conditions.

The scale is a series of numbers from six to twenty. A seven, for example, is a "very, very light" rate of exertion. Nine is "very light." The general idea is to feel like you're working between eleven ("fairly light") and thirteen ("somewhat hard"). Once you get into the region of fifteen ("hard") to nineteen ("very, very hard"), your chances of injury are high, and so are the odds that you will drop out.

Obviously, compared to low-intensity exercise, vigorous, intense exercise increases the strength of your heart muscle and allows it to pump out more blood. But researchers have learned that the dropout rate in the intense group is more than 40 percent higher than in groups doing less stressful exercise. One of the psychological traps of treadmills and resistance machines is allowing yourself to think you should keep progressing, getting faster, going longer.

The most important thing about any workout is to *feel good* while you're doing it. A constant struggle to do better guarantees you'll end up hating the very idea of exercise. So just cool it and zone out.

Twenty-One

A gym isn't just about physical fitness, I have discovered. It is a touchstone for my therapeutic and spiritual requirements—again, not unlike a church—a place that I go when I feel too depressed or weak or unloved or fearful to go anywhere else. It becomes my last and most faithful refuge, a shelter against the worst in the world and in myself. Spiritual and mental progress isn't as easy to measure as muscle mass or body fat percentage, but in many ways it is more important.

I've seen the magic at work time and again—people rising to new levels, conquering what once seemed the unconquerable, overcoming debilitating fears, doubts, and weaknesses by the simple process of concentrating on the positive. I use my two and a half hours at Big Steve's not merely to work my muscles but to work the part of my mind that is hardest to reach under ordinary circumstances. Frequently I meditate or pray as I exercise. After the first fifteen or twenty minutes of sweating, I start to "zone out," forgetting my ego, freeing myself from the snare of selfish trappings, disappearing into the pleasant, pain-free, abstract tide of the subconscious. Sometimes I solve problems without really trying or fully understanding the process. Other times I concentrate on specific flaws of character that I have discovered in myself—being too judgmental or insensitive or selfish, for example—and attempt to arrive at ways to moderate them. It's hard to explain to someone who hasn't been there, but there is in the dynamics of hard physical work something approaching a state of grace.

Bob Guest, a retired sixty-five-year-old accountant, had been a runner most of his life and didn't get into weight training until he was fifty-one. "I used to be a mean, arrogant, hostile little bastard," he told me. "Coming to this gym kept me out of a lot of trouble." About three years ago, Bob learned that his wife was dying of lung cancer. As her pain got worse, he remained almost constantly at her side—except for the three afternoons each week when he came to Big Steve's Gym. He never complained or asked for special consideration. When you asked Bob how his wife was doing, he would give you a candid update, but he never burdened anyone with his private suffering or indeed exhibited the countenance of one who was losing the person most dear to his life. When his wife finally died in the fall of 1996, we didn't see Bob for several weeks, then he returned to Big Steve's ready for new challenges. He recently took up home-brewing and began dating. I don't know anyone who meets life more head-on, without regret or apology.

Darlene Utos, a lean and sexy thirty-four-year-old biker, joined Big Steve's after a long, abusive marriage that nearly devastated her. "I was afraid all the time," she admitted. After she'd spent a few months at the gym—with some help from experienced weight lifters like Peggy Box—Darlene's fears began to subside. She married a second time and seemed sublimely happy. Then in the late summer of 1996, maybe a year after she joined, Darlene stopped coming to the gym. Nobody knew why. Five or six weeks later, we learned that she had been nearly killed in a motorcycle accident in New Mexico. Coming over the crest of a hill at night, Darlene and her husband, Michael, had hit a black cow standing in the middle of the road. Both were thrown eighty-three feet (the cow sailed sixty-three feet). Michael was pronounced dead at the scene, and Darlene suffered multiple injuries to her body and head, including permanent nerve damage to her face and an eye that was nearly torn from its socket.

After two operations, she's still legally blind. She suffers almost constant pain in her back and hip. On top of everything else, Darlene learned that her insurance wouldn't pay for her physical therapy. Six weeks after the accident, against the advice of her doctors, Darlene returned to the gym. She was almost demonic in the way she attacked the weights. You could sense the anger and the anxiety of her loss. Sometimes there were tears in her eyes. Sometimes she crumpled into a fetal position on one of the mats. But she always got up, she never quit. "I'm not afraid of anything now, not even death," she told me. In April 1997, Darlene married a third time. Again, she seems sublimely happy, and one assumes that if tragedy strikes again she will deal with it.

Darlene and a number of others at our gym learned the power of positive thinking from Peggy Box, a forty-year-old who has been working out most of her life and has been a member at Big Steve's since the place opened in 1982. "You can do absolutely amazing things," Peggy assures younger bodybuilders. "Don't think of yourself as flesh and blood. Think of yourself as energy." Under Peggy's guidance, Darlene rearranged her routine so that she lifted more weight for fewer hours and staggered her workouts so that she exercised different muscles. After a year, Darlene had improved her squats from forty pounds to 120 pounds, more than her body weight. "I still hear Peggy's voice," Darlene tells me. " 'Push, Darlene, you can do it!' I use the memory of her voice as motivation." As Peggy instructed, Darlene has set as her goal to be the best she can. "I can't be any taller or younger or have a bigger chest," she says, "but I can feel good knowing I'm the best I can be at my age."

No one at this gym commands more respect than Peggy Box, who was world-class in the squat lift until she quit competing in 1988, disillusioned by the rampant use of drugs among power-lifters. The last straw, Peggy told me, was a moment in the women's locker room at the national meet in Utah when one of the contestants undressed to reveal a body completely covered with hair.

In her prime, Peggy weighed only 103 but could squat with 370 pounds of iron on her back. A ruptured disk in 1995 almost ended her days as even a noncompetitive power-lifter—her doctor told her she would never squat-lift again—but Peggy is as a tough as a twenty-five-pound dumbbell. By 1997 she was again squatting two hundred pounds and looking at more. Any woman who worries about becoming muscle-bound needs to meet Peggy. Built along the lines of a pint-sized Coke bottle, she is unusually attractive and unfailingly perky and pleasant—she's all woman. On the other hand, if I was in a dark alley in the bad part of town, the person I'd most want with me is Peggy Box.

Jim Peters is our resident hypochondriac, but he hasn't allowed the condition to deter him. When I first met Jim in 1992, I thought this guy ought to be playing Tarzan in the movies. I'd never seen a better physical specimen. In his late forties, Jim was six feet three, 230 pounds of rock-hard muscle. His body fat must have measured under 10 percent. Tanned and uncommonly handsome, he had a beautiful wife, a talented teenage daughter, and a number of successful business operations, including four grocery stores, a liquor store, a laundromat, and a mini-storage-and-car-wash facility. And yet he seemed habitually depressed and constantly worried about dying. He read dozens of self-help books and all the health magazines he could find. Jim was the first one to alert me about the dangers of free radicals.

I gradually became aware that over the previous five years Jim had experienced a staggering number of very serious medical problems. His doctors were baffled—he was something of a textbook case. In 1986, he ripped a biceps out of one arm at the gym, attempting to bench-press with excessive weights. Later, he ripped out the opposite biceps while dragging his powerboat from Lake Austin. A lump the size of a football appeared in his abdomen and turned out to be an enlarged spleen, which surgeons removed, along with his gallbladder. He began experiencing chest pains. An angiogram revealed that one of his major coronary arteries was 60 percent blocked. He started having problems urinating, due apparently to an enlarged prostate. It's not unusual for a man in his late forties to experience an enlarged prostate, but there were complications that suggested something more sinister was at work—Jim was a bleeder. Even small cuts would pour blood and keep pouring. After his second biceps operation, the wound began bleeding under the cast, which had to be cut away. Three trips to the operating room were required to check the bleeding.

Doctors finally discovered that Jim's core problem was myelofibrosis, a cancerlike disorder in which excess platelets are produced in the blood. Normally, excessive bleeding is caused by having too *few* platelets, but Jim's problem was that he had too many. The doctor had misdiagnosed his prostate problem—the reason for its enlargement was that the prostate had been infiltrated by platelets.

Shortly after we met, Jim began to deteriorate. I didn't notice at first, but little by little he was shrinking, losing muscle mass and body definition. The drug that he took to control platelets, interferon, caused great fatigue and made him generally miserable, somewhat as chemotherapy does. Rather than advise Jim to cut back temporarily on the amount of iron he was pumping, his doctor told him to stop lifting altogether. It would have been impossible to give worse advice to a man like Jim Peters. Weight training had sustained him through all those terrible and terrifying months. Without the gym, I feel certain, he would have wilted and died.

Jim's physical condition was complicated by a perpetually negative attitude that predated his medical problems. A classic Type A personality, Peters was an overachiever who felt compelled to be the best at everything. He needed to feel in control. He needed to drive the fastest car, own the biggest boat, live in the finest home, lift the heaviest weights. And yet he lived in constant fear of failure. "I've never been able to do my best," he confessed one day. "No matter what I do, I feel I should have done better."

"That's ridiculous," I told him. "I don't know many people who are more successful."

He shook his head and said: "But I still feel like I've failed at everything I've ever tried."

"By whose standards are you judging yourself?" I asked. "This isn't the Olympics. You're competing against a phantom in a game of no-win burnout!"

"I know you're right," he said. "I'm going to try to do better."

A few weeks after our conversation, on a family vacation in Hawaii, Jim's teenage daughter Amanda challenged him to a footrace. Despite his chronic fatigue and an energy supply below sea level, Jim couldn't let Amanda beat him. Fifty yards down the beach, straining like a madman, he felt a searing pain in his chest and collapsed on the sand. Naturally, he refused to interrupt his vacation to see a doctor. Back in Austin a few days later, he learned that the pain hadn't been a heart attack but a small stroke.

He had a second stroke a few weeks later, causing some memory loss and problems with speech. All of his doctors in Austin were stumped. So were his friends, who urged him to seek treatment at the famous Mayo Clinic in Rochester, Minnesota. I was concerned that Jim might literally *worry* himself to death. I mentioned this to Roy Farr, Jim's business partner and best friend. Roy was a direct opposite personality, as upbeat and confident as anyone I know. "I want it to say on my tombstone: 'I'll be right back!' " Roy told me, laughing. "I guess Jim's tombstone ought to say: 'See, I told you I was sick.' " The two old friends worked out together most afternoons, Roy prodding Jim about his negative attitude and Jim telling Roy that his was the only smart attitude to have.

During a business meeting one time, Peters told his partner: "Roy, your problem is you're too optimistic!"

"Too optimistic!" Farr exploded. "You think I'd be better off if I was a pessimist?"

"Absolutely!" Jim told him.

Farr was also becoming concerned that Jim was acting out a self-fullfilling prophecy of doom. Roy knew something of the syndrome. He was a recovering alcoholic, one of the meanest and toughest barroom fighters in central Texas in his drinking days. Once he got into Alcoholics Anonymous and stopped drinking, Roy was magically transformed into a near-opposite of his former self. In his fifteen years of sobriety, he worked tirelessly with other reformed drunks, routinely climbing out of bed in the middle of the night to help some poor devil stay off of the sauce. Farr still attends three or four AA meetings each day, not because he needs them but because "we need each other."

What he had observed about his business partner is that Jim had the classic symptoms of an alcoholic, even though Jim never touched the stuff. But Jim's father had been an alcoholic, which could explain his irrational fear of failure.

"Jim suffers from what they call anticipation anxiety," Roy told me. "In effect, Jim creates what he most fears. I try to tell him: 'If you think you're having a heart attack every time you have a little gas pain, you'll end up having a heart attack. What you think about, you talk about. And what you talk about, you become.' "

With the help of Big Steve, another recovering alcoholic, Farr finally persuaded Jim to attend a meeting of Adult Children of Alcoholics, in the company of another friend who had a similar problem. On the way to the meeting their car was nearly rammed by a van that ran a red light. Jim and his friend had identical reactions: "Let's catch the bastard and beat the stuffing out of him." To their humiliation, the driver turned out to be an eighty-year-old woman. If the drive over was bad, the meeting was worse. Jim told me later, "I kept sitting there listening to all that stuff and thinking, What am I doing here with all these *losers*?"

Jim smiled as he told me this story, which I took as a positive sign, one of the first I'd seen in a long time. The return of a sense of humor, an ability to laugh at yourself, is the first step toward permanent attitude adjustment. Jim had started to see himself as we saw him, as a man who had been amply blessed by life but who had this problem that needed addressing. But before addressing the problem, it was necessary to admit he had it.

In July 1996, Jim and his wife traveled to Rochester, Minnesota, and checked him into the Mayo Clinic. For several days doctors ran tests. They took him off the interferon that had caused him so much grief and gave him a new combination of medications (one of them experimental) with no side effects. He started feeling better almost instantly. The chronic fatigue vanished, and his stamina surged. All that negative energy that had taken him under for so many months seemed to drain away like last night's dishwater.

Until now, Jim had believed that that anyone who saw a psychiatrist was by definition weak and spineless. But he changed his mind. He began regular sessions with a psychiatrist and a psychologist, a husband-and-wife team who were both weight lifters. They prescribed antidepressants, which worked almost at once. They also told him to keep pumping iron, the best advice possible for a man in his condition. Within a few weeks, Jim's gloomy-but-predictable disposition had returned to a safe, comfortable level, and his muscles began to respond.

"I learned something interesting from my doctors," he told me one day as we were dressing for our workout. "I learned that depression is just a disease. Nothing to be ashamed about, nothing embarrassing."

"You were ashamed and embarrassed about being depressed?"

"I thought it was a weakness."

Jim looked like Tarzan again. He had gained back all but five of the thirty pounds he had lost and was nearly as strong as when I first met him. He had changed his diet, limiting saturated fats and eating more fruits, vegetables, and grains. His business, his marriage, his life—everything about him appeared in harmony. Oh, the superego was still there, the imperative to prove the unprovable; it's a constant threat to life and limb, and will be for the foreseeable future. From time to time Jim feels the irrational, irresistible challenge to attempt a bench press well out of his range, and the following day, more than likely, he is horrified to discover blood in his urine. These unfortunate traits of character may in time vanish altogether, though more magic will be required before all of the old attitudes surrender. But Jim is on the right track. We all are.

A television reporter interviewing Willie Nelson on the occasion of his sixty-fourth birthday asked, "How does it feel to be a year older?"

Willie treated the young woman to one of his always gracious smiles and replied, "That's the whole point, isn't it?"

Twenty-Two

*I*n July 1996, the same month that Jim Peters went off to the Mayo Clinic to begin his long road back to health, I was jolted from my comfortable routine of life by a completely unexpected turn of events. My son, Mark, telephoned from Atlanta with the startling news that he had been diagnosed with acute leukemia. His type of leukemia was extremely difficult to cure and usually fatal. His only chance, I was told, was to have a bone marrow transplant, and even then the odds of survival were not good.

I was stunned nearly speechless. If my son had been killed in a car wreck, I would have been devastated, but the news would have at least seemed familiar and within the scope of my experience. The idea that he might be dying of leukemia was so alien that I found it hard to believe. I'd never known anyone suffering from leukemia.

"Don't worry," I told him once I had digested the news. "We'll beat this thing."

"I'm sure of it," he said.

"So am I!" And I was. I had no doubt we would find the answer. In times of great crisis, I have the ability to think and act logically— and with enormous energy—and I began reading everything I could find about the disease. "Leukemia" means "white blood." Mark had M-5 leukemia, the most severe type of adult acute myelogenous leukemia (AML), in which immature white blood cells called blasts take over the bone marrow and prevent it from making enough normal white and red cells and platelets. The blasts overwhelm the mature white cells that fight infection, the red cells that carry oxygen, and the platelets that help blood clot. They spill into the bloodstream, infiltrating organs and glands until the process of life shuts down. M-5 is particularly nasty and extremely resistant to chemotherapy.

Scientists don't know what causes leukemia, only that there are different types that react differently to treatment. Children's leukemia, for example, can be cured far more easily than adult leukemia. Less than 20 percent of all AML patients live longer than five years, though the figure is higher for patients under sixty. While chemotherapy can induce complete remission in the majority of AML patients, the leukemia frequently returns, and once this happens, the patient almost always dies. Victims of chronic leukemia sometimes live for years because the blasts are more mature and progress more slowly, but eventually the production of immature white cells quickens and chronic leukemia progresses into acute leukemia.

Dr. E. Aubrey Thompson, a friend at the University of Texas Medical Branch at Galveston who has done leukemia research for twenty years, told me that Mark may have had chronic leukemia for the past ten or even twenty years, even though no one had detected it. "What makes adult leukemia so extremely difficult is that the cancer cells come and go, hiding out most of the time," Aubrey told me. "You go along for years, having a few bad days when you feel tired or run-down or flulike, but most of the time you feel fine. Then one day it explodes into acute leukemia. In childhood leukemia, by contrast, the cancer cells are very active. They come out of hiding and grow rapidly, and therefore they are sensitive to certain drugs and can be wiped out."

Mark's doctor immediately placed him on a program of intense chemotherapy at Northside Hospital in Atlanta. Once the cancer was in remission, the doctor told us, the disease might be cured with a bone marrow transplant. But the transplant process was long and dangerous, littered with formidable obstacles and treacherous ifs— *if* a matching marrow donor can be located; *if* chemotherapy can force the cancer into temporary remission. The expense of the transplant procedure is enormous—up to $250,000—and it is highly risky. Between 40 and 60 percent of those who undergo a transplant survive, but some of the survivors later succumb to fatal complications from graft-versus-host disease.

Unfortunately, no one in our family was a match for Markie's bone marrow. From July through the fall of 1996, our family watched and waited as doctors scanned the National Bone Marrow Registry, looking for someone in the world with six matching antigens or markers. Six is the magic number, the perfect match. It is possible to do a successful transplant with five or even four matching antigens, but the already long odds of survival drop sharply. There were more than three million people on the National Registry, but the best we could find was a five-out-of-six mismatch.

Between chemotherapy sessions, Markie came to Austin several times in the autumn. Though I knew the sessions had been rough, he looked much the same, except that his hair was gone. In typical Mark fashion, he hadn't waited for it to fall out from the effects of chemotherapy but had called in his personal hair stylist to shave his head. I told him that he looked like Yul Brynner. He had lost just enough weight to look trim. Though he didn't have much of an appetite, we ate at our favorite Mexican joint and drank a few pints at the Dog & Duck.

It was great to see him, almost but not quite like old times. Normally when he came to Austin the two of us would work out together at Big Steve's. Never were workouts so pleasurable as when Markie was there with me. But this time he didn't feel up to it. We took the dogs down to the hike-and-bike trail, but even that was almost too much for him.

Working through my own exercise routine that fall, I did a lot of praying. I asked God to help us find a bone marrow donor and to make the cancer go into remission, at least temporarily. I asked Him to help us be strong and to not lose hope. In long moments of reverie, I remembered things that Mark and I had said or done, the uniqueness of our relationship, the way it grew out of our long absences from each other, and the depth and layers of love that our years together had fashioned.

We were never like father and son—more like brothers or best friends. He always called me by my nickname, Jap, never Dad or Daddy. Markie was six when his mother and I divorced. She moved to Chicago, then to Los Angeles, then to Atlanta, so I saw Mark and Lea only in the summer or at Christmas. I remembered a time that Markie visited me while I was in Philadelphia, writing a sports column for the *Inquirer* and doing some freelance magazine work. He must have been around ten—this bright, resourceful, resilient, uncommonly stubborn kid—and he was dogging me to take him along on a business trip to New York. I explained that I didn't have time to show him the sights, but he wanted to tag along, and I couldn't say no. Dan and June Jenkins and their kids were out of town, so Markie and I had their entire apartment on Park Avenue to ourselves. Our first night in the Big Apple, in a hurry to make an appointment, I gave him twenty dollars and a key to the apartment, then dropped him off at Times Square. I remembered asking him if he'd be okay. His cocksure reply was: "Sure. Nothing to it!"

My cab hadn't gone half a block when the stupidity of what I'd done slapped me upside the head: I'd deposited my ten-year-old son in the geographical center of the evilest, most sinister square mile in America! I threw open the door and raced back into oncoming traffic, but by then he'd been swallowed up in the crowd. For the next few hours I was nearly sick with fear, imagining what had happened. But when I got back to the apartment there was Markie, propped up on the king-size bed, a cat on his lap, eating a bowl of ice cream and watching a John Wayne movie.

"Are you okay?" I asked, badly shaken.

"Sure," he said, grinning at me as though we were co-conspirators in a plot to overthrow the world. "Nothing to it!"

In the summer of 1975, just after I'd moved back to Austin from New York—and before I'd started dating Phyllis—Markie graduated from high school. A week later he was on his way to Austin, to attend the University of Texas. For the first year he slept in my large walk-in closet. These were the best of times for both of us. We hung out together, shopping, cooking, eating, listening to music, having adventures. We even bailed each other of jail a time or two. I was sitting in the Scholz Garten one Friday night with my friend Warren Burnett, the prominent west Texas lawyer, when Markie called from the jail in Bastrop. Along with several hundred other UT students, he had been arrested for picking magic mushrooms in a cow pasture. It wasn't the magic mushrooms that brought the law but the fact that the students had knocked over a fence and allowed the farmer's prize bull to collide with a passing Cadillac, to the great detriment of all concerned. Burnett eventually persuaded the local district attorney to dismiss the drug charges in exchange for a plea of trespassing.

Markie dropped out of school for a while and opened his own nightclub, the Third Coast. That was a dream of his, to own his own club or restaurant. My dad had passed on to me an appreciation for cooking and eating well, and I handed it down to Mark. Before long he was cooking gourmet meals that took three days to prepare and five hours to eat. Phyllis and I nicknamed him Maurice. After he married Helen and moved into the professional world, Maurice's seated dinners became legendary in Dallas and Little Rock. Journalists and politicians (among them Bill and Hillary Clinton) jockeyed for invitations. For one of my birthdays, he whipped up a five-course dinner that included rack of lamb, dove breasts wrapped in bacon and sautéed in wine sauce, roasted ancho peppers with salmon and goat cheese, and an unbelievable dome-shaped dessert with layers of crushed Heath Bars, fudge cake, ice cream, and toasted butterscotch crust. Naturally, Maurice selected the appropriate wine for each course.

Sometimes we wrote songs, Markie strumming his guitar and me jotting down the words. We could compose an entire opera in an afternoon. When my friend Sue Sharlot graduated from UT Law School, we wrote a number for her graduation party called "All You Gotta Do Is Know the Law, Then Boogie Till You Puke." Another all-time favorite was "Beat Me Like the Bitch I Am." We wrote alternate lines, laughing so hard we could barely get the words out: "Reel and rod me / Marquis de Sade me / Make me feel so fine / But beat me like the bitch I am / And tell the world you're mine!"

All of our time together, he found it easier to express his love than I did, and in his effortless manner he taught me to express my love too. He taught me to appreciate his favorite expression: "Nothing to it!" It was a manifesto of the indomitable spirit, an attitude that recognized no limit. I just naturally assumed Markie could do anything he set his mind to, and I guess he felt the same about me. Together, we thought of ourselves as unconquerable. And for many years we were.

When Markie visited us between Christmas and New Year's, he had just completed his fourth intensive session of chemotherapy, and he looked as if he'd been drug a thousand miles behind a freight wagon. The chemo had been worse than any of us had ever imagined, inducing not only extreme nausea but pain and debilitating fatigue. After each session, it got harder and harder for him to recover. Though we still hadn't found a perfect match, his doctors in Atlanta had decided to go ahead with the bone marrow transplant in early January, using the five-out-of-six mismatch. I didn't like the sound of it: had they given up hope? Markie, however, was optimistic as always. I opened a good bottle of red wine and we toasted a successful transplant and a better 1997.

The doctors had assumed that the most recent jolt of chemo would force the cancer into remission, but they were wrong. Two days into the New Year we learned that the cancer was still there, stronger than ever. Mark's doctor, Daniel Dubovsky, compared cancer cells to cockroaches. "You might kill ninety-five percent of them," he told us, "but the remaining five percent emerge stronger and more resistant." Dubovsky and the doctors in Atlanta acknowledged at this point that indeed they had done all they could. We arranged for Mark to be admitted to the University of Texas M.D. Anderson Cancer Center in Houston, where the newest experimental drugs were available. Though none of us talked about it, we knew this was our last hope. Even as we slept, even as we prayed, the clock was ticking.

In January and February, various friends and family members staged testing drives in Atlanta, Little Rock, and Austin, adding another fifteen hundred people to the national registry, yet still there was no perfect match. Nothing had worked in our favor. Among Caucasians, a match exists for a given patient about 80 percent of the time; among minorities, the figure drops to about 50 percent. Why weren't we in the ball game? One doctor speculated that finding a match for Mark was so difficult because there were traces of Native American blood in our family, but he was just guessing. Anecdotal evidence suggests that genetic tissue typing for bone marrow is a crapshoot. In 1993, Ann Connally, the daughter-in-law of former Texas governor John Connally, turned out to be the world's only perfect match for a sixteen-year-old Japanese girl who is alive and doing well because Mrs. Connally was tested and added to the national registry in 1990.

In seeking a donor, we cast as wide a net as possible, appealing to college students, employees of the state of Texas, Native American tribes, and everyone on every mailing list any of us could locate, including the Texas Institute of Letters, the Austin Board of Realtors, and the *Texas Monthly* subscription roster. Phyllis and I ran a full-page ad in *Texas Monthly*—publisher Mike Levy donated the space—pleading for help. People from all over the country called, volunteering to be tested, extending their support, contributing money to the Leukemia Society of America. Rosalind Wright, sister of Austin writer Lawrence Wright, telephoned from Lexington, Massachusetts, where she had rallied thirteen tribes of Native Americans and personnel from a military base to get tested. My old friend Brother Jonathan—aka Marvin Schwartz, the movie producer from our Mad Dog days—sent a seed blessed by the Dalai Lama with instructions on how Mark was to ingest it. When I presented the seed to Markie in his room at M. D. Anderson, he accepted it without hesitation. "This is the best offer I've had lately," he told me.

Markie's fortieth birthday was February 11, 1997. About eight days before that landmark occasion, he completed his second and final session of experimental chemotherapy—and his sixth chemo session since being diagnosed the previous July. "This last week was the worst I've ever been through," he told me one morning just before he was released from the hospital. Throughout the ordeal, he had never complained or solicited sympathy, but I could tell that the long grind was getting to him. He looked haggard and beaten, his voice straining to rise above a whisper. He had lost twenty-five or thirty pounds and was a pale ghost of the strapping young man who had been my workout partner at Big Steve's and my best buddy through countless high adventures.

We celebrated his birthday the following weekend, in two large condominiums that I had rented on the beach in Galveston. Markie's ex-wife, Helen, brought their two children, Katy and Malcolm, from Little Rock. Lea flew in from Atlanta, and Shea and his wife, Lisa, drove down from Houston. In all, several dozen relatives and close friends gathered for the weekend, including Mark's current girlfriend, Susan Shaw. At one point Phyllis pointed out that three of Mark's former lovers were at the party. We cooked a giant pot of seafood gumbo and bought heaps of fresh shrimp and oysters. For two days the family ate, drank, and enjoyed being together. It was a vintage Cartwright moment except for one thing—for most of our time in Galveston, Markie stayed in his room, sleeping or fighting back the sickness.

The two of us sat together one afternoon on the balcony, enjoying the sun and the Gulf breeze, but unable to find much to say. Our silence had become awkward and unnatural. We had shared so many good times, talking of our hopes and dreams and frustrations. I kept looking across the street at the ocean and grasping for something profoundly philosophical to say. But every time I formulated a thought and tried to put it into words, it came across as shallow and foolish. Maybe silence was the final way to communicate. I kept remembering my own fortieth birthday in Mexico City, and I imagine Mark remembered it, too, though neither of us mentioned it. Twenty-three years ago the future was so bountiful and limitless, our happiness so complete and secure, that we took everything else for granted. Now it was all too sad for words.

In early March, Mark and I took our final trip together, to the Chihuahuan Desert east of Van Horn, Texas, to search for the new top leaves of the creosote bush. When brewed into a tea, I had learned, the leaves were considered a cure for leukemia and other diseases by some Mexican *curanderos.* I had learned this in a letter from a man named E. Leslie Thompson, who was doing twenty-five years on a drug charge in state prison. In my years as a journalist I had received hundreds of letters from people in prison, but they always wanted something from me. This guy just wanted to do me a favor. We knew that it was the longest of long shots, but long shots were all we had.

The trip was long and arduous, and it sapped what little strength Mark had left. The letter explained that the two of us had to travel together, and leave a "gift of water" for the creosote plants. We flew from Austin to Dallas to Midland, then drove 125 miles to an isolated spot within sight of the Davis Mountains, two liter-size bottles of Evian on the seat between us. Mark slept almost all the way, racked with fever, chills, and nausea. At the road marker mentioned in the letter, I parked well off the highway. With our bottles of water and a canvas bag stuffed with smaller plastic bags, we crawled through a barbed-wire fence and walked several hundred yards into a desert

covered with the foul-smelling creosote bush. Except for a few cac-
tuses, nothing else grew out here. After a short time, Markie had to
return to the car. I stayed until I'd collected three bags of leaves, then
we headed back in the direction we'd come.

We spent the night in a Midland hotel, the kid so sick that I wondered if he'd make it through the night. I was awake until two in the
morning, talking long-distance to friends and family, trying to figure
out our next move. Mark was adamant that he wanted to fly back to
Atlanta—not Houston as we had planned. The transplant was still
scheduled in ten days, at Atlanta's Emory University Hospital,
though we both knew that a transplant was out of the question unless
or until the cancer was in remission. One thing was clear—he
couldn't survive another round of chemotherapy. The deadly toxin
that was supposed to destroy cancer cells had instead destroyed his
immune system and probably done irreparable damage to his liver
and other organs. I suspect that one day we'll look back at this
wretched procedure the way we look back with revulsion at frontal
lobotomies, but at the time chemotherapy was the best medical science had to offer.

The worst day of my life—worse even than the day Mark died
six weeks later—started early the next morning, when I drove Mark
to Midland International Airport for a flight to Atlanta. Until then I
hadn't understood how far the disease had progressed. He was so
weak that I doubt he could have walked unassisted to the gate. I
helped him into a wheelchair and pushed him. He had eaten almost
nothing for the last four days, so we stopped at the coffee bar. I
bought him a Coke and a banana, and he was able to keep them
down. For two days he had said almost nothing. A question that
needed a response got a nod or a shake of the head. Looking at him
then, as pale and weak as a newborn puppy, I couldn't help but remember that just a year earlier we'd worked out together at my gym
in Austin. He had corrected my technique, pointing out that I was
jerking rather than lifting the weight—and in danger of injuring my
shoulder. He had looked so strong, so able, so confident: now you
could almost see his life leaking away.

When it was time for him to board the plane, we hugged and
kissed, knowing it might be our final good-bye. I was close to tears.

Watching my son shuffle slowly down the ramp to his plane, his hair-less head bowed in agony, his clothes hanging off his emaciated frame, a kid who had just turned forty but looked ninety, I kept think-ing: Why him? Why not me? When a child dies, "Why?" is the last question to go away.

About a week later, Phyllis and I flew to Atlanta for the death-watch. It was obvious now that Markie had been doomed from the very beginning: all that chemotherapy never came close to forcing his cancer into remission. We didn't know how many days remained or how we would handle them, but we trusted that Markie would set the style.

Getting reacquainted with his longtime group of pals, we real-ized he had set the style years ago. In high school he had put to-gether a combination rock band and chili cookoff team called the Chain Gang, and they were with him until the end, honoring his wish that nobody feel sorry for him or for themselves. Tom "Meat" Smith, Markie's oldest friend, sat at the foot of his bed and regaled us with stories about the Great Cartwright. It seems that the women of Atlanta were not *quite* unanimous in their adoration. Meat told us about one woman that Mark had jilted when he worked for the Turner Broadcasting System. To this day, she is unable to speak his name without pausing to spit on the floor. Meat demonstrated, feign-ing a high-pitched voice: "Oh, you must be referring to Mark— *hock, spitooey*—Cartwright." Sick as he was, Mark doubled over with laughter.

Also on hand was the latest and last of Mark's girlfriends, Susan Shaw. She was as tough and tenacious as they come. Almost single-handedly she had organized a drive that put five hundred new names on the bone marrow registry. She could have bailed out at any time—no one would have blamed her—but Susan wasn't the type to bail. The only time she lost it was the day Dr. Dubovsky told the family it was over. "It wasn't supposed to be that way," Susan said later, her eyes swollen and red from a day of crying. "I had imagined our twi-light years, sitting on the porch watching our grandchildren. Sud-denly, I just went to pieces. I was crying and calling out to God, saying, 'Why Mark? Why me?'" Soon after, Susan got a call from the National Marrow Donor Program, telling her that she was a partial match for a fifty-four-year-old man from the Midwest. "God works in mysterious ways," she concluded.

What got us through those last few weeks was the remarkable courage, grace, dignity, and measured good humor with which Markie faced death. He had resolved to put his affairs in order, and that's what he did. He dictated a will, and made it known that when the end came he didn't want the paramedics to resuscitate him. He asked that his body be cremated and his ashes scattered in the Gulf of Mexico. (One exception: Some of the ashes would be handed over to the Chain Gang, whose members would select an appropriate urn—most likely a cowboy boot—and take them each year to the chili cookoff in Athens, Georgia.) He selected a Cajun friend, Jonathan "Gator" Ordoyne, as his replacement in the Chain Gang.

One morning while I was helping him shower, I asked Markie if he was scared. "No," he said, "strangely enough, I'm not." He had been sick so long that what he really wanted was just "a few good days." That became my prayer: "If you can't give us the miracle of sparing his life, Lord, then grant our fallback position: a few good days, then let him die quickly, without pain or fear."

My prayer was answered. Markie seemed to get better by the day. He climbed out of bed and spent several hours sitting in the sun, watching a titmouse build a nest in a tall Georgia pine. He was able to eat solid food and even hold down cups of the creosote tea. He went to a couple of movies with Susan, and the three of us spent an afternoon at the Atlanta Botanical Garden. We drove the rural back-roads, where spectacular explosions of azaleas, redbuds, and dogwoods seemed to have blossomed specifically on Mark's behalf, and had dinner at his favorite Mexican restaurant.

Phyllis had already returned to Austin to take care of business, and now it was time for me to go home, too, Markie and I agreed. "You've got to go sometime," he said, not unaware of the double meaning. My last night in Atlanta we had dinner at his favorite Thai restaurant, then Mark and Susan drove me back to my hotel. Standing there face-to-face in the parking lot was the hardest part, just as I knew it would be. Neither of us wanted to drag it out. Mark kissed me and said he loved me. I said I loved him too. "I can't bring myself to say good-bye," I told him. "So, until I see you again."

"Until I see you again," he told me back. I turned toward the hotel entrance, knowing it wouldn't be in this lifetime.

After that we talked daily by phone. Mark told me that he and Meat were driving to Augusta for the opening round of the Masters golf tournament. On Friday, April 11, he flew to Little Rock to visit his children, nine-year-old Katy and seven-year-old Malcolm. It was an act of sheer will: his fever had returned, signaling that the brief reprieve was over. He somehow made it back to Atlanta on Sunday afternoon.

At four-thirty the next morning, Mark's mother called us and told us he was dead. His last words were to Susan. "I think this is it," he said softly, closing his eyes. "I'm packing 'em in."

Phyllis and I lay together in the cold darkness, holding each other, drained but glad it was over. At daylight, I climbed out of bed, dressed, and drove to Big Steve's. I didn't know what else to do. I worked out for more than three hours, the pain and anguish gradually subsiding. I thought of Markie and heard his voice: "Jap, you're jerking that dumbbell again! What you want is a slow, even movement!" Right, Markie, I got it now. Slow and even.

I had been coming to this gym for a little more than six years, in good times and in bad, and it had become a necessary part of my life. It had given me balance and staying power and an inner peace that equipped me for harshest realities. It had permitted me to keep going.

That's what I have to practice now, I kept telling myself: the art of keeping on.

Part Six:

GETTING BETTER, NOT OLDER

Twenty-Three

I will tell you in some detail about Frenchy and Monique and their week in Paris, not to be voyeuristic but to make a point that has until recently been overlooked by scientific research. It is this: that the willingness and capacity for love, both physical and spiritual, does not diminish with advancing age but, properly courted, can reach levels of passion and intensity never imagined in the urgent, sticky lust of youth.

At the time of their magical week in Paris, Frenchy and Monique had been married to each other for more than eighteen years, and each had been married more than once before. Monique, in her early fifties, was Frenchy's third wife. Frenchy was about to turn sixty and was her fourth husband. They came together with no illusions. For about a year before they decided to marry, they shacked up, along with their two teenage sons from previous marriages. Their vows were spoken in October 1976 in the backroom of the Texas Chili Parlor, in a ceremony presided over by the Reverend Bud Shrake, card-carrying doctor of metaphysics of the Church of Universal Life.

Frenchy and Monique were both blessed—cursed, some might argue—with strong sex drives developed during their teens. Both had been sexually active in high school and college and had had numerous lovers before and between marriages. Not surprisingly, both had been unfaithful to all of their previous marriage partners, though this was pretty much the norm among the people they knew. In fairness, Frenchy had been far more flagrant than Monique when it came to sleeping around. But they knew of each other's past and in fact shared a degree of pleasure in acknowledging this bond of selfishness and weakness of the flesh. It solidified them as lovers and explained something profound about their relationship. They had been looking all their lives for a sense of fulfillment, looking but not finding. Almost from the start of their relationship, they suspected that they might find it in each other, but the proof was still some years away.

Mostly, their marriage had been very good. They trusted and respected each other and enjoyed being together almost at the exclusion of being with anyone else. They were both good cooks and enjoyed creating together in their kitchen. They shared a love for spicy foods, for adventure, for travel. They could find black humor in the bleakest and most morbid circumstances and wondered why others couldn't. They were bonded by an indomitable resiliency. They accepted what happened and made the best of life. Both were raised as Christians, and though they did not attend church regularly each had a private accommodation with God that served them in good times and bad. Their fallback was each other, but their ultimate fallback was God. They had no doubt that God had put them together, that each was the answer to the other's prayers.

And, of course, they loved sex and had learned to be its master rather than its slave. "At least we have mastered its slavishness," Frenchy observed. He sometimes thought of sex the way he thought of shrimp, as something he'd never get enough of. He was surprised and pleased to find that Monique loved it as much as he did. From the beginning their sex was hot. Sometimes it was so hot they felt faint afterward, the sort of light-headed rapture that endangers people who soar too high or plunge to unbelievable depths. Instinctively, they knew that even small changes in their routines brought new intensities to their love life. Gradually, they began to see a ratio between change and pleasure: the more exotic the first, the greater the second.

Each spontaneous discovery uncovered new layers to their relationship. Once while driving through a remote part of the Rio Grande Valley on their way to Brownsville, they got so turned on they had to stop in a cornfield and make love. This was one of their landmark frolics. One Valentine's Day some years later, Monique found a photograph they had taken that day of her standing in a cornfield—holding, as though it were a trophy, a pair of panties. She signed it "Monique of the Cornfield" and gave it to Frenchy as her gift of love. He keeps it tacked to the wall of his closet, so that he sees it several times every day. He bought a large pink piggy bank, which Monique decorated with red flowers. Each time they made love, they put ten or twenty dollars in the piggy bank, toward future adventures.

The changes of scenery that really stoked the furnaces of their libidos, that threatened them with meltdown, were vacations to distant and exotic places like Mexico or Europe. It was as though they boarded an airplane in one country and emerged hours later not only in a different place but as different people, younger, wilder, more open to possibilities, and committed in their indifference to everything except each other and the pleasure of the moment. These were, without fail, can't-keep-my-hands-off-you experiences that would have embarrassed both of them if they had been thinking straight.

Consider, for example, Frankfurt, after a twenty-hour flight from Texas. No oversexed teenagers in the history of the world ever experienced more frenzied lovemaking than Frenchy and Monique that magic morning, in an antique German bathtub the size of a pickup truck and overflowing with bubbles, a freshly opened bottle of champagne on the floor beside the tub and their sexual appetites stretched almost beyond endurance by the kisses, nudges, and secret strokes stolen during their long overnight flight over the Atlantic. There had been similar moments in Budapest, in front of a large window overlooking the Danube and the Chain Bridge, and in that small room above the Grand Canal in Venice. But Paris was something else, an interlude of passion that would alter their lives forever.

The apartment that they rented was at 3 Rue Volta, in the recently gentrified Marais, on the fifth floor of what was said to be the oldest inhabited building in the city. According to some documents they read, the building was constructed in 1282, a claim apparently verified by the plumbing. The apartment was owned by a famous French opera singer who leased it while she was on tour. Her name was also Monique. The first four floors of the building were half-timber with stone, but the top floor—their floor—was slate—part of the mansard roof, actually—slightly angled away from the street, with two dormer windows looking down on the Rue Volta. They had been warned that there was no elevator and had exercised their legs for many weeks in preparation for climbing the tight, narrow spiral staircase ascending to their apartment. Frenchy counted 182 steps that first day as he struggled to drag and shove Monique's trunk-size suitcase upstairs. Once they had settled in, however, the 182 steps became part of their fortress, a moat to discourage visitors.

The apartment was small and deliciously romantic—a living room with high ceilings, beams, and a skylight (also a grand piano, which they had sworn never to touch), an efficiency kitchen with a window overlooking a courtyard, a roomy bath with overhead pipes that made threatening noises night and day, and a bedroom in which the bed extended almost wall to wall. The view from their bedroom was to another bedroom in another fifth-floor apartment across the street. Frenchy placed both pairs of binoculars on the window ledge.

Once she had put away her things, Monique slipped a disk of their favorite opera, Puccini's *La Bohème,* into the cassette player and turned it up full volume. The weather was warm for November, so she opened the dormer windows, allowing the smells and sounds of the Paris street to sweep the room. Frenchy found some logs and kindling in the alcove and started a small fire in the living-room fireplace, then went to the kitchen and opened a bottle of good red wine, which he placed on a tray with two glasses and some bread, cheese, and olives. Strange how they worked together, independently and yet as a team, all the while speaking not a word but reading each other with military-like precision.

When he returned to the living room, Monique was curled like a kitten on the overstuffed couch in front of the fire. She had changed into one of the many seductive costumes in her sexual wardrobe— a white see-through blouse, knotted just below her bare breasts, and white bikini panties trimmed with lace. This particular number was called *The Warden's Daughter.* There were at least two dozen costumes collected over the years, each with a name and history. A long black silk gown with deep cleavage and a slit up the side had been labeled *The Black Maria.* A short gold slip with black trim was called *Goldstuff.* A very short and sexy red cocktail dress purchased from Neiman-Marcus had been dubbed *The Mexican Hooker* (and was always worn without panties). An off-white slip with a minimum of lace and some suspicious stains near the crotch was called *Poor White Trash.* Two different outfits were made of white gossamer, one held loosely at the waist with a gold sash, the second worn under a transparent negligee. The first was called *The Sirens:* it was purchased in a shop on the Amalfi Coast of Italy, near the mythical Grotto delle Sirene from which Sirens lured sailors to their deaths by the beauty of their songs. The second of the gossamer outfits was labeled *The Love Goddess:* it had first appeared at a memorable wedding anniversary soirée at a suite in the Melrose Hotel in Dallas. In addition to these old favorites there was *Valentine Surprise, The Cheerleader, The TCU Pompom Girl, Nioka the Leopard Girl,* and various others, each evoking its own mood and style. Sometimes Monique would ask Frenchy to select her costume. Other times, like now, she would surprise him. Frenchy was never disappointed. Just thinking about the many costumes drove him half mad with desire.

He poured her a glass of wine and watched her sip it, her eyes locked to his, her little smile hungry and eager. He settled down next to her, working an arm under her back so that he could bring her lips to his with a minimum of effort. She was light as a feather. Her lips tasted like dark cherries with hints of spices, a vintage that he automatically began to catalog. He could feel her legs wrapping around him. From the ancient ceiling beams, the magnificent voices of Mimi and Rodolfo singing the duet from the first act of *La Bohème* made them tremble with anticipation. The autumn sun slanting through the skylight stirred the colors and made them dance. He felt himself being sucked under, carried away by beautiful and terrible creatures of love, encapsulated by the white sound of pleasure until he had lost all connection with the outside world.

They decided that first day to name their apartment La Bohème. The other Monique, the one who owned the apartment, was an attractive women with dark hair and burning eyes, about fifty judging from the photographs posted around the living room and in the hall. Showbills established that in her time on the stage she had sung many roles, including Mimi in Puccini's wonderful love story set in the Latin Quarter of Paris in the seventeenth century. In one photograph this Monique posed with some French dignitary in a top hat and red sash, on a platform near the Place de la Concorde, where she no doubt thrilled a nation with her rendition of the "Marseillaise" at a Bastille Day celebration. The shelves of the living room were crowded with her books and recordings and memorabilia, and there was the smell of lavender in the room. Forever after, Frenchy would associate that exotic smell with the two Moniques.

They spent most of their days exploring Paris on foot or by Métro. From their apartment they walked down the wide, clean Rue Beaubourg, spotting interesting cafés and restaurants for future reference, pausing to watch the fire-eaters, dancers, and jugglers outside the Pompidou Center. They crossed the busy Rue de Rivoli, dodging the honking taxis, and walked in front of the Hôtel de Ville, a Gothic monstrosity that reminded Frenchy of sixteenth-century Paris when nobles and aristocrats dominated life in the Marais.

They followed the quais of the right bank, passed the Louvre, which they had visited on previous trips, then crossed the the river at the Pont des Arts and found the steps down to the water's edge. Somehow the air smelled lustier down here, more full of life, and the river flowed swifter than they remembered. There is something soulful about being under one of the famous bridges of the Seine, something basic. Across the river they could see the ancient Pont Neuf and the delicate spire of the Sainte Chapelle. An old fisherman with a bottle of wine and a can of bait at his side napped in the sunlight. Monique waved to a small girl aboard a tourist barge. A couple young enough to be their children walked with their arms around each other, smiling at them as though they were old friends. Monique took Frenchy's arm, and he turned to kiss her. The kiss took on a life of its own. For seconds—maybe minutes—they lost themselves in each other, exploring each other's body with no thought of where they were or who might be watching. Only in Paris did lovers feel so uninhibited, able to behave in rhythm with their feelings rather than the dictates of convention.

It was still early. The cafés would just be opening for lunch. "Would you like a glass of wine?" Frenchy asked.

"Soon," she said, taking his arm again as they returned to the street.

They strolled along the quais of the *rive gauche,* stopping at the bookstalls, lingering at the shops that sold plants and exotic birds, headed nowhere in particular, enjoying each other and the renewed vigor of being in Paris.

On the Boulevard St. Germain, Monique took a photograph of Frenchy posing with a statue of Danton at his back. Farther down the boulevard, they found the famous Brasserie Lipp, where they had eaten their first Parisian meal four years earlier, shortly after arriving on the train from Frankfurt. Everyone has a magical first night in Paris, and theirs was dinner at the Lipp, at a table just inside the front door where they could watch people come and go. He had once read that famous authors were seated by the windows and, true or not, was pleased to note a window just behind them. They ordered steak and English peas, two items that they were able to identify on the French-language menu, and a carafe of red wine from Cahors. Monique said that she had never eaten fresher, more wonderful, pea-er peas. Just after midnight, two young men who appeared extraordinarily euphoric made a dazzling appearance at the Lipp, waltzing through the front door to music they alone heard. Frenchy recognized one of them as Michael Moriarty, the American actor. They had admired him in *Bang the Drum Slowly* and were apparently starring like starstruck tourists, because Moriarty walked over to their table and bowed deeply from the waist. He kissed Monique's hand and inquired with a theatrical flourish: "And how are the children?"

"They're fine," Monique told him. "One's in prison and the other's just escaped from a leper colony in French Guiana."

That was one of the things Frenchy loved most about Monique— her quickness with the right quip, sassy but never mean-spirited. After that, every time they saw Michael Moriarty on the screen, they thought of that night at the Lipp. "Our dear friend Michael Moriarty has found work!" Monique would chirp happily.

Crossing the street from the Lipp, they took a sidewalk table at the Café des Deux Magots and ordered *vin rouge* and espresso. Frenchy speculated that Hemingway might have sat at this same table, scribbling in his blue-backed notebook. Frenchy couldn't resist discoursing on Paris in the twenties—recalling Hemingway, Fitzgerald, Ezra Pound, Ford Madox Ford, *une génération perdue,* almost as though he had known them personally. Monique held his hand, loving the lyrical passion that always overtook him at such moments.

One day they walked to the Quartier Latin, returning by way of the Boulevard St. Michel to seek out such literary landmarks as Shakespeare & Company, Sylvia Beach's rental library and bookstore, where Hemingway had read all of Turgenev, and Gertrude Stein's studio apartment at 27 Rue de Fleurus, where Hem and Ms. Stein had argued the merits of D. H. Lawrence and Aldous Huxley. Frenchy was simultaneously rereading Hemingway's *A Moveable*

Feast and Victor Hugo's *Notre Dame of Paris* during his time in the city. Sometimes he would read sentences or paragraphs aloud to her. They spent more than an hour searching for what Hemingway had called "one of the best cafés in Paris," the Closerie des Lilas, which in the twenties was near the flat over the sawmill at 113 Rue Notre-Dame-des-Champs where Hem and his wife, Tatie, lived. He guessed that it had been torn down years ago, but to his surprise they located it on Boulevard Montparnasse, only to find it closed for repairs. It didn't matter. The search itself had put him back in that place and time.

Just as Frenchy lost himself in the memories of the great writers, so Monique identified with the great painters, in particular the impressionists—Monet, Degas, Manet, Cézanne, Renoir. They spent most of a day at the Musée d'Orsay, working slowly though the old train-station-turned-art-museum. Monique was fascinated by a van Gogh painting titled *Bedroom in Arles,* painted in 1888 just after van Gogh moved to Arles from Paris. She stood looking at it for a long while, loving the bright colors of the spare, empty bedroom. "I think van Gogh was trying to express his loneliness, his powerful need to love and be loved," she told Frenchy. "See the way he has paired objects in the painting? Two pillows on the bed, two chairs, even the pictures hung in pairs!" In the gift shop she purchased a reproduction of *Bedroom in Arles,* which she would later frame and hang in the living room of their home.

They took the Métro to Montmartre and tried to find the garret where van Gogh had lived and painted during his short time in Paris. According to their guidebook, the apartment, which he shared with his brother Theo, would have been on Rue Lepic. Their search took them down the steep, narrow streets of Montmartre, amid small shops and bohemian apartments, but they never found van Gogh's studio. "He was here," Monique said at one point. "I can smell him." They stopped at an art supply shop like the one where the starving artists of Paris used to hang their works. Supposedly, van Gogh had met Cézanne in such a shop as this, and supposedly Cézanne had told him, "You paint like a madman!"

They stopped at the famous Montmartre cabaret Lapin Agile and ordered *eau-de-vie,* the fragrant, colorless liqueur, this particular one made from wild raspberries. This was a neighborhood where great painters like Toulouse-Lautrec and Utrillo had lived and worked, and it spoke directly to Monique, translated in terms she understood what it meant to be in Paris. She had read and imagined herself at the wild and famous dinner party that Picasso staged at his Montmartre studio for Rousseau, a party in which donkeys wandered about freely while the best of Parisian society fell face forward into the pastry and one guest ate a woman's hat. It reminded them of the parties they had attended in Austin.

At the bottom of the hill below the Sacre-Coeur basilica, they ate lunch at a sidewalk café with no sign identifying its name. Monique struck up a conversation with an old French woman who carried a cat in her floppy canvas bag. It was a strange conversation, because neither of them spoke the other's language, and yet both seemed to understand completely and, in general, agree on the priorities of life. Monique bought the woman a glass of wine and the woman repaid the kindness by giving Monique a cheap ballpoint pin.

Working their way back toward the Métro stop at Place Pigalle, they strolled arm in arm through the gaudy red-light district where every manner of amateur and professional sin had flourished for more than a century. Frenchy stopped in front of a theater advertising, in both French and English, *Live Sex Show,* marveling at the enormous breasts of a showgirl pictured on the poster. Monique flirted with the barker who was trying to lure them inside. Frenchy insisted on taking her photograph posing in front of a sex shop's sign. She took one of him in front of the Moulin Rouge, where a hundred years ago Lautrec had sat for hours, drinking and sketching the dancers and clientele.

"Think of La Goulue!" she told him as she steadied the camera. La Goulue was one of their many private jokes. She had been a featured attraction of the Moulin Rouge in the 1880s, the naughty dancer La Goulue, her thighs swathed in sixty yards of foamy lace, famous for a high kick that could knock the hats off gentlemen in the audience—not the least of whom was Edward, Prince of Wales. Frenchy had given Monique the nickname La Goulue years ago, on his first visit to her hometown of Wetumka, Oklahoma. On the way, he'd started asking studious questions about the economic base of this part of the state—was it cotton, or oil, or cattle, or what?—to which she had famously replied, "I don't know about stuff like economic bases, I was just a high kicker."

Each afternoon late, they would return to La Bohème, exhausted and happy, their arms loaded with sacks of groceries and bottles of wine. They ate most of their evening meals at the apartment, listening to their opera and to the jazz of Miles Davis, John Coltrane, and the Modern Jazz Quartet. Though no city in the world has better or more famous restaurants than Paris, they much preferred to be alone, delighting in each other's company and in the faded luxury of their love nest. A few blocks from their apartment, just off the Rue du Temple, they discovered a narrow street lined with great bakeries, wineshops, fruit and vegetable stands, flower stalls, and butcher shops where they could buy roasted game, beef, and chicken and prepared pasta and vegetable dishes better than any they could have cooked themselves. Frenchy made friends with a man at the wineshop, who spoke just enough English for them to discuss the qualities of various bottles and agree which were the best bargains. Monique got to know the two young women who ran the Vietnamese restaurant on their block and was hugely impressed by the graciousness they demonstrated the day she dropped and broke a liter of olive oil on the sidewalk directly in front of the restaurant entrance. In a way, they had become part of the neighborhood, not two strangers on a visit. The Rue Volta was their street, their place, their discovery—and always would be.

Late at night after they had finished dinner and were on their second or third bottle of wine, they would stand by the open window, drinking in the nightlife along the Rue Volta, watching young people mingling in small groups in front of the Tchatch Tango, a jazz club on the corner, or couples strolling toward Le Tipaza or one of the several neighborhood restaurants, or taking shortcuts to the Pompidou Center, where there was some kind of folk music festival. At this time in their life, they much preferred to watch nightlife from the comfort of a living-room window or balcony. Sometimes the kids at the jazz club would call out to them and Frenchy would call back, using one of the phrases that he had committed to memory, hoping it was appropriate. What impressed Monique was the uncommon cleanliness of the Paris streets. All hours of the day and night the green street-sweeping truck would pass under their window, men in coveralls trailing with brooms.

Toward the end of the week, Frenchy began concentrating on Monique's birthday, always one of his great dilemmas. For one thing, he was never able to remember the exact date—it was either the 3rd, 4th, or 5th of November. This problem was solved by celebrating all three days. Then there was the greater obstacle of the gift. Monique had impeccable but severely eclectic tastes in clothes and jewelry, and Frenchy had learned long ago that he was no match for the challenge. They had more or less come to the understanding that Monique would select the gift, then act appropriately surprised when he presented it as his own idea. In time, this understanding had taken on a special magic. Without fail, they always found exactly the right gift, not just for Monique but for them both.

On November 4, he took her shopping on the Champs-Elysées, the famed promenade crowned by the Arc de Triomphe—a street world-famous as the final word in *haute couture*. To his surprise, Monique did not seem comfortable. They strolled both sides of great street, stopping at interesting windows and poking their heads into interesting shops, but Monique seemed hesitant—even intimidated—in a way he'd never seen before. She had in mind a particular type of hooded raincoat—she'd seen it once in a catalog, or maybe she'd dreamed it—but as clear as it was on the rear screen of her mind there was no way she could describe it to the impatient clerks on the elite Champs-Elysées. "I'm running out of hand signals," she whispered to him. She was about to cry. A day that had started so optimistically, with such unbounded happiness and promise, was being swept away by the blackest despair. "How do you say 'Shop till you drop' in *français*?" he asked, hoping to change her mood with his little joke. But it only made things worse.

He spotted a Burger King directly across the street. Though they were in the middle of the block, he obeyed his impulse and grabbed her arm, pulling her into the flow of the swift and deadly traffic, dodging a speeding Ford, kicking at cyclists who deliberately tried to run them over, racing the final few steps to miss a fast-approaching truck. Out of breath, he said at last, "A burger and a plate of fries should revive our sagging spirits!"

Halfway through lunch she remembered reading about a famous Parisian department store, Au Printemps. "I think I'd be more comfortable there," she admitted. The Champs-Elysées was great, but only in theory.

"That's my girl," he said, squeezing her arm. "Don't let the Frog bastards get the best of you!" He looked up Au Printemps in a phone book. It was on the Boulevard Haussmann, a short Métro ride away.

As soon as they emerged from the Métro station, they spotted Au Printemps: it took up a city block and then some. Hurrying to beat the traffic light at the corner, they felt the rush of excitement of a day being reborn. They took escalators to the third floor and immediately spotted the racks of coats. While she inspected the coats, he drifted over to admire the lingerie. The mere thought of lingerie in Paris gave him vertigo. He must have been daydreaming, because he didn't hear Monique come up beside him. She was holding a black lacy slip to her body, sizing it. "Do you like this one?" she asked. His throat was so dry he couldn't speak. Finally he managed to nod.

"I do too," she said. "It's *très sexy, non?*"

"I thought you wanted a coat," he reminded her.

"Don't worry," she said, taking a credit card from her pocketbook as they headed toward the cashier's counter. "I always find what I'm looking for."

The next morning he woke before she did. Moving softly so as not to disturb her, he dressed, descended the 182 steps, and hurried to their shopping street off the Rue du Temple. At the bakery, he bought fresh croissants. At the grocer, some pears and a bottle of fresh orange juice. His friend at the wineshop helped him select an excellent bottle of Laurent-Perrier champagne. At the flower stall, he bought three dozen tulips in assorted yellows and pinks. Barely able to see behind his load, he headed home, humming and singing: "The last time I saw Paris, her heart was warm and gay . . ."

Monique was watching from the dormer window with her camera as Frenchy came down their street, his arms loaded with sacks and bundles of tulips. The photograph of him surprising her would be his surprise—one of them. She had only pretended to be asleep. When she heard his footsteps descending the stairs, she climbed out of bed, slipped into a sexy white negligee, made coffee, put away the dishes from their meal the previous evening, and slipped the cassette of *La Bohème* into the stereo so that it would be playing when he burst through the door with the flowers. Of course, she acted surprised and pleased, expressing her gratitude with a long, passionate kiss that promised great rewards. "Don't be impatient," she scolded him, then gave him another kiss even hotter than the previous one. She was taking his patience to the limit and knew it.

While he opened the wine, she drew her bubble bath. One of his greatest pleasures was watching her in the leisure of a bubble bath. At the Hôtel d'Europe in Avignon a week earlier, he had photographed Monique in her bath, mounds of bubbles discreetly positioned to conceal her breasts, bringing a wineglass to her glistening lips. Now he sat on the edge of the tub, keeping her glass filled, making small talk, occasionally kissing her, both of them very much aroused but in no hurry. When she was finished, he held out a giant towel for her to step into, then used a second towel to dry her all over. She could feel his lips brush against the back of her neck.

The lacy black slip, still in its Au Printemps wrapper, waited on a shelf by the mirror. She motioned for him to hand it to her. Then she said, "While I get cosmetically correct, why don't you start a fire and set out some juice and croissants."

It was going to be a great day, even by their lofty standards. A great, great day!

Their final day in Paris was a Sunday, and they spent it exploring the narrow sidestreets near the busy Rue des Francs-Bourgeois, working their way gradually to their ultimate destination, the Place des Vosges. Built by order of Henri IV in 1605, the so-called royal plaza was a square of identical pastel buildings with a small, pretty park in the center. In the seventeenth century this was a very exclusive community of dukes and duchesses and cardinals like Richelieu, who celebrated their greatness at the expense of everyone else and raised offspring who themselves raised offspring who presumably lost their heads at the time of the French Revolution. What at-tracted Frenchy and Monique was the apartment at No. 6, which had once been the home of Victor Hugo.

After a tour of No. 6, they sat in the park, sharing a bag of warm chestnuts. Frenchy had brought one of Victor Hugo's books for the express purpose of reading her this one passage: *"Supreme happiness is the conviction that we are loved."*

"Read it to me again," she said, pleased at the message and the way he delivered it.

"Supreme happiness is the conviction that we are loved," he repeated, this time more slowly and with extra feeling.

"I think you got it exactly right."

"Me and Victor Hugo."

"Do you know what I'd like to do now? Go to the Ritz. Drink a lot of champagne. Eat a fabulous meal. Then go home and make mad love for the rest of the day."

So that's what they did.

Twenty-Four

They call Paris the City of Lovers for good reason, but it is not the city that makes them love so passionately and so well, it is the trust and devotion and openness that the lovers bring with them. The city doesn't matter, only that it is someplace new, someplace out of the ordinary. New York or Chicago or even Cleveland can seem light and gay if you will let it. Love is not a place but a pleasure—the pleasure lovers take in bringing pleasure to the other, their willingness to give, their certainty that what they receive is pure and honest and ordained. Lovers live and grow separately according to the life they have made together, and they presume that it will never end.

By the way, Monique got the coat she had dreamed of; he had never doubted that she would. She designed it herself and had a dressmaker in Austin sew it to her specifications. It's bright red, with a hood, and it's the envy of all who see it. Two years after their adventure in Paris, she wore the red raincoat to Italy. In their collection of wonderful moments is a photograph of Monique posing at the National Museum of Archaeology of Naples, with the famous Farnese *Hercules,* her wonderful red raincoat in the foreground.

And the sexy, lacy black slip from Au Printemps? It is now part of their permanent collection, known simply as *Monique's Paris Slip.*

The great philosopher Satchel Paige once reminded us that age is simply a question of mind over matter: if you don't mind, it don't matter. Researchers have proved again and again that the three secrets of staying young are attitude, attitude, and attitude. People who like themselves, who think positive, and who believe that loyalty, fidelity, and generosity are good things have a much better chance of good health and long life than people who don't. People who live in despair, who hate and fear their neighbors, who harbor grudges and earnestly believe that this country and indeed the world are a malevolent conspiracy of greed and evil intent, are already dead and buried—they just haven't realized it.

As we age, we sometimes allow our minds to slip into autopilot, worrying about the future or reliving the past while the present slips away unappreciated. Older people forget what children know instinctively, that each moment is new and alive with possibilities. The years have a way of numbing us to new experiences, of blinding us to anything that happens outside our self-imposed shells. It's the old been-there-done-that syndrome. We give up on life, not because life gives up on us but because our attitude becomes so insular, so restrictive and self-centered, that our spirits began to atrophy.

It doesn't have to be this way. There is a simple, effective technique called "mindfulness," which requires nothing more than attention to details. Watch the birds. Listen to a stream. Walk alone in the woods. Pay attention to people other than yourself. Perform a kindness to a stranger. Get laid in the middle of the day. Take a nap. Ask yourself: What do I really want to do with the rest of my life? Then make a list. Do something beside feeling sorry for yourself.

Corinne Wise, director of Heartwise Monitoring Service, where I get my pacemaker checked every three months, has observed that new clients invariably believe that their pacemaker is the beginning of their end. She employs several strategies to convince them otherwise. The silk screen that separates the testing area from the office is papered with postcards mailed by clients from such exotic locales as Hong Kong, the Yucatán, Kruger National Park in Africa, Moscow, Venice, Nîmes, Assisi, Paris, New Zealand, the Czech Republic, Japan, Taiwan, and the Great Wall of China. When a new client inquires about the possibility of obtaining a handicapped sticker for his car, Corinne points to the postcards. "Wearing a pacemaker doesn't make you an invalid," she tells them. "It keeps you from being one!"

A growing body of medical evidence links a positive attitude to healthier, happier, and longer lives. People who enjoy happy marriages and a good relationship with the folks around them and with the Almighty do not despair for significant periods, nor do they waste time on paybacks and other negative activities. A study by Dr. David B. Larson, president of the National Institute of Health-Care Research, demonstrates clearly that fidelity in marriage and faith in God can make you live longer, weigh less, earn more, make less trouble, and enjoy far higher self-esteem. Another study asked a group of people what attitudes they thought defined "the spark of life." At the top of the list was "being very optimistic," followed by "having a strong belief in a higher power."

Polls show that 87 percent of us believe that someone or something up there answers prayers. The big exception, wouldn't you know, is scientists. Only about 45 percent of scientists believe in God. Schooled in materialism, scientists require "proof," even though many elements of science are clearly unprovable. Relativity, evolution, black holes—merely theories, scientists' best explanations for observable phenomena. Gandhi wrote once to Einstein and asked him what he did. Einstein replied: "I'm a scientist. I trace the lines that flow to God." Einstein saw in the vastness of space and infinitesimal smallness of subatomic particles the work of a mind greater than his own.

I think that where the concept of God is concerned, people tend to either overintellectualize or dogmatize. If an intelligence higher than our own is at work in the universe, how can we be expected to grasp the magnitude of His work with our own limited brains? How can we possibly conceive of infinity? What was here before heaven and earth? What happens after eternity? In the unshakable conviction that they are right, atheists seem hell-bent on disproving their own faith—but then so do Christian fundamentalists. Why else do the True Believers find God and the theory of evolution so incompatible? If you believe that God created the universe, why is it so difficult to see evolution as simply another manifestation of His creativity? Indeed, the fundamentalists must think that God is as vain and shallow as they are.

What almost everyone overlooks is the simple message at the core of almost all religions: that we pitifully vulnerable creatures alone on this small planet desperately need a higher authority to deliver us from the human failings of intolerance, cruelty, selfishness, self-indulgence, and self-pity. If there ain't a God up there, pal, you'd better invent one damn quick!

Framed and hung on the wall of the guest bedroom at Warren and Kay Burnett's home near Galveston Bay is this poem or prayer, which I read again every time I stay there.

A Prayer

Lord, thou knowest better than I know myself
that I am growing older and will someday be old.
Keep me from the fatal habit of thinking I must
comment on every subject and on every occasion.
Release me from craving to straighten out everybody's
affairs. Make me thoughtful but not moody; helpful
but not bossy. With my vast store of wisdom it
seems a pity not to use it all, but thou knowest,
Lord, that I want a few friends at the end. Keep
my mind free from the recital of endless details . . .
give me wings to get to the point. Seal my lips on
my aches and pains. They are increasing and love of
rehearing them is becoming sweeter as the years go
by. I dare not ask for grace enough to enjoy the
tales of others, but help me to endure them with
patience. I dare not ask for improved memory but a
growing humility and less cocksureness when my
memory seems to clash with the memory of others.
Teach me the glorious lesson that occasionally I may be
mistaken. Keep me reasonably sweet . . . a sour old person
is one of the crowning works of the devil. Give me the
ability to see good things in unexpected places and
talents in unexpected people. Give me the grace
to tell them so.
Amen.

—*Author unknown*

I assume that Kay put the prayer on the bedroom wall because
Warren devoutly does not believe in God. Warren is one of my oldest and best friends, and his loathing of all things religious wouldn't
be a problem except that he feels compelled to heap abuse on anyone who does believe, particularly Kay and me. The two subjects that
most often engage his brilliant legal mind are his unshakable con-

viction that God and right-wing politicians have conspired to destroy the ethos of America, and his sincere belief that his own mean childhood in the coal-mining community of Austin, West Virginia, makes him the last word on God and Country.

Late at night when we've all had numerous glasses of wine, Warren will start talking about his "people" in West Virginia as a prelude to some moral conclusion. "My people," he'll say, "read the Bible twenty times a day, but they had neither the time nor the inclination to consider Shakespeare or Blake." Kay and I usually indulge him, but sometimes my own contrarian nature gets the best of me. "My people ate nothing but flies, rocks, and dirt," I'll say casually. "On Christmas, as a treat, we'd each get a small sack of rusty nails, which we'd eat like hard candy."

One Sunday while we were having lunch at a Greek restaurant on the waterfront, Warren launched into a diatribe about how the elite of Galveston society had climbed to their lofty positions on the backs of African-Americans and had made it their mission to "keep the niggers from being anything except niggers." (In Warren's mind, the racial pejorative wasn't a slur but a social comment because it came out of the mouth of a card-carrying Wobbly.) I made some sort of feeble objection that such remarks were overly general—Kay called them "bumper-sticker philosophy"—but our objections just caused Warren to turn red in the face and pound on the table with his fist. "Damn you!" he shouted in a voice that could be heard all across the room. "If it wasn't for God, we wouldn't have so goddam many niggers!"

I mention Warren's overtly negative attitude toward God and religion to call attention to a little-known disease that afflects mankind just as drastically as clogged arteries and high blood pressure: hardening of the cerebral arteries. This kind of attitude is an almost willful effort to transform that which is sunny and upbeat to something bitter and toxic. It is easy, fashionable, and even fun to deny the existence of God when you are young, but atheism in anyone of advancing years seems to me the ultimate conceit.

Leonard Pitts, a funny and talented columnist for the *Miami Herald,* reminds readers of an old "Far Side" cartoon by Gary Larson. The caption reads "Agnostic fleas" and the cartoon shows two fleas standing in a thicket of canine hair, one saying to the other: "I'm not so sure there really is a dog."

Believing in the existence of God isn't always easy, but it's not nearly as hard as some people make it out to be. Most of us come by our beliefs as a natural process of growing up, much as we learn to accept that the Constitution is a wonderful document, that Popeye eats spinach, and that John Wayne fought at the Alamo. If you love life and love your fellow man, it's not hard to see God everywhere. I understand that some people's experiences of life are contrary to my own, and that they associate their own hardships and bitterness with proof that God does not exist. If there is a God, I've heard it argued, how could He possibly allow His name to be used for such cruel and stupid pursuits as the Crusades, the Inquisition, or the endless holy wars in Ireland, Bosnia, Afghanistan, and countless other lands? I don't know the answer. There have been a lot of crimes committed in the name of God. But that doesn't mean that God signed off on any of them. God cuts the world a lot of slack, it seems to me.

We make our own happiness; and similarly, we make our own unhappiness. In his autobiography, Willie Nelson tells coauthor Bud Shrake: "Our creative imagination tells us to get on the ball and use the higher mind to create positive conditions. The purpose of suffering is to make us understand we are the ones who cause it. The possibilities live within each of us. 'Let this mind be in you that was also in Christ Jesus,' is how Paul put it."

People are actually predisposed to either happiness or unhappiness. Whatever happens in anyone's life—whether it's good or evil—the effect is only temporary. In a short time, usually a few weeks, all of us return to a mood state that is natural for us. Scientists have studied lottery winners and found that almost none of them were happier a year after winning the lottery than they were before they won. The flip side is equally true: setbacks don't last all that long. Divorces, family deaths, the loss of a job, the loss of a pet—we bounce back to our normal level within three months.

Nothing has ever rocked me the way Mark's death did. Dealing with the "why" question was my ultimate test of faith. I came to understand that God is not there to answer "why" questions, though He can help ease other emotions that overwhelm a parent whose child

dies: the guilt, the frustration, the anger. What could I have done differently? What *should* I have done? Phyllis told me that when her son
Robert was dying of AIDS in 1994, she had an irresistible urge to
hold him tightly, as though she might transfer her energy and her
wellness to him. I felt that same urge.

Anger was the emotion that hit hardest and lasted longest. I was
angry at his doctors and the hospitals for allowing him to waste away:
there must have been something else they could have done, I
thought. I hated the entire pharmaceutical industry for wallowing in
its obscene profits while its researchers consistently failed to find
cures. I even called my friend the leukemia researcher Dr. Aubrey
Thompson to vent my anger. He assured me that research was doing
the best it could. After a few weeks, the guilt, anger, and frustration
had run their course. When he was dying, Markie didn't blame God
or fate, and neither would I. Life ain't fair, but none of us has time
to worry about it.

As we age—as loved ones die and fortunes shift and fate seems
sometimes to be dealing from the bottom of the deck—we rearrange
priorities and take new looks at the things that make us happy. Phyllis is my happiness. She is the only one I couldn't do without. What
we do together, what we learn, and what we are forced to deal with
are the substance of my life, all that I am or can be.

Losing two sons was a blow neither of us could have imagined
surviving, but we did survive. In a way their deaths validated what
we believed, that those whom we love are always with us. We carry
Robert and Mark constantly in our hearts, and we honor their memories and keep their spirits alive. I talk to Markie a lot, and sometimes I think I hear him talking back. I'm sure Phyllis has the same
line of communication with Robbie. By coincidence, Robbie is
buried a few hundred feet from the spot where my dad is buried, at
a cemetery in Arlington. Someday my mom will be buried there, too.
When we can, we visit the cemetery and place flowers on both
graves. In the summer of 1997, we carried Markie's ashes to Galveston and scattered them at the opening of the ship channel, from the
deck of the Bolivar ferry.

The scattering of Markie's ashes was one of those magic moments when you know that God is in His heaven and all is right with

the world. We boarded the ferry just before sunset, with our Galveston friend Pam Diamond. We had brought along a Bible and a bottle of full-bodied Shiraz from southern Australia—Maurice would have said that the tannins needed more time to settle—and Pam brought four crystal wineglasses and four linen napkins, the extra set for Markie. I read from the first chapter of Ecclesiastes—"All rivers run to the sea, yet the sea is not full; unto the place from where the rivers came, there they return again"—then allowed the ashes to flutter over the side of the ferry. Watching them float across our wake, I poured the four wineglasses half full. We shared Markie's glass, tossing the final corner into the water. "Markie," I said, raising my glass in a toast, "we'll always know where to find you." As we drained our glasses, a V-formation of twenty-one pelicans flew low across the horizon, between us and a huge, blistering red-orange sun that was just touching the sea. As the sun sank slowly into Galveston Bay, the pelicans peeled off into a straight line—as though saluting—then reformed themselves into a V as the last slice of sun melted into the Gulf. At that moment, Phyllis and I both knew that when our times came, we wanted our ashes scattered in this exact place, with those same words and that same wine, and that same formation of pelicans, if they would be so kind.

I see now that as life becomes shorter, it also becomes simpler. Appearance matters less than before. Ambitions are thankfully modest. Accomplishments retain a degree of satisfaction but are, all in all, overrated and quite temporary. Experience has allowed me to see with new eyes and enabled me to find redemption in the faded and worn. If I look closely, I can see a lot of gray hair mixed in with the dark brown, and yet in certain lights it makes me appear thoughtful and resolute, the way I once imagined smoking a pipe made me look. I haven't just accumulated years, I've accumulated sharper instincts and scattered bits of wisdom, if only the knowledge of how truly unknowledgeable I am.

Phyllis has taught me to be more flexible, more adaptable, more likely to understand, forgive, and forget. She's got me organized, instilled in me the value of using time well. She is my joy and fulfillment. More than her I dare not ask. We get by just taking life one day at a time. We try to get a good night's sleep, take our medications, eat our broccoli, go to Big Steve's, walk our dogs, answer our mail, pay our bills, do our work. We pray daily—nightly, too—and attempt in our pathetic way to be better Christians. We don't let ourselves become consumed by guilts and try to tell others that the blame lies not in ourselves but in the stars.

Most of all we do not take anything too seriously, especially ourselves. We sound so ordinary, and I guess we are. But we're happy and complete, and if there are good things ahead we're ready for them.

We were talking life and death with a friend not long ago and he broke us up by casually remarking: "I want to die peacefully in my sleep like my ninety-two-year-old grandpa. Not screaming in terror like those four poor devils in the car with him."

Me? I'd prefer something less cumbersome. I'd like to die in August 2033, on my hundredth birthday, in my sleep, after working all day, having wine and dinner with Phyllis, and making passionate love. And if there's a late movie with Bogart or Sean Connery on TV that night, I'll take that, too.